Gehlen
The politics of coexistence

Date Due

Printed in U.S.A.

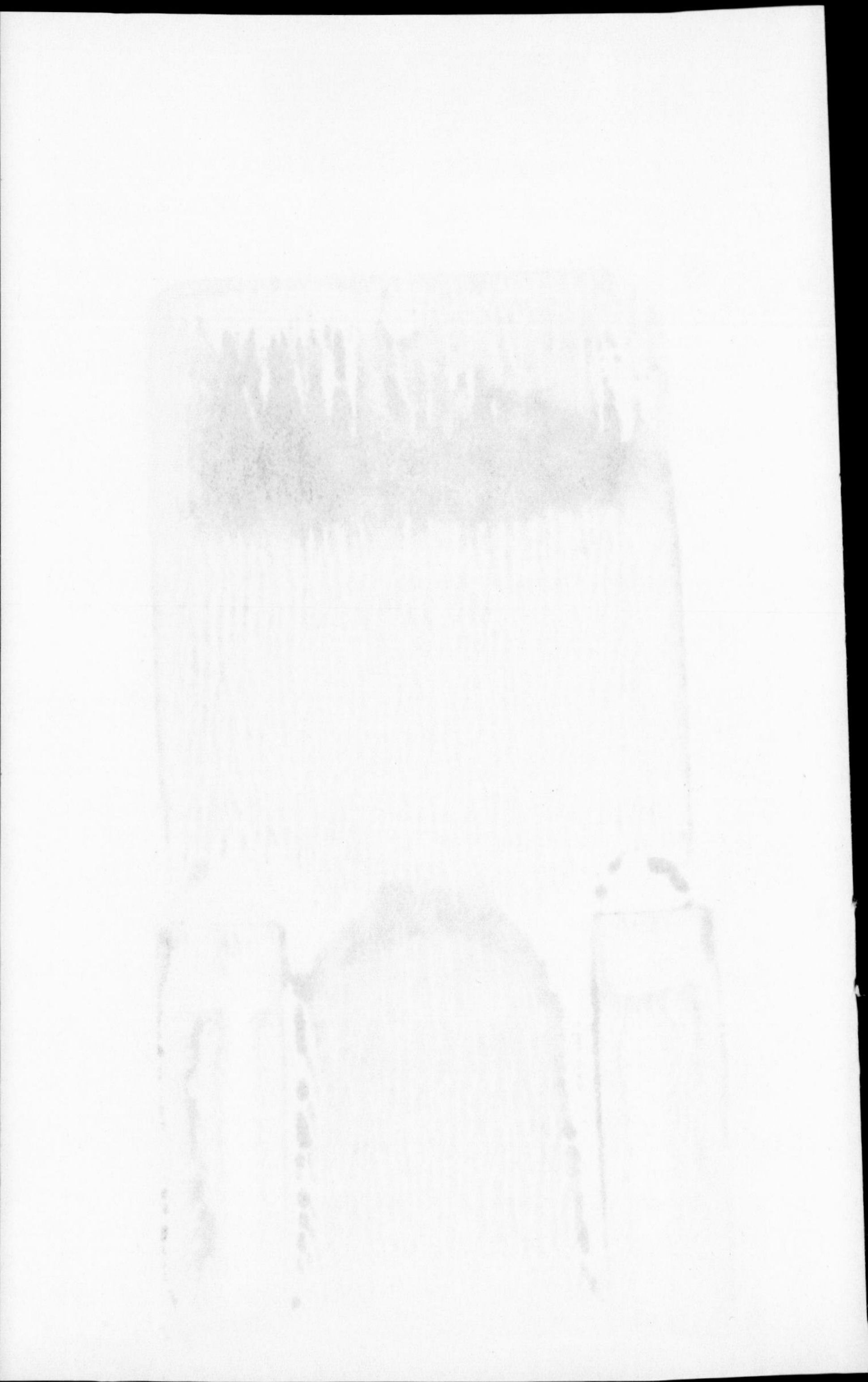

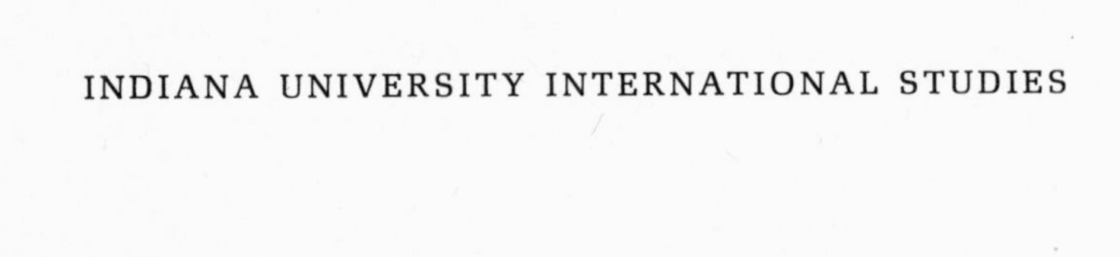

INDIANA UNIVERSITY INTERNATIONAL STUDIES

THE POLITICS OF COEXISTENCE

THE POLITICS OF COEXISTENCE

SOVIET METHODS AND MOTIVES

by Michael P. Gehlen

INDIANA UNIVERSITY PRESS
BLOOMINGTON & LONDON

Library of Congress catalog card number: 67-13023
Manufactured in the United States of America

TO MY PARENTS

CONTENTS

ACKNOWLEDGMENTS

THIS MANUSCRIPT has undergone a great deal of evolution since the first draft was prepared in 1962. There are four scholars to whom I am particularly indebted for having read all or parts of the manuscript during its preparation. Without associating them with the interpretations and conclusions contained in *The Politics of Coexistence*, it is appropriate to recognize the valuable advice given me on the organization, documentation, and general content. These Sovietologists are Jan F. Triska of Stanford University, Edward Taborsky of the University of Texas, George Barr Carson of Oregon State University, and Sidney I. Ploss of the Foreign Policy Research Institute of the University of Pennsylvania. In addition, I wish to express my gratitude to Virginia Radatz Stewart for her services in preparing the final revision of the manuscript. Finally, the Slavic Languages Division of the Hoover Institute at Stanford University deserves a special note of appreciation for assistance in obtaining many of the materials used in this study.

THE POLITICS OF COEXISTENCE

INTRODUCTION

THE PURPOSE of this study is to examine the assumptions behind the policy of coexistence and the methods employed by the Soviet Union to achieve her foreign policy objectives. The first chapter presents in both factual and theoretical form the domestic context of Soviet decision-making in the period from the death of Stalin to the 23rd Party Congress. Following this statement of decision-making patterns in the Soviet system are four principal divisions involving different aspects of Soviet foreign policy and the politics of coexistence. First, we shall examine the theoretical basis of the concept of coexistence, noting the modifications of Leninism and the general shift in emphasis in the post-Stalin period away from the more bellicose and martial elements of Bolshevik thought. The second division is concerned with the relation of military policy to the politics of coexistence. Here we shall consider the principal assumptions pertaining to military strategy and the internal circumstances within which military policy is formulated. In order to compare strategic concepts with actual policy and to assess the impact of domestic conflict over military policy on Soviet behavior in world affairs, a study of risk-taking and of disarmament and arms control policy follows the consideration of military strategy. The third main section of this work involves an examination of the methods of Soviet policy as it has sought to implement a program of economic, political, and ideological competition with the United States. Fourth, although Soviet officials claim that coexistence applies only to states with different social systems, we shall consider the effects of diversity within the Communist system of states on Soviet foreign policy, which have in effect imposed a kind of coexistence among the members of the system. In all areas where it can be clearly established, we shall be concerned with the relationship between the domestic political and economic situation of the Soviet Union and the objectives and methods of foreign policy. Finally, general conclusions will be drawn on the basis of the data and interpretations presented in the body of this study. We are hopeful that the conclusions drawn in each chapter and at the end of this study will be found to be meaningful statements about the importance of controversy among the members of the Soviet elite on foreign policy methods and objectives as well as about the degree of permanency that may be expected from recent developments in the politics of coexistence pursued by the leaders of the U.S.S.R.

PEACEFUL COEXISTENCE: INTERNAL DEVELOPMENTS

Comrades: We must abolish the cult of the individual decisively, once and for all. . . . It is necessary for this purpose: First, in a Bolshevik manner to condemn and to eradicate the cult of the individual . . . and to fight inexorably all attempts at bringing back this practice in one form or another.

—N. S. Khrushchev

THE DOMESTIC SETTING IN THE POST-STALIN PERIOD

I

One of the cardinal principles of world politics is that the nation-state operates as the basic unit of global affairs. The commonly used term *international* politics serves to underscore that fact. Conflicts, compromises, and coalitions among states are widely held to stem from the various interpretations of individual governments of the national interests of each member of the nation-state system. The methods employed by the public decision-makers are shaped by the values and goals of the national system as well as by the power available to promote those interests and the limitations imposed on the uses of the various forms of national power.

In 1917, when the Bolsheviks assumed control of the Russian state, Communist theory officially disclaimed the possibility that the interests of the nation-state could supersede in any way those of the working class. Communists viewed the international revolutionary movement as the primary force in world affairs. Loyalty to the movement and its credo was expected to replace the loyalty to the nation-state which the bourgeois order had ordained. Events, however, failed to confirm the expectations embodied in the theory and, increasingly, the leaders of the Soviet state came to monopolize the right to define and apply the tenets of Communism in all situations and to all Communists, regardless of nationality. As time progressed, the interpretation of Communist doctrine reflected ever more strongly the interests of the Soviet Union as a national state. The seemingly monolithic nature of the Communist movement, embracing parties in and out of power, was maintained under Stalin only by the heavy preponderance of Soviet power. This included the exclusive right of the Soviet hierarchy to declare the appropriate party line, not only for the Communist Party of the Soviet Union (C.P.S.U.) but for all national parties. The assertion of national independence by Yugoslavia in 1948 was the single blemish that marred the record of overt unity and solidarity on major issues. Internally supported by an elaborate system of terror under a gigantic security police apparatus and externally abetted by nationally organized Communist parties known more for their obedience to Moscow than for their political ingenuity, the Communist empire successfully managed to convey the image of a massive, monolithic movement steadily extending its tentacles around the globe.

The myths proclaimed in self-description by the elite Stalinist guard were often accepted as facts by observers in the non-Communist world. Two developments unfolded in the years after Stalin, however, that made the perpetuation of the myths impossible to continue in theory or in fact. In the first place, the expansion of Communism in Asia and eastern Europe brought with it the inevitable erosion of unity as peoples with vastly different cultural and economic backgrounds were brought within the Communist system. In the second place, the gradual maturation of the Soviet economy and the substantial modification of the system of terror introduced new trends and forces in Soviet life. Both of these developments encouraged the growth of diversity within the international Communist movement and within the Soviet Union itself. That the party hierarchy in Moscow neither planned nor desired this trend is not a serious point of contention. But that the forces of change were unleashed and have often escaped the control of the ruling elite is also easily documented. The development of diversity has influenced the theory and policies as well as the underlying ideology of the Soviet state, for the changes have slowly brought alterations in the conception of the interests and goals of Soviet Russia.

As in the case of any non-Communist country, the foreign policy of the Soviet Union cannot be understood as something completely separated from the domestic politics of the nation. Foreign policy represents the convergence, conflict, and amelioration of internal interests insofar as domestic groups are affected by foreign policy developments. Such policy decisions cannot be made in a vacuum or by considering only ideological or external factors. The changing demands on the policy commitments of the U.S.S.R. are, therefore, closely associated with domestic pressures. The evolution of Soviet society, particularly those fundamental alterations that have occurred in the post-Stalin period, provides the context in which the nation's foreign policy is formulated and without which a meaningful appraisal cannot be made.

The principal developments in domestic affairs may be summarized in four parts. The first is the denigration of Stalin and Stalinism. This process was set in motion before Khrushchev's formal denunciation of the erstwhile Soviet dictator and is reflected in all the major facets of Soviet life. Perhaps de-Stalinization has been most commonly associated with the end to the indiscriminate use of terror. The reorganization of the police apparatus and the diminution of its authority were, however, only the beginnings of the process. Theory had to be brought into line with practice by the rejection of Stalin's claim that the class struggle sharpened as the transition to socialism progressed, a theory which had served as the justification of the system of terror. These modifications of Stalinism set in motion a force that has been less discussed, but that may prove to be of greater long-range significance than the modification of the use of terror. The leadership of Malenkov and Khrushchev gradually brought new techniques of decision-making to government. This is not to contend that the structure of government itself has been drastically reshaped, for, in spite of some reorganization, it has not. But the methods of governing have indeed changed from the arbitrary rule of one man to techniques of discussion and persuasion within an expanding group of party and government officials. The voices of the branches of the military services, of the bureaucracy, of scientists, and to a rising degree of the consumer have attained sufficient stature to exert independent pressure on the Soviet decision-makers. As a consequence, de-Stalinization represents the guarded opening of the political processes to groups within the shifting power structure of the U.S.S.R.

The elimination of terror as the principal instrument of maintaining internal control and the modification of the techniques of rule to include the recognition of diverse groups with differing interests have required the reorganization and strengthening of the Communist Party in order to protect the position of the ruling elite. The post-Stalin era has witnessed the re-emergence of the party, rather than the police, as the dominant instrument of control and as the channel through which competing groups must operate. Khrushchev carefully revitalized the party machinery, broadened the membership of the Central Committee and gave it new importance, and reorganized the party structure to parallel more closely the economic divisions of the country. The party serves in the capacity of a control and processing system for the various interests in Soviet society, permitting greater discussion of problems before decisions are made while preventing the development of liberal representative institutions in the Western sense. *Partiinost,* more in the spirit of Lenin than Stalin, has been the second chief feature of the new period of Soviet history.

The third feature has been an increased measure of personal and cultural freedom accompanied by a rising standard of living. The strikingly different atmosphere of the Russian society of 1950 and that of 1966 can perhaps best be characterized by the present air of confidence and security of the Soviet citizen. The slow but steady growth of consumers' goods industries and the criticisms and hopes voiced in publications and orations testify to the discernible transition of the Soviet nation from a *have-not* to a *have* society. While these changes may not be fully appreciated by those who insist on comparing them to British or American experience, they stand out plainly in comparison with the recent past of the U.S.S.R.

Fourth, and last, changes have been reflected in the officially accepted tenets of Communist theory. Some of these changes are only shifts in emphasis. Others have been formal modifications of assumptions long considered permanent features of Leninism. Recognition of the possibility of nonviolent transition to socialism, rejection of the inevitability of war, and admission of different roads to socialism other than the Soviet road are only the more dramatic examples. At the same time, theory has become increasingly descriptive rather than prescriptive, even to the point that Khrushchev did not find it necessary to distinguish between theory and ideology. The result has been that social and economic changes within the Soviet Union, coupled with modifications of theory, required the further rationalization of ideology. In short, the seeds of ideological erosion were planted. Precisely what the harvest will be or how the Soviet leaders will deal with it cannot be foreseen. But it can be safely predicted that they cannot long succeed in suppressing the problem of gaping divergencies between theory and practice on the one hand and ideology on the other.

The development of these four patterns in the Soviet political system has made it increasingly possible for functional groups to exert influence in the decision-making process. These groups stem from the social structure of the system and play important roles in its operation. Groups are identified here as collectivities of persons associated through activity directed toward the achievement of political goals. Group political activity ordinarily consists of attempts to influence public policy. Group goals are the product of evaluations made on the basis of shared norms. Groups may be thought of as highly organized and relatively stable (as in the case of the rigid hierarchical command structure of the military or of the attempt to institutionalize artistic discretion through the Writers' Union) or as less highly organized with significant instability of membership (as in the case of the generalized pressure for increased availability of consumers' goods). For analytical purposes, a political group exists if some degree of self-awareness of goals and of activity directed at influencing public policy is manifested.

In the Soviet Union groups must operate within a system that purportedly rests on a set of explicitly stated political values. These generalized values or goals are set forth in the postulates of Marxism-Leninism as interpreted by the contemporary party elite. Values stated as doctrine are a principal instrument of the leadership in controlling the Soviet public through indoctrination, in establishing highly stylized channels within which groups must operate, and in providing the rationalization for the perpetuation of the system. The authority to interpret doctrine and to set general goals therefore constitutes a fundamental part of the power available to the decision-makers. Consequently, any group that has as its aim some basic modification of the system, such as some religious groups, is not likely to obtain direct access to the high-level decision-making process.

On the other hand, the societal context is such that groups that have specific aims or grievances, and that do not challenge the general value system, already exist in the Soviet Union. They attempt to alter existing norms either directly or by persuading competent decision-makers to do so. Their own norms are derived from the functional roles that they play in society. The existence and effectiveness of normative-oriented groups in the U.S.S.R. appear to stem largely from three factors: (1) their utility in the social system, (2) their ability to establish access to or membership in decision-making bodies, and (3) their ability to concentrate their energies on trying to change specific normative patterns without demanding fundamental modification of the general values. It is, therefore, possible for the army to bargain for larger allocations and for an economic ministry to argue against decentralization, although it is difficult for either to demand the abandonment of the system itself. While the general value system supports the existing order, it does not prevent group manifestation of specific normative values and goals.

The location of legitimate high-level decision-making power to which most groups must have access in order to be effective is not found in any one person or body. National decision-making power is generally attributed to the Politburo of the Communist Party, with some members occupying positions somewhat "more equal" than the others. It can be established that in some instances a smaller number than are in the Politburo and in other instances a larger number participate in making basic national decisions. During the Cuban crisis of 1962, a select body of the Politburo rather than the whole membership appears to have been responsible for decisions. In other circumstances, such as the decision to decentralize most of the national economic ministries and the "anti-party crisis" of 1957, a large group of individuals, including the entire Central Committee, participated in the resolution of differences over leadership and policy. These variations in the location of political authority and the legitimacy of high-level decision-making power, however, should not obscure the fact that the weight of all available evidence supports the assumption that the members of the party hierarchy share the responsibility of making and approving general policy. It is appropriate, therefore, that the study of domestic and foreign policy decision-making in the Soviet system centers on the party elite. It is not appropriate, however, to treat the members of the higher party organs as a monolith, for the party elite is in fact a composite of various elite groups.

It is the composite nature of the higher party organs that enables the policy-makers to acquire the information that enables them to make functional decisions. It has been common to assume that both the degree of independence and the scope of jurisdiction of the decision-makers are relatively "total" in the Soviet system (i.e., their exercise of power is relatively unencumbered by considerations of who may be affected and how a given policy may be implemented). While the use of terror during the Stalin era lent some credence to this view, studies of the Khrushchev period have failed to support such wholesale contentions. Indeed, the requisites for making functional decisions in other societies suggest that it is not plausible to assume that principal policy decisions can be made over an extended period of time in such a fashion, sealed off from those who must put them into effect and those who will be significantly affected by their administration. Functional decisions require an input process. They require an inflow of information from competent technical, administrative, and general sources. Decisions can be functional primarily because of reliable information about the environment of groups affected by those decisions and reasonable estimates of the relationship between groups and between groups and the policy-makers.

Political decision-making in a complex industrial society, including the Soviet Union, is essentially competitive. The degree of competitiveness and the style in which it is conducted, of course, vary from system to system. But whatever the methods that are permissible in the pursuit of their goals, organized groups (e.g., the bureaucracy, the military services, scientific research establishments, writers, etc., and their various subdivisions) acquire vested interests. These interests are primarily the outgrowth of the functions that the groups perform. Group concern over productivity and the allocation of specific goods, services, and rewards can be expected to produce attempts to influence the decisions of the ruling elite in a maturing industrial society. What is being suggested, therefore, is that the development of group awareness and group access to the decision-makers is of increasing importance in the analysis of the Soviet political system.

Since it can be fairly assumed that the upper echelon of the party makes the general policy decisions for the regime, groups must be able to make their interests known to the party elite. To be effective, they must have access to the party hierarchy either through party channels and party membership or through other contacts with high-ranking party personnel. This becomes possible, even in a rigid hierarchical arrangement operating under the practice of democratic centralism, largely as a result of the need of the ruling elite to make functional decisions. The shift in party membership from the generalist to the specialist illustrates the evolution of the C.P.S.U. from the Leninist party of revolutionaries who were willing to undertake the most divergent types of assignments to Khrushchev's party hierarchy of highly trained specialists closely associated with the groups of their particular specialization. Preliminary surveys of the membership of the Central Committee of the party indicate that the selection of members of that body is based at least in part on the tacit recognition of the existence of group interests. To call these persons "representatives" in the sense that they are politically responsible to occupational groups may be premature. However, even in Western democracies the fact of representation exists by action and not merely by formal

TABLE I

Higher and Specialized Educational Backgrounds of the Members of the Central Committee (1961)

	Full Members	*Candidate Members*
Military	16	18
Technical & scientific	102	83
Other	36	28
None	21	26
	175	155

Functional Positions of Members of the Central Committee (1961)

	Full Members	*Candidate Members*
Party apparatus	62	46
Agricultural party work	15	11
Party and state work	29	22
Bureaucracy	43	46
Military	14	17
Writers	3	3
Scientists	2	4
Trade unions	4	1
Other[a]	3	5
	175	155

[a] The category of "Other" includes workers and officers of the Council of Consumers' Cooperatives.

Source: These tables are taken from Michael P. Gehlen, "The Educational Backgrounds and Career Orientations of the Members of the Central Committee of the CPSU," *The American Behavioral Scientist*, April, 1966.

delegation of representative authority from some constituency.

The political interplay that stems from the competition among the principal groups and subgroups is most easily detectable in regard to conflicts over domestic issues. However, differences among factional alliances, particularly those in which the military participates, also have an impact on the formulation of foreign policy. As in other countries, the values, politics, and economics of the domestic system influence the choices of the decision-makers and shape the objectives and methods of Soviet foreign policy. The decisions of Khrushchev and his entourage of associates were made not only in the context of world events but in the midst of, and frequently on the basis of, domestic political controversies. Kosygin and especially Brezhnev are essentially the products of the political conflicts that developed within the Soviet elite in the post-Stalin period. They, like Khrushchev, spoke out to defend the policy of coexistence and their leadership is likely to reflect a continuation of both the domestic and international politics of coexistence and the internal conflicts associated with such politics. Under Khrushchev the principal general characteristics of coexistence were experimentation in methods and re-evaluation of objectives of Soviet foreign policy. His successors may reach different conclusions on specific policy questions but cautious experimentation and re-evaluation characterized the collectivity of leadership through the 23rd Party Congress in March-April, 1966.

IDEOLOGICAL FOUNDATIONS OF POLICY

All of us Communists are united by the great Marxist-Leninist ideas. The source of our Party's strength and invincibility lies in its indestructible ideological and organizational cohesion.

—N. S. Khrushchev

THE THEORETICAL FOUNDATIONS OF COEXISTENCE

II

THE NATION-STATE system sets the stage on which the foreign policy of any country's decision-makers must be acted. The way a nation's decision-makers interpret international events, the objectives they hope to attain, and the methods they are prepared to use in order to attain them are fundamental elements of the policy process. The Soviet policy-makers express their interpretation of world affairs, enunciate their objectives, and justify their methods in the terminology of Marxism-Leninism. Any analysis of Soviet behavior in foreign affairs would be incomplete and possibly misleading without consideration of the theoretical basis of the general strategy pursued by the Soviet elite and the role of theory in maintaining the stability of the system.

The extent to which Leninist theory clarifies or confuses analyses of Soviet foreign policy depends largely on interpretation of the role that Marxism-Leninism plays in the Soviet system. Sovietologists are not agreed among themselves on what role or combination of roles official doctrine performs.[1] Since it has not been possible to conduct extensive interviews with the members of the Soviet elite, there has been no way to determine with great confidence the precise significance of Communist thought on the formulation of public policy and on the general values common in the system. At this point we can only set forth a tentative hypothesis concerning the role of theory and ideology in the Soviet Union.

In the first place, Marxism-Leninism may be interpreted as cognitive theory providing to its adherents a rational, though not necessarily accurate, frame of reference. In this sense Marxism-Leninism is understood as basically a dialectic of history which contains tools of analysis for interpreting societal developments. The principal utility of this theory is that it gives decision-makers a framework within which they may analyze developments of the past, present, and future. The very act of decision-making within this framework is a theoretical as well as an operational act, for, by definition, there is unity between theory and action. To the extent, then, that every act of the Soviet elite is justified on theoretical grounds Marxism-Leninism may be construed as the conceptual framework within which this justification is formed. If theory and action are, in fact, treated as one, there is no way to assess to what extent Marxism-Leninism as an operational code limits the range of alternative courses of action considered by policy-makers who justify their choices as validations of the theory. This means that in practice cognitive theory is married to normative theory, thereby complicating the task of analyzing the functions of either aspect.

Marxism-Leninism, therefore, has ideological as well as cognitive functions. Ideology is interpreted here as the normative theory of the Soviet system. As ideology, Marxism-Leninism takes the form of an elaborately constructed system of beliefs that provides the basic norms of behavior for individuals and groups operating under its precepts. In this capacity, the normative part of Leninism verbalizes the basic values that are set forth as guidelines for behavior and as general goal directives. Acceptance of the vanguard role of the Party, the value assigned to labor, the kind of social responsibility emphasized, and the norms governing intergroup relations are some of the products of the normative theory contained in Soviet Leninism. These may be designated as *functional norms.* They perform two kinds of integrative tasks. First, they help to integrate the operational units of the social and economic system. Second, they have the function of assuring the synthesis of new or revised values in the theoretical structure. As integrative devices, functional norms serve as system-stabilizing mechanisms for the whole social structure.

Illustrative of this factor is the close association of normative theory in the Soviet system with the processes of political socialization and legitimation. In fact, the role of ideology most widely agreed on by students of the Soviet Union is the functional use of Marxism-Leninism as an instrument of control over the general population. In this regard there are actually two levels of primary communications in which the ideology plays a paramount role. First, the normative aspects of Marxism-Leninism are used to indoctrinate the Soviet citizen, teaching him to accept the values of the social and political system. Similarly, ideology is employed as a means of regulating the behavior of groups (military, bureaucrats, peasants, etc.) that perform functional roles in the system. Such regulation is often accomplished by prescribing the legitimate goals and procedures of groups in ideological terms. Threats to the stability of the regime are reduced, at least in part, by reliance on the integrative power of effective propaganda, which in turn is predicated on the normative values expressed in the vocabulary of the Marxist-Leninist lexicon.

Second, both the normative and the cognitive aspects of Leninism play a major role in the communications network, especially at the higher levels in the power structure. Marxism-Leninism provides a vocabulary for political discussion to a much greater and more precise extent than was once thought possible. One of the major reasons, if not *the* major reason, for sending high party and state officials to schools of Marxism-Leninism is to train them in semantics derived from the theory. In these schools they learn how to engage in debates over policy through subtle changes in words and word order of what often appear to be stereotyped phrases of Party doctrine. In this way extensive discussion of policy problems is usually successfully restricted to those few who are skilled in the semantic usages of Marxist-Leninist words and phrases.

Whether or not Leninism serves as the major determinant of the decisions reached by the Soviet elite, normative theory is something which the rulers cannot do without. It is a device that helps them to remain in power. This reliance on ideology as a stabilizing factor greatly strains the long-range viability of cognitive as well as normative theory. Except for the members of the higher echelons of Party, state, and group organs, knowledge of alternative policies and interpretations must be kept at a minimum for reasons of internal control. Also, the theory must be accepted and applied with what at least appears to be a great degree of consistency, for if it is changed too drastically or too often, the professed creed may cease to be applicable at all and become little more than verbal baggage.

The scope and usage of Leninism in the Soviet system predestine it to include inconsistencies in theoretical statements and to be subject to conflicting interpretations. However, the purpose here is neither to consider the contradictions within the body of Leninist theory nor to reconstruct its principal tenets in detail. Rather, it is to attempt to recreate the general tenor, the tone, of Leninism as it was developed by a man who deemed himself the architect of revolution in a time of revolutionary ferment. The changes in the Leninism professed by the Soviet leaders of the post-Stalin era can then be placed in better perspective.

THE REVOLUTIONARY PAST

Lenin placed great emphasis on the importance of theory as a guide for revolutionary practice. "Without a revolutionary theory there can be no revolutionary movement," he wrote in *What Is To Be Done?* Theory is necessary for the maintenance of unity within the movement. Although Stalin's reliance on personal dictatorship probably reduced the influence of the cognitive aspects of Marxism within the Party, he earnestly affirmed Lenin's belief that theory

> alone, can give the movement confidence, the power of orientation, and an understanding of the inherent connection between surrounding events; for it, and it alone, can help practice to discern not only how and in which direction classes are moving at the present time, [but] also how and in which direction they will move in the near future.[2]

In Marxist-Leninist terminology, theory, therefore, is the expression of reality that guides those who have a scientific understanding of the course of history in choosing actions that will promote the end of history—communism. Theory and practice are conceived as one, not as separate entities. Theory is reality.

The political significance of this concept is that it plays both a unifying and a directing role for the whole movement within which the party—the one organ deemed capable of determining what is real—serves as the official interpreter and provides the discipline to enforce its acceptance. Theory thus becomes an instrument of party control, for that select group alone can correctly understand the course of history and thereby assure the ultimate victory of the Communist movement. It was only natural that, as theory was put into practice by this technique, patterns were set in motion that eventually transformed Leninism, by its own definition, into an ideology which provided the party apparatus the rationalization needed to justify its existence and to increase its power in a campaign to restructure and modernize Russian society. In short, the normative value system was partly the outgrowth of cognitive theory.

Rigid conformity to the ends of the revolution not only permitted but required Lenin to repudiate all conventional ethics and morality that might retard the revolutionary process. Since the goals were all-important, morality had to be made subordinate to them. According to Lenin, "morality consists entirely of united discipline and conscious mass struggle against the exploiters."[3] Morality is, therefore, determined by submission to a disciplined movement and by unquestioning loyalty to the goals of Communism as they are defined at any given moment. This view permitted great flexibility in the methods of attaining communism while, at the same time, it demanded complete acceptance of the ultimate aims.

The ability of his followers to effect the proper combination of dogmatism and flexibility was of particular concern to Lenin. While expecting Communists to be steadfast in their loyalty to the ideas and spirit of the official doctrine, he warned them that they must never allow ideology to become a political straitjacket, a vise in which flexibility of tactics had to be sacrificed to dogma. They must have the political sagacity, he insisted, to know when to take "two steps backward" in the interest of the ultimate realization of that doctrine. According to the tenets of "creative Marxism," the "strictest loyalty to the ideas of the Communist must be combined with the ability to make all the necessary practical compromises. . . ."[4]

Among the most important theoretical concepts to which the "strictest loyalty" is demanded are the class struggle and its international implications. Relying on Marx's theory of the emergence of antagonistic classes under capitalism, Lenin and Stalin considered the great conflict of modern history to be the struggle between the proletariat and the bourgeoisie, the exploited and the exploiting classes. Capitalism itself was described in simplistic fashion as a system in which the owners of the means of production were in a position to exploit the workers. Capitalism contained the seeds of its own decay, however, for the proletariat would grow whereas the number of capitalists would decline until the struggle ended in the victory of the proletariat. Marxism-Leninism is characterized by the glorification of the proletariat over other social classes and by belief in the inevitable rise of the workers to a position of numerical and moral dominance in the social and economic structure of society. This proposition logically led to the expectation that nationalism as a conscious emotional force would eventually be replaced by a class consciousness that would transcend national loyalties and spark the growth of a truly international movement.

Lenin, however, had one great reservation about the virtues of the working class that Marx had not been prepared to accept. Economic status alone, he argued, was not sufficient to make the proletariat aware of its revolutionary potential in spite of the capitalists' exploitation of the workers. In *What Is To Be Done?* he argued that without leadership workers are capable of developing only "trade-union consciousness." Socialism has to be brought to them from the outside. "A small, compact core, consisting of reliable, experienced and hardened workers" must organize into a highly centralized party capable of operating in "strict secrecy." The party becomes the vanguard of the proletariat, acting in its behalf as the most class-conscious part of the working class. The vanguard is the instigator of revolutionary action, the political leader of the workers, and the official protector and interpreter of the Marxist creed. It is above all a party of the proletariat capable of waging "a class struggle for socialism even against the most democratic and republican bourgeoisie. . . ."[5]

Making another adaptation of Marxism, Lenin contended that sympathetic nonproletarian elements in society should be drawn into the revolutionary picture in order to increase the popular support of the movement. Aware of the potential power of the peasantry in Russia, Lenin argued that peasants had much in common with the proletariat and insisted that it was the duty of the Bolsheviks to support "unequivocally" the revolutionary struggle of any section of the peasantry.[6] The party, Stalin claimed after his assault on the kulaks, must "rely on the proletarian and semi-proletarian strata of the rural population. . . ."[7] To broaden the spectrum even further, the "progressive" bourgeoisie and the "revolutionary" intelligentsia could be made the allies of the proletariat. But whatever alliances the vanguard party made, the aim remained the same—victory in the class struggle and destruction of the capitalist system.

In Marxist-Leninist thought there are actually two revolutions which are expected to occur in the modern world and in which the proletariat plays different roles. In the semifeudal and backward countries where capitalism has never fully developed, a bourgeois or national revolution is normally expected to precede the socialist revolution. As a means of quickening the revolutionary pace, the proletariat was encouraged by Lenin to work in the bourgeois revolution and wrest the leadership from the bourgeoisie at the opportune moment. Fearing that this tactic might be interpreted by some as reformism, Lenin carefully spelled out the purpose of proletarian participation as part of the class struggle. The intent was to develop the class conflict "by extending its scope, its consciousness, organization and resoluteness." He insisted that

> Marxism teaches the proletarian not to keep aloof from the bourgeois revolution, not to be indifferent to it, and to allow the leadership of the revolution to be assumed by the bourgeoisie but, on the contrary, to take a most energetic part in it, to fight most resolutely for consistent proletarian democratism, for the revolution to be carried to its conclusion.[8]

Hence the first task is to overthrow the established order and then to weaken the position of the new leadership.

Once the bourgeois revolution has been completed, the principal task is to move as swiftly as possible toward the triumph of the socialist revolution. All of the energy of the restive masses must be exploited. After all, Lenin asserted, "revolutions are festivals of the oppressed and the exploited." The proletarian party must direct the revolutionary energy of the populace into the most propitious channels, using whatever tactics are necessary to take the power of the state from the bourgeoisie.

Approaching the question from the viewpoint of the committed revolutionist with an unbending distrust of capitalism, Lenin did not envision the possibility of any capitalist state surrendering its political power peacefully in the transition from bourgeois democracy to proletarian dictatorship. He wrote, in 1917, that "the substitution of a proletarian for the capitalist State is impossible without a violent revolution. . . ." To make this point emphatically clear, Lenin insisted that the phrase "the inevitable violent revolution" be taken literally, by explaining that its use was "by no means a mere 'impulse,' a mere declamation or a mere polemical sally. The security of systematically fostering among the masses this and only this point of view about violent revolution lies at the root of the whole of Marx's and Engels' teaching."[9] Furthermore, the coming of the revolution was no longer dependent on the ripeness of capitalism. The revolutionary elite, organized into the highly disciplined party of the workers and peasants, could hasten the arrival of the Communist victory. Knowing the objective laws of history, not only could the vanguard undertake action, but it was its duty to bring about the downfall of bourgeois democracy. Political consciousness, as the result of such tactics, became more important than economic development in Leninist theory and practice.

Significantly, Stalin did not change the tone of violence in his interpretation of the transition to socialism. The only method of attaining political power which Communist parties could rely on, he argued, was revolution. The dialectical process made it clear that "revolutions made by oppressed classes are a quite natural and inevitable phenomenon." As a result of this, he contended that "the transition from capitalism to socialism and the liberation of the working class from the yoke of capitalism cannot be effected by slow changes, by reforms, but only by a qualitative change of the capitalist system, by revolution."[10] This emphasis on violence was softened during the 1930's when the Comintern promoted participation in popular fronts as a means of averting Nazi aggression. However, after the second world war Soviet pronouncements and ideological works resumed the martial fervor of Leninism by insisting even more strongly that "violent overthrow" be considered a "general law of the Socialist Revolution."[11]

Marxist-Leninist theory, therefore, clearly forecasts an inevitable progression of qualitative changes in the world, each change resulting in a higher stage replacing a lower one. Qualitative change is considered the result of the revolutionary transfer of power from one social class to another. In the modern epoch, which is seen as a struggle between the ruling classes of capitalist states and the socialist system of states, each revolution is but a stage in the global transition to an international Communist system. Consequently, the revolutionary theory of orthodox Marxism-Leninism places emphasis on the international character of the class struggle.

While the class struggle within capitalist states would lead to the inevitable violent overthrow of the exploiters, the international class struggle assumed increasing importance as a result of international trends set in motion by the capitalist system itself. Lenin's views on this subject were first elaborated on extensively in his work, *Imperialism, the Highest Stage of Capitalism*. The purpose of this study was twofold: to explain the reasons for the continued rise of capitalism, contrary to the expectations of Marx, and to explain the causes of World War I. Probably no theory has served more as a justification of Soviet actions in the international arena than Lenin's interpretation of the international significance of modern capitalism.

Capitalism, Lenin contended, had found a way to delay the

inevitable revolutionary breakdown that would result from the contradictions within it. This way was paved by the growth of monopolies and the development of finance capitalism. "The coalescence of bank and industrial capital . . . and . . . a transformation of the banks into institutions of a truly 'universal character' " results in the establishment of international financial oligarchies which, in turn, result in imperialism. Industrial monopolies superimposed themselves on the system of competitive enterprises. In order to organize production on a more rational basis and to protect their interests from the uncertainties of the competitive market, the owners of industry are compelled to join forces through cartels, syndicates, and trusts. This union of effort requires an increasing reliance on money capital. The principal agent in supplying this capital is the bank. Under the old form of capitalism, the most common feature was the export of goods. Now the main export is capital. The appearance of this type of finance capitalism is greatly facilitated by the manner in which banks could manage capital investments in monopolies, on both a national and an international scale. The international character of this development becomes more manifest as internal crises increase and the rate of profit declines. The monopoly capitalists then seek to direct their compliant governments into helping them obtain new markets abroad. When referring to the purely economic aspect of imperialism, Lenin used the term "finance capitalism." The alliance of monopolies and government, however, he gave the name of "state-monopoly capitalism." It was under this alliance of government and monopoly that capitalist states had begun to develop their foreign markets peacefully by dividing the world into spheres of influence and by the acquisition of colonies. Soon there is a "crystallisation of a small number of financially 'powerful' states from among all the rest." These states, having been successful in their economic and territorial expansion, are able to postpone their inevitable revolutionary destruction.

The emphasis on the economic and political division of the

world is highly significant to Lenin's theory. The establishment of trusts with international interests has the effect of drawing an economic division of the world in the form of spheres of influence and exclusive trade agreements. These developments signify the intensification of competition between rival economic groups of capitalist states. However, Lenin strongly stressed the importance of the political division that is already completed. Capitalist governments readily make political alliances with other states that will increase the profits and advance the security of their own investors. Therefore, while economic monopolies are the original villains, politics becomes the principal means for conducting the impending struggle.

Monopoly has been fed by colonialism, Lenin argued. In order to sustain itself, it must, not from choice but from necessity, intensify its appetite for greater economic advantage through expanding its colonial empires in an era of bitter international competition. The conflicts over redistribution of colonial possessions can be resolved in only one way—by war. In Lenin's words,

> Imperialism is the epoch of finance capital and of monopolies, which introduce everywhere the striving for domination, not for freedom. The result of these tendencies is reaction all along the line, whatever the political system, and an extreme intensification of existing antagonism in this domain also. Particularly acute becomes the yoke of national oppression and the striving for annexations, *i.e.*, the violation of national independence.[12]

War resulting from these antagonisms signifies that capitalism has reached its highest and last stage—imperialism. Capitalism had laid the groundwork for its own overthrow by transferring competition from a free domestic economy to the realm of world politics, where there is little restraint on the activities of nation-states. In order to arrive at the Communist utopia, it is necessary to understand the existing laws of the hostile world—the world as it is juxtaposed against the world as it ought to be.

The theories of class struggle, revolution, and imperialism provide the key to that understanding of orthodox Leninism.

Buttressed by the conviction of the imperialistic and militaristic nature of the capitalist countries, Lenin and Stalin persistently avowed that only the violent upheaval of the governments of imperialist states and global Communist victory could assure world peace and the long-term security of the Soviet Union. Although aware of the importance of national sentiments, Lenin kept as his ideal the dictatorship of the world proletariat that could recognize, in Stalin's words, "that national autonomy is contrary to the whole course of the class struggle."[13] This world dictatorship, the Communist International declared at its Sixth Congress,

> can be established only when the victory of socialism has been achieved in certain countries or groups of countries, when the newly established proletarian republics enter into a federal union with already existing proletarian republics, when the number of such federations has grown and extended also to the colonies which have emancipated themselves from the yoke of imperialism and when these federations of republics have grown finally into a World Union of Soviet Socialist Republics uniting the whole of mankind under the hegemony of the international proletariat organized as a State.[14]

The political goal was, then, the federation of all countries and the transference of loyalties from national states to an international social and economic system.

While aspiring to foment world revolution, however, both of the first two Soviet dictators found it necessary to recognize the continuing impact of the nation-state as the basic unit in international politics and to undertake measures to safeguard the security of the Soviet state. Indeed, in the absence of world revolution and with the decision to build "socialism in one country," the national security of that state assumed paramount importance, not only to the Russians, but to the Communist movement as an international phenomenon.

Addressing the Seventh All-Russian Congress in 1919, Lenin laid the theoretical basis for Soviet foreign policy by emphasizing the "fundamental antagonisms between the capitalist and socialist systems." The Russian Republic, he warned, must expect and be prepared for another intervention from the West. While domestic industrialization was being undertaken to build up the strength of the Soviet Union, the Kremlin strategists were instructed to concentrate on supporting other national Communist parties in a united endeavor to undermine the strength of capitalist countries. Lenin predicted that the next era would usher in a transitional stage of history marked by wars and revolutions. In the midst of these upheavals, the Soviet state had to be prepared to defend itself and to direct the individual parties of the Communist movement in a coordinated effort to further the cause of revolution without endangering Soviet national security.

This situation caused Lenin to expand his concept of war. He had long asserted that wars between capitalist states were inevitable. Now, with the existence of a Communist state in their midst, he extended this theory to apply to relations between states with different social systems. Speaking to the Eighth Congress of the Communist Party in 1919, he predicted that "a series of frightful collisions between the Soviet Republic and the bourgeois states will be inevitable." In order to forestall this inevitable war until his country grew stronger, Lenin, and Stalin after him, advocated making minor accommodations with Western nations. True to his revolutionary commitment, however, Lenin was careful not to give the impression that a lasting accord could be reached between capitalist and communist states. "It would be a mistake to think that concessions will mean peace," he warned, for the new policy merely represented "a new form of war." Even though the change from the military to the economic battlefront might bring some "indirect guarantee of peace," Lenin insisted that "we have not forgotten that war will return again. While capitalism and socialism exist, they cannot live in peace; either one or the other, in the last analysis, will be victorious; either a requiem will be sung over the Soviet Republic, or over world capitalism."[15]

It was in this context that the term "peaceful coexistence" came into use to describe the tactic advocated by Lenin. To him as well as to Stalin, the guarantee of the final victory of Communism required that the Soviet Union design its policy to postpone the inevitable conflict until Communist states had become sufficiently strong and sufficiently dominant to enforce their will on the rest of the world. There is more than ample documentary evidence to refute Khrushchev's contention that Lenin envisioned coexistence as either a theoretical or a long-term strategic concept. His own words and those of the Comintern repeatedly declared that coexistence was "merely—under present conditions—a more advantageous form of fighting capitalism." The peace policy of the U.S.S.R., the Comintern declared in 1928,

> rallies all the allies of the proletarian dictatorship around its banner and provides the best basis for taking advantage of the antagonisms among the imperialist states. The aim of this policy is to guard the international revolution and to protect the work of building up socialism—the progress of which is revolutionizing the world. It strives to put off the conflict with imperialism for as long as possible.[16]

In an interview with Harold Stassen in 1947, Stalin noted that, while he believed cooperation between the two systems was possible, there did exist "capitalist encirclement and danger of attack on the U.S.S.R. If one party does not wish to cooperate then that means that there exists a threat of attack."[17] The burden of cooperation was, therefore, placed on the capitalist side by Stalin's interpretation of coexistence. The first two heads of the Soviet Republic accepted the tactic of coexistence as a necessary expedient in Soviet foreign policy that permitted them to cooperate with capitalist states in order to advance the internal economic construction of the U.S.S.R. or when the safety of the Russian nation was in jeopardy. In spite of the significance the tactic assumed during the popular front period of the late 1930's and during World War II, the concept was never construed as a permanent feature of Communist ideology; it was only a tactical device.[18]

Temporary coexistence with the capitalist states dampened revolutionary enthusiasm but by no means drowned it entirely. After accepting the possibly disastrous consequences that a military confrontation with the Western powers might have had on the Soviet Union and the world revolutionary movement, Lenin and his successor turned their eyes toward the colonial empires of the East as the objects of immediate revolutionary expansion. While continuing to believe that the West would eventually become the heart of a socialist world, Lenin became convinced that the path to revolution in the advanced capitalist states lay in the East.[19] The theoretical justification for this view was found in implicit form in Lenin's theory of imperialism. Imperialist countries exported capital to colonial possessions in order to industrialize them. This in turn gave birth to a working class in the semifeudal areas of the world. But rather than assuring the stability of capitalism, imperialism merely intensifies the class struggle by making it truly international. Monopoly had fed its appetite for greater economic advantage by expanding its colonial empires. By their own action monopolies had made the class struggle a truly international phenomenon. What better way to weaken the capitalist states of the West existed than to undermine their position in their colonies and deprive them of that important economic advantage?

As Lenin saw it, imperialism had succeeded in temporarily stifling the class struggle in the great capitalist countries but had accentuated that struggle in the underdeveloped nations.

These backward lands had come to fulfill a role corresponding to that of the workers in classical capitalism. They had become the exploited. In his report to the Second Congress of the Communist International in July, 1920, Lenin explained the importance of this development to the cause of revolution.

> The imperialist war has helped the revolution; the bourgeoisie tore soldiers out of the colonies, out of backward countries, out of isolation, in order to take part in this imperialist war. . . . The imperialist war has drawn the dependent peoples into world history. And one of the most important tasks that confronts us now is to ponder over how the foundation-stone of the organization of the Soviet movement can be laid in the non-capitalist countries. Soviets are possible in those countries; they will not be Workers' Soviets, but Peasants' Soviets, or Soviets of Toilers.

The bourgeois and the proletarian revolutions could be telescoped into one, following the Russian example, by having the workers join the movements of national liberation in the underdeveloped and oppressed nations. Not only would this strategy provide a theoretical justification of Bolshevik behavior, but it would help transform the Communist movement into a powerful force for modernization.

Lenin took particular care to stress to his followers that conflict within the "backward" countries was much more complicated than in the more advanced countries of the West. The struggle of the proletariat against the bourgeoisie grows simultaneously with the struggle of caste against caste, peasants against landlords, nationality against nationality, and bourgeoisie against the traditional rulers who align themselves with the imperialists. In the West such conflicts had occurred in different stages. In backward areas they had been superimposed on each other simultaneously by the transplantation of modern industrial society resulting from the policies of the imperialist powers. Marxism, Lenin held, could provide the leaders of these backward countries with the direction necessary to carry their national revolutions to promising socialist conclusions.

The crystallization of this concept in Lenin's mind had a profound bearing on his perspective of Russia. Since industrialization in the U.S.S.R. was being imposed on a peasant society by the Communists, Lenin realized that for the time being the Russian experience could prove little or nothing to the advanced countries in the West. Instead, it could serve as a model for nations in the incipient throes of industrialization. It could form a bridge between the East and the West. In fact, in his report to the Second Congress of the Comintern, Lenin went so far as to declare that with the aid of the proletariat of the advanced countries, the underdeveloped nations could "pass to the Soviet system and, after passing through a definite stage of development, to Communism, without passing through the capitalist stage of development." Thus Lenin set the stage for Communist concentration on producing revolutions in underdeveloped nations.

Although Stalin's directives to Communist parties in colonial and backward countries greatly exaggerated the role and strength of the workers and underestimated the power of an organized peasantry, his writings and public statements on colonialism reflect the same recognition of the necessity of highly flexible revolutionary tactics in these areas that was seen by Lenin.[20] Stalin, however, did not heed his own advice. His leadership of the Communist movement in colonial areas was notably unsuccessful. Military miscalculations and failure to attract a large segment of the restive peasantry into the revolution as Lenin had advocated resulted in serious setbacks for the Soviet-led parties in China in 1927 and in India, Malaya, and several countries of the Middle East after World War II. Stalin did not alter the theoretical and strategic precepts set forth by Lenin on the colonial question, but he failed to recognize the more subtle implications of the theoretical framework developed by Lenin.

Under Lenin the Communist Party showed a remarkable capacity for theoretical adaptation and innovation. Remaining true to most of the broad principles of Marxist-Leninist thought, the Bolsheviks could still accommodate a wide variety of tactics and strategies. Lenin had in particular an extraordinary genius for making modifications in theory to meet the demands of new conditions. The inclusion of the peasantry in the ranks of the revolutionary movement, the theory of imperialism, the effort to bring revolution to the West through colonial revolts in the East, and the peculiarly Bolshevist interpretation of nationalism all demonstrated Lenin's willingness to adapt new precepts of prescriptive theory and strategy. To him political theory was an organic instrument and could never be compressed in its entirety between the covers of books. The debates over broad policy designs in the early years of the Soviet regime were, to Lenin, debates over cognitive theory. The aim of theory was practical in nature—the development of an analytical framework from which operational designs could be created. The momentum of the revolutionary movement in the few years he served as head of the Soviet state enabled him to continue to make the classical Marxist distinction between theory and ideology.

With the gradual loss of the initial zeal and Stalin's increasing exercise of personal power, the Stalinist era witnessed the gradual convergence of theory and ideology. The cognitive and prescriptive aspects of Communist theory became indistinct from the descriptive nature of the ideology, which had become a crucially important means of controlling potentially powerful groups in Soviet society as well as an instrument designed to control the thought processess of the ordinary citizen. The doctrinal adaptability and the party debates on questions of theory that had been so characteristic of the Lenin period slowly disappeared from practice as an era of intellectual dullness set in. Such important developments as the breakup of colonial empires and the establishment of Communist regimes in eastern Europe and Asia did not result either in new theoretical clarifications or in consistent application of the formally enunciated theory. The significance of the growing tide of nationalism in the underdeveloped areas of the world was often underestimated and sometimes completely overlooked. Stalin's failure to recognize the import of these changes in the postwar world left his successors in an ideological quandary. To them fell the responsibility of making what had become known as Leninism more amenable to the new conditions existing in the second half of the twentieth century.

By the end of the Stalin period the theory and practice of Soviet foreign policy had developed two striking and contradictory characteristics. The zealous revolutionary tone of Lenin still existed and found expression not only in public statements and official party and government documents but in the establishment of the Cominform, in the network of espionage and subversion, and in the ill-conceived efforts to stage revolutions in supposedly vulnerable underdeveloped countries. On the other hand, the acceptance of "socialism in one country" and the gradual linking of the revolutionary movement with Russian national interest engendered a defensive attitude on the part of the Kremlin strategists. This feeling was greatly exacerbated by those tenets of Leninist theory that purported to explain the nature of imperialism and the behavior of capitalist states. Every strategy was adopted as a form of struggle against the enemy as defined by theory. While leaders of the great revolutions in the West have not ordinarily been defensive in attitude, in Soviet Russia internal historical development, cultural environment, and international conditions combined to bestow upon Soviet Communists a defensive mentality that has often bordered on the paranoiac. Theoretical concepts undoubtedly played a significant role in effecting this condition. By the time of Stalin's death the Soviet Union had developed a clear case of schizophrenia—a compulsion toward universalism countered by a highly zealous concern for the vital interests of the Soviet Republic.

THE DEVOLUTION OF REVOLUTIONARY THEORY

Under Khrushchev, ample opportunities existed for the formal elaboration of changes in Marxist-Leninist doctrine. In the first place, three Party Congresses were held within the short span of a mere six years. Of these, the 20th Congress in 1956 was the most momentous in regard to ideological and theoretical problems. Not only was the formal repudiation of Stalin announced, but innovations in the theories of the transition to socialism and the inevitability of war were officially made. The 21st Congress in 1959 was basically Khrushchev's personal affair, affording him an opportunity to demonstrate his firm grip on the party machinery. The announcement of the Seven-Year Plan heralded a stepped-up reliance on economic factors in the struggle between Communism and capitalism as the Soviet Premier stressed the importance of economic growth as the key to achieving superiority over the United States during the era of peaceful coexistence. The 22nd Congress in 1961 was the natural, though delayed, sequel to the de-Stalinization campaign begun in 1956. It also served as the platform for hailing the adoption of the new Party Program. In addition, leaders of Communist parties throughout the world met in 1957 and 1960. Finally, a major conference on ideological problems was held at the Marx-Engels-Lenin Institute in 1961 under the supervision of the Central Committee of the C.P.S.U.

In varying degrees, all of these events included efforts to

clarify or to amend Communist theory and strategy in order to make them conform more realistically to contemporary circumstances. Evidence stemming from these meetings and other sources indicates that the Kremlin is well aware of the importance of ideology as an instrument of control over the Russian populace and as a necessary means to rationalize and justify the existence of the Soviet system. The major question for Khrushchev and the Soviet regime was whether or not the changes would be great enough to meet the demands of new conditions without being so great that they might undermine the authority of the party and the government.

Throughout his tenure as head of the C.P.S.U., Khrushchev stressed the theme of "the return to Leninism" as the way to restore the ideological vigor and the revolutionary élan of the early Bolshevik period. Much effort went into a concerted attempt to invigorate the party and other institutions through reorganization and renewed concern for ideological questions. Assailing the anti-party group of Molotov, Kaganovich, and Malenkov in his concluding speech to the 22nd Party Congress, Khrushchev insisted that Stalinist methods of leadership be "resolutely" rejected and reminded his comrades that "the Party's strongest weapon is its ideology. . . ." This approach was incorporated into the new Party Program, which was designed to lead the C.P.S.U. along the only correct course, "the course of the restoration and further development of Leninist norms of Party and state life, the course of raising the leading role of the Party and the creative activeness of the popular masses. . . ."[21]

In spite of this professed concern with Leninist theory, the extent to which Khrushchev was genuinely interested in Leninism *as theory* is open to question. On February 3, 1959, *Pravda* claimed that Molotov's attack on Khrushchev in June, 1957, included the accusation that the First Secretary was guilty of "practicism and utilitarianism." This suggests that the old guard thought that Khrushchev merely used the jargon of Leninism as a doctrinal veil to conceal his empiricism as well as his attraction to experimental schemes. The aforementioned references to Khrushchev's concern with Leninism indicate that he was more conscious of the ideological than of the theoretical facets of Communist thought. In his secret speech at the close of the 20th Party Congress, Khrushchev's most violent attack on the former Soviet ruler centered on the effect that arbitrary personal leadership had on the Party and the morale of the people. He accused Stalin of abandoning the "method of ideological struggle for that of administrative violence, mass repressions and terror."[22] In order to combat this aspect of Stalinism, Khrushchev announced that the cult of the individual must be abolished once and for all and a re-examination of the relationship of ideology to practical work must be undertaken. This could be accomplished only by a return to "the most important theses of Marxist-Leninist science" concerned with the role of the people and the party in the transformation of society and the victory of Communism.

In the program of returning to Leninism, Khrushchev attempted to emphasize the dynamic aspects of Communist thought rather than the fixed stereotypes of dogma and strategy. In his heralded address before party workers at the Institute of Marxist-Leninism in 1961, the Soviet Premier noted that the Party was able to lead the U.S.S.R. in the construction of Communism precisely because it treated Marxism-Leninism as a "creative, constantly developing doctrine."[23] With this attitude, the Khrushchev regime embarked on a re-examination of ideological precepts that resulted in slightly modifying some of the tenets of official doctrine and producing significant innovations in others. In effect, Khrushchev rendered Lenin's theory of inevitable war nonoperational, thereby striking out one of the cardinal principles of the cognitive theory of Leninism as it related to Soviet foreign policy.

Ideological tenets with a high degree of continuity

The Marxist-Leninist goal of completely remaking society has always included the assumption that morality is a product of the economic structure at any given stage of history. Morality reflects the values resulting from that economic basis. The Khrushchev regime continued to embrace this traditional Communist view by drawing a distinction between bourgeois and socialist morality. Soviet statements repeatedly claim that Communism fosters a new type of human relationship in both the private and the social context. They further claim that the Soviet experience proves that "human nature can be refashioned, that the new man, the new mentality and morality, are not myths but realities." Whatever governmental policy enhances the development of this "new man" and the achievement of a communist society is considered an appropriate course of action.[24] The theory has clearly not been altered, but in post-Stalin Russia the practical implementation of highly flexible strategic and tactical policy measures has been hampered by different opinions concerning just what attributes of character this new man should have.

Another major doctrinal concept which has remained relatively unaltered concerns the relationship between the proletariat and the party. Following the orthodox Leninist pattern, the leadership of the workers in the class struggle continues to be vested in Communist parties. At the 20th Party Congress Khrushchev declared that whatever the form of the transition to socialism, "the decisive and indispensable factor is the political leadership of the working class headed by its vanguard." The 1961 Party Program also reaffirmed the conviction that Communist parties alone are the vanguard of the world revolutionary movement. Consequently, there has not been any significant deviation from the view set forth by Lenin in *What*

Is To Be Done? While the character and higher organization of the party have been reshaped under Khrushchev, the theoretical premises from which it operates have not been revised.

Perhaps the most constant feature of Communist thought has been the interpretation given imperialism and the foreign policies of capitalist states. It is one of the cardinal principles of Marxism-Leninism that a state's external policy can only be an expression of the correlation of its internal economic, political, and social forces. The current stage of imperialism is known today, as in Lenin's time, as state-monopoly capitalism. Communist interpretations label this development "profoundly reactionary" and claim that it is based on "militarization." The union of monopolies and the state has two ends: to prolong the existence of the capitalist system and "to provide enrichment to the monopolies with the help of government by means of the redistribution of national incomes."[25] The activity of the state in economic matters is not able to change the nature of imperialism. The new Party Program warns that it only widens the gap between the interests of labor and capital, between the majority and the owners of monopolies.

With N.A.T.O. confronting any Soviet drive into western Europe, the U.S.S.R. had no real alternative, short of war, to focusing attention on the newer and less developed nations of Asia, Africa, and Latin America. The drive to draw newly developing nations under Soviet influence required a plausible theoretical explanation for the relatively voluntary dismantling of colonial empires by the "imperialists." The Kremlin's interpretation was in the form of a simple rationalization: because of the power of the Communist states and their support of national liberation movements, the imperialist powers found themselves compelled to grant "political" independence to many of their colonies.[26] The imperialists, however, have developed new forms of domination. Aid programs and Western-owned industries are used to plant capitalism on the soil of former colonies.

The struggle for liberation shifts to the economic sphere, where imperialists still attempt to exploit underdeveloped lands. Therefore decolonization is "false and hypocritical," for only the forms, not the substance, of classical colonialism are thought to have changed.

Nevertheless, the crisis of capitalism has been sharpened by the disintegration of the colonial system. The achievement of independence by former colonies has gradually reduced the noncompetitive markets depended on by the imperialists. Consequently, there has been an intensification of economic competition among the remaining capitalist countries. According to the 1960 Declaration of Communist Parties, "the narrower the sphere of imperialist domination, the stronger the antagonisms between the imperialist powers." The growth of the socialist camp and of movements of national liberation is, therefore, thought to have the effect of hastening the inevitable destruction of the capitalist system by playing on the antagonisms inherent in it. The Western world is already bankrupt of ideas and dependent on negative slogans of anti-Communism. Eventually the West will be economically and politically bankrupt as well and a world socialist order will be established in its place.

It is interesting that in spite of this tendency to downgrade non-Communist economic systems and in spite of the distrust of and hostility toward capitalism, Khrushchev condemned Stalin at the 20th Party Congress for failing to take into account the technological progress made under capitalist systems. The idea of the "complete stagnation" of the capitalist economy is alien to true Marxism-Leninism, he claimed. Recalling passages from Lenin's works to substantiate his interpretation, Khrushchev pointedly remarked that the general decay of capitalism does not preclude technical progress. "We must study the capitalist economy attentively and not take a simplified view of Lenin's thesis of the decay of imperialism," he noted, "but study the best that the capitalist countries' science and technology have to offer in order to use the achievements of world technological progress in the interests of socialism." The thesis of the "bottling up of productive forces" was condemned as an "unscientific theory." The essence of the decay of capitalism was held to be not the failure to produce but the failure to provide a system of widespread utilization and distribution of the goods that are produced. This interpretation was given formal sanction by its incorporation into the new Party Program of the C.P.S.U.

Khrushchev's revisions of Leninism

Although the bulk of Leninist theory went without formal change, three important theoretical innovations were proclaimed officially at the 20th Party Congress in 1956, in order to bring the theory into line with the strategic design of peaceful coexistence. The Leninist emphasis on violence in the transition to socialism and on the inevitability of war was altered, along with Stalin's unbending insistence that the Soviet path to socialism was the only path. In all three instances changes in policy had already preceded the formal modifications in doctrine. Indeed, Stalin himself had implied in his last work, *Economic Problems of Socialism in the U.S.S.R.*, that war may no longer be inevitable, and Malenkov had hinted that this interpretation was the basis of his expressed fear that nuclear war could greatly damage the Soviet Union. However, whatever the background of the innovations, Khrushchev now insisted that all of the changes in Leninism were predicated, in theory at least, on an optimistic appraisal of the international significance of the growing military and economic strength of the Soviet Union.

After the successful launching of the first sputnik in the fall of 1957, confidence in the scientific, technological, and military strength of the Soviet Republic climbed rapidly. The spirit of certain victory generated by the accomplishments of this period was undoubtedly a factor in the formal burial of the theory of capitalist encirclement when the new Party Program was announced in February, 1961. On that occasion the Kremlin served notice to the West that it no longer had the power to compel the U.S.S.R. to live in isolation from the rest of the world, since the new alignment of international forces compelled the capitalist states to recognize the power and interests of the Soviet Union, the system of socialist states, and, to a lesser extent, the underdeveloped nations. Moscow claimed that it could now use its position to attempt to neutralize the countries around its perimeter. This campaign was accompanied by a heightened stress on anti-colonial, anti-imperialist propaganda and by efforts to weaken the alliance systems of the West and to create a neutral, atom-free buffer zone in central Europe.

The new assessment of the radical changes favoring the Communist states in the international balance of power prompted the new Soviet leadership to proclaim that new prospects had arisen in respect to the transition of countries to socialism. Lenin's thesis that violent revolution is inevitable in transforming a capitalist society into a socialist one was formally replaced by acceptance of the possibility of peaceful transition to socialism. It was small wonder that the Chinese Communists raised their eyebrows at the idea of a revolutionary movement demanding no revolution.

In altering the formerly fundamental tenet of Leninism, Khrushchev and Mikoyan carefully explained to the 20th Congress that a new correlation of forces existed in the world. The strength of the socialist camp, the influence of the peace campaign, and the present degree of organization and class consciousness of the working class were responsible for creating this new correlation. These conditions make it possible in a number of capitalist countries for the Communist parties and their allies "to gain power by peaceful means, using existing parliamentary institutions, without an armed uprising or civil war."

In toning down Lenin's emphasis on violence, Khrushchev attempted to produce a new formula that would help him to reach the long-denied rapprochement with socialist and leftist parties in the West and at the same time not alienate the old-line dogmatists within the Communist movement. While Mikoyan told the old-guard Communists at the Congress that "revolution—peaceful or otherwise—will always be revolution," Khrushchev emphatically denied to the socialist and leftist parties of non-Communist countries that "we regard violence and civil war as the only way to remake society." The forms of social revolution vary according to country and circumstance, he declared. Furthermore, since the modern proletariat will turn to arms only in defense of its own interests, according to Khrushchev, the responsibility for the use of violence must be levied on the "resistance of the exploiters" rather than on the revolutionaries. In addition, Soviet theoreticians have insisted that the possibility of "victorious peaceful socialist revolutions *in a number of capitalist countries*" is not predicated on the assumption that imperialism is changing its nature but on the basis of the preponderance of forces working for socialism and peace.[27]

Departing from Lenin's strong dislike of parliamentarism, Khrushchev also accepted the possibility of peaceful transition to socialism through the parliamentary method. Considering the present correlation of international forces, he argued that

> the working class, by rallying around itself the toiling peasantry, the intelligentsia, all patriotic forces, and resolutely repulsing the opportunist elements who are incapable of giving up the policy of compromise with the capitalist and landlords, is in a position to defeat the reactionary forces opposed to the popular interest, to capture a stable majority in parliament, and transform the latter from an organ of bourgeois democracy into a genuine instrument of the people's will. In such an event this institution, traditional in many highly developed capitalist countries, may become an organ of genuine democracy, democracy for the working people[28]

Subsequently, the view was even expressed that opposition parties could be permitted in a future Communist United States, since that country would no longer be encircled by capitalist states.[29] The recognition of the possibility of the use of legislative bodies to effect the transition to socialism allowed the popular front concept to be revived with the hope of employing democratic institutions to advance the expansion of Communism.

The possible ways of effecting the transition to socialism in underdeveloped states was a troublesome point for Soviet theoreticians for several years. During the Stalin period many leaders of national revolutions, such as Gandhi and Nehru, had been criticized for being lackeys of the imperialists. Those who were not clearly on the side of Communism were generally placed in the category of enemies of the revolution. In 1954-1955, Soviet policy shifted as Moscow began to court the favor of the leaders of the newly established governments through a series of personal exchanges of high-ranking dignitaries and the beginning of the Soviet foreign aid program. The shift in policy called for a shift in theory.

Khrushchev made general theoretical remarks concerning the status of the less developed states in his address before the 20th Party Congress in 1956, but the first thorough examination of the question came in an authoritative article published in *Kommunist* in December, 1956. V. Semyonov, the author, attempted to provide an elaborate theoretical statement of the status of former colonies and underdeveloped nations in general in the contemporary period of world history. Semyonov divided the former colonies into three groups, all between the two poles—the Soviet Union and the United States. In the first group, that closest to the U.S.S.R., were the states that have won "complete liberation"—China, North Korea, and Vietnam. The second group was composed of nations now possessing national independence and not participating "in military blocs with the colonial powers." This division included India, Indonesia, Egypt, Syria, Burma, and others. Undoubtedly this category has been enlarged since the publication of the article. Finally, there was a group of states with "formal state independence" but linked tightly to imperialist powers by "unequal treaties." The Philippines, South Korea, and Iran fell into this category. The "liberation" of the states in the first category and the "independence" of those in the second has been made possible, according to Semyonov, solely by the existence of the "powerful world system of socialist states." Their leaders may correspond to the bourgeois nationalists of Lenin's day, but in the present epoch they are the heads of national liberation revolutions which are distinctly "anti-imperialist" though not necessarily pro-Communist in character. They are progressive because they are transitional leaders in a revolutionary period that will have the function of weakening the imperialist camp by wrecking colonial empires.

Soviet analysts contend that there will be an eventual polarization of forces in the national liberation movements that will make it possible for the progressive forces to form a national front in which the working class will have a leading role.[30] These forces can direct their nations to socialism, bypassing the capitalist stage regardless of the level of their economic development, by depending on the assistance of the Communist states. This form of transitional state is labeled National Democracy and can be brought to completion only by conducting a "decisive struggle against imperialism and internal reactionary forces." In a National Democracy the state sector of the economy is large and plays a progressive role, agricultural cooperatives are developed, and efforts are made to construct heavy industry. The socialist and general democratic tasks of the national liberation forces are held to be closely interwoven in the attempt to achieve these goals. The traditional Stalinist opposition to nationalism was abandoned to the point of declaring that the basic task at the present time is the completion of the anti-imperialist revolution of national consolidation, giving full recognition to the national aspirations of the people and to progressive leaders of national revolutions. The formal transition to socialism will come later.

Beginning with the first rapprochement with Yugoslavia in 1955, the Khrushchev regime accepted the possibility of different roads to socialism as well as peaceful means of starting down that road. By "creatively applying Marxism-Leninism" to the conditions of each nation, local divergencies in the domestic affairs of Communist states are now held to be permissible. This is due to recognition of the varying levels of development that each nation had reached before falling under Communist control. The Stalinist requirement of absolute conformity not only in foreign but in domestic policy was discarded to allow for differing national applications of socialist principles. It was possible for Khrushchev to say, as Stalin never could, that the "collective treasury" of the Communist parties had been enriched by the diversity "without which . . . one cannot possibly conceive the building of socialism by different peoples."[31] While this modification of Stalinism had its greatest significance for the countries within the Communist system, it also helped pave the way for a revival of the popular front tactic and a broadening of the international "peace movement" by alleviating some of the fear of non-Communists who were potential participants in popular front alliances.

The theory of different roads to socialism implicitly involves the question of nationalism. Here Khrushchev appeared to find himself torn between the visionary hopes of Communist mythology and the hard realities of modern circumstances. Expressing the idealistic side of the question, the Premier told the March 1959 workers' conference of Leipzig that as the socialist system progressed, "the old concepts of borders as such will gradually disappear." Only ethnic borders are expected to survive and those only as a convention. The development of a common economic system will eventually create a single world order in which national variations and national loyalties will be remembered only on the pages of history.

In contrast, *Pravda*, on June 22, 1960, reported the Prime Minister as emphasizing that countries already in the process of building socialism will continue their construction of the new order with a "great diversity of techniques and forms." National variations not only would be permitted but should be expected and encouraged whenever they contribute to the stability of the regime and the building of socialism. Perhaps the clearest recognition of nationalism in advanced countries was contained in Khrushchev's address to the East German Party Congress in January, 1963. There he declared:

> The struggle in the capitalist countries is a domestic problem for their working-class movement. Only the party of the proletariat of the capitalist country in question—and not other countries or other parties—has a right and is in a position to specify the tactics of a revolution and the forms and methods of its struggle.[32]

This statement is not only a concession to domestic control of each national party (verbally at least) but overtly gives national class conditions priority over the proverbial loyalty normally demanded to the international class movement.

Still another tenet of Leninism to undergo reinterpretation by Khrushchev is the concept of inevitable war between the forces of capitalism and those of Communism. Like the innovation of the theory of peaceful transition to socialism, the alteration of the doctrine of war is based partly on an optimistic appraisal of the power of the Soviet Union and of favorable conditions toward the further expansion of its influence without resort to warlike operations and partly on fear of the results of any war in which nuclear weapons are employed. The basis of the change in orthodox Leninist theory and the Communist view of the meaning of the change were announced at the 20th Party Congress and were most authoritatively elaborated on in Khrushchev's address before the meeting of party workers at the Marx-Engels-Lenin Institute in January, 1961.

The causes of war are still explained in the traditional Marxist-Leninist fashion. War is the continuation of the domestic policy of states. Warfare is not brought about by evil rulers or the bellicose spirit of a nation; rather, it is due to the existence of antagonistic classes. The source of all "predatory wars" lies in imperialism, the system in which there is the sharpest class struggle. The struggles for profits and new markets, aggravated by the uneven development of capitalist states and by their hatred of socialism, "in their totality impel imperialism to the path of aggression and war."[33] By their very nature, capitalist states cannot conduct peaceful relations over a long period of time since their foreign policy cannot avoid reflecting the force inherent in the "exploiter-exploited" order of its domestic system as revealed by the struggle for markets and greater profits.

However, Khrushchev asserted that war is not purely an economic matter. Whether or not there is a war "depends in large measure on the correlation of class, political forces, the degree of organization and the awareness and resolve of the people."[34] In other words, politics is the paramount factor in resolving the issue of war. Khrushchev conceded that as long as imperialism exists, the economic basis for the outbreak of war exists. But the "mighty social and political forces" of the Communist states were thought to provide the military means and the intellectual resolution to frustrate the "adventurist plans" of the imperialists. Hence "war is not fatalistically inevitable."

On the other hand, Khrushchev was careful to explain that, although they were no longer necessary in the sense of being inevitable, wars were still quite possible. In January, 1961, he wrote in *Kommunist:*

> Wars appear with the division of society into classes. This means that the soil in which wars are originated will be liquidated once and for all only when there is an end to the division

> of society into hostile, antagonistic classes. With the victory of the working class in all the world, with the victory of socialism, all the social and national causes of wars will be eliminated and mankind will have the possibility of being eternally delivered from this terrible evil.

The possibility of world war is, therefore, considered a continuing feature of the modern world. Only the inevitability has been removed. But even this is a major theoretical concession.

Local wars fall into the same category as world wars in Communist pronouncements of the post-Stalin period. Soviet spokesmen have violently attacked the theories of limited warfare disseminated by such American scholars as Henry Kissinger on the ground that wars begun with limited strategic aims can rapidly escalate into a "world thermonuclear rocket war." The new power advantage of the Soviet Union and her allies is judged as barring the West from engaging in efforts to contain Communism by means of local warfare.

While toning down the martial element in Leninism, however, Khrushchev persisted in openly sanctioning one type of war—"just, progressive wars of liberation." He termed revolutionary wars of independence both right and inevitable as long as imperialism exists and announced the unreserved support of such wars by the Soviet Union. Drawing a distinction between local or interstate wars and internal wars for national independence, the Soviet Premier insisted that the latter do not threaten international peace; hence they will not precipitate the same dangers of thermonuclear war that conflicts between states may engender. Consequently they may be sanctioned and even encouraged.

Modification of the theories of violent revolution and inevitable war was essential to make the grand design of Soviet foreign policy more plausible to the outside world. This design is peaceful coexistence, the theme song of the post-Stalin era. Although Lenin and Stalin had used the term "coexistence," both applied it to temporary conditions as a tactical necessity. The phrase was revived with new significance during the two-year interregnum of Malenkov and particularly at the Geneva Conference of 1955. However, it remained for Khrushchev to expand the concept of peaceful coexistence, formally to make it a fundamental principle of Soviet policy at the 20th Party Congress, and to elevate it to a tenet of Leninism by virtue of its incorporation in the new Party Program of 1961.

Peaceful coexistence

Leninist theory has traditionally assumed that the world is divided into two opposing forces—Communist and capitalist. The experience of the cold war helped to intensify that conviction. The competing "camps" have different social systems representing the progressive forces, whose work is yet to be completed, and the reactionary forces, whose social utility has ended. Lenin contended that the mutual hostility of the leaders of the two systems would inevitably result in a violent showdown that would end in the global triumph of Communism.

The inclination to see the forces of the world divided into clearly drawn groups of black and white with no permanent shades between the two extremes persisted in the theoretical pronouncements of the post-Stalin period. The current international situation is held to reflect "two systems, two worlds, two ideologies, two politics."[35] However, Khrushchev sought some means to keep the conflict and the sense of struggle alive, while at the same time reducing the tension that resulted in large measure from fear that a military confrontation was necessary to resolve the differences between the competing systems. This modified form of struggle between capitalism and Communism was given the name of peaceful coexistence. According to the official Soviet version, the principle of peaceful coexistence "assumes that the historical conditions of struggle between the two systems must take place in economic, political, and ideological areas, and not grow into armed conflict, threatening the annihilation of mankind."[36]

Peaceful coexistence, Khrushchev repeatedly contended, means the repudiation of war as a means of resolving controversies between states with different social systems and the acceptance of negotiations for the consideration of "mutual concessions" and compromises. Coexistence is possible for two basic reasons, Soviet leaders claim. In the first place, the balance of world forces is deemed to have changed with the result that the Soviet Union together with the "peace-loving peoples" of the world "can curb and neutralize the imperialist groupings that are striving to unleash military conflicts." The military might of the United States and the Soviet Union is sufficient to accomplish mutual destruction and, therefore, is unacceptable to both sides as a means of resolving disputes. In the second place, "scientific, technological and cultural progress has immensely increased the overall mutual interdependence of countries and events in various parts of the world." As a result of these factors, peaceful coexistence, "although still lacking completeness and stability, has already become a fact." The possibility of mutual annihilation and the development of economic interdependence have made peace and coexistence far more than "merely a truce between world wars."[37]

In spite of the recognition of significant changes in the world and the rather unorthodox emphasis on scientific and technological interdependence of all nations, Khrushchev was still prepared to insist that "imperialism is imperialism, and its nature has not changed." He also argued that it was the times that had changed and not the capitalist system, denying that there was a contradiction between his insistence that "imperialism is imperialism" and his declaration that coexistence was both possible and necessary. It remained for the Chinese Communists to point out the incompatibility of Lenin's theory of imperialism and the possibility of long-term coexistence and peace. Translating Peking's charges against the Soviet Premier from Communist jargon, the accusations read that the First Secretary of the C.P.S.U. was guilty of subduing the revolutionary aspirations of his own party in order to make accommodations with imperialist states as a result of his lack of faith in the inevitable triumph of Communism.

Ignoring the Chinese commentaries on his theories and policies, Khrushchev proceeded to emphasize that he contemplated "not only the negative pledge of forgoing war as a means of resolving conflicts but positive goals of cooperation, recognition of territorial integrity, disarmament, and the liquidation of military blocs."[38] Particular stress was placed on cooperation through the expansion of trade between East and West. Mikoyan noted at the 20th Congress that coexistence is "unthinkable" without increased trade, and Khrushchev asserted that it could receive a firm foundation only with an increase in "an extensive and absolutely unrestricted international trade." The application of peaceful coexistence to international trade "means that economic relations must be put into practice without any discrimination, without imposing unequal conditions on anyone, and the basis of equal advantage and equal sides."[39] The further strengthening of peaceful coexistence is also held to demand "the recognition of the principle of non-intervention in the internal affairs of other states—particularly the banning of counter-revolution and interventions. This means that it is necessary to repudiate the export of revolutions and also counter-revolutions."[40] The latter point has been repeatedly stressed in Soviet statements since 1956, suggesting that the Kremlin elite may have been genuinely fearful of Western intervention in the Hungarian revolution of 1956 and is anxious to secure a guarantee against support of revolts in east European states. The call for nonintervention may, therefore, be considered an effort to secure recognition of legitimate Soviet interests in the affairs of other members of the international system of Communist states. Another part of the coexistence theme is general universal disarmament. Coexistence and disarmament are held to be "inseparable one from the other." Finally, there is emphasis on the liquidation of military "blocs" and the removal of all foreign military bases.

The strength of the Soviet-led campaign for coexistence is considerably augmented by a "vast Zone of Peace," including both socialist and nonsocialist nations of Europe and Asia. This zone includes not only the neutral countries but a large percentage (as seen by Moscow) of the populations of many advanced Western states as well. "There is plenty of scope for initiative on the part of any country, party, political force or individual in the peace movement." To demonstrate his conviction on this point, Khrushchev singled out the Roman Catholic Church for praise, noting that in spite of sharp ideological differences, "we Communists nevertheless uphold the statements of the heads of the Catholic Church—Pope John XXIII in the recent past and Pope Paul VI today—in favor of peace and the solution of international disputes through negotiations."[41] Moscow persistently encourages nonparty "forces of peace" to be active, to organize, and to engage in politics. The consolidation of this Zone of Peace is thought to be particularly important for enabling former colonial countries to conduct an independent foreign policy. In addition, by uniting with the Communist states in a struggle for peace, the supporters of peace can dominate the course of world politics and restrain the imperialist powers from taking action against any member of the peace forces.

It can readily be seen that the Soviet concept of peaceful coexistence is basically an explanation of conflict between two opposing systems in a period when technological advances have made warfare and violent revolution extremely hazardous means of resolving disputes and implementing programs of territorial aggrandizement. Coexistence is not intended by the Soviet rulers to be a repudiation of struggle but merely a refinement of the means of struggle. The expression, therefore, describes a shift in strategy from an emphasis on violence to a more sophisticated design for achieving the goals of the Soviet regime. *Kommunist* aptly explains the hope contained in the theme of peaceful coexistence in this way:

> Under conditions of lasting peace, and all the more of disarmament, all the advantages of the world system of socialism would develop to an enormous extent; it would obtain new possibilities of advancing the economy and culture and of winning the competition with capitalism in historically short periods of time.[42]

The grand design of Soviet foreign policy in the Khrushchev period placed a premium on providing time for the Soviet Union to strengthen itself by striving to overtake the United States in economic productivity. According to Khrushchev, it was founded on the assumption that "the socialist mode of production possesses decisive advantages over the capitalist mode of production." The concept of coexistence is, therefore, closely associated with the new appreciation of the real and potential economic and technological strength of the states governed by Communist parties.

The economic aspect of peaceful coexistence deserves special attention as a result of the great stress laid on this type of competition with the West at the 21st and 22nd Party Congresses and in the new Party Program. Khrushchev announced that the world struggle was entering "a new stage of economic competition" in which the aim of the socialist states must be "to overtake and surpass the most highly developed capitalist states." The resolutions approved by the 21st Congress declared that the superiority of the socialist system will be proved by producing more than half the world industrial output by the end of the 1960's.[43] By advancing the economic development of the U.S.S.R. at the rapid pace envisioned by the Seven-Year Plan, the resolutions further declared that Communism would simultaneously be winning the world wide competition with capitalism. The adoption of the new Party Program in 1961 at the 22nd Congress merely reasserted this thesis in bolder form by linking these economic goals with the establishment of communism in the Soviet Union by 1980. By that time the ability of Soviet Communism to provide the people with an abundance of material benefits is expected to set an example that will overwhelm the world. Certainly, neither Lenin nor Stalin could seriously entertain this hope so often expressed by Khrushchev.

The relationship between the policy of peaceful coexistence and Soviet domestic policy has always been officially recognized but has received enlarged attention since the development of acute economic problems in 1961-1963. The Soviet journal, *Mirovaia ekonomika i mezhdunarodnye otnosheniia,* published an article in 1963 declaring that "the politics of peaceful coexistence represents an *important prerequisite* for comprehensive economic construction, indispensable for the creation of the material-technical base of Communism in the U.S.S.R., for the construction of a socialist society and for the realization of the transition to Communism in other socialist countries." (Emphasis supplied)[44] The drain of the Soviet military budget on the general economy appears to have prompted recognition of the importance of relatively stable international conditions if allocations are to be geared to "comprehensive economic construction." Problems resulting from military expenditures have also encouraged reaffirmation of the disarmament theme in the hope of diverting a larger portion of defense funds to meeting that "important prerequisite" for economic construction. In his article, "On Peace and Peaceful Coexistence," written for the Italian Communist Party press, Khrushchev noted:

> Another effective means of combating the threat of war would be to make drastic cuts in military expenditures, which are, in effect, unproductive expenditures that, in principle, create no

> new benefits for the people. . . . The money made available by this measure could be used to solve internal problems, such as improving the economy, public health and culture; or to aid nations whose economy is less advanced due to colonial oppression.[45]

The policy of coexistence is, therefore, closely associated with economic policy. Confidence in the ability of the Soviet Union to broaden its economic base is tempered by the awareness of the often conflicting demands placed on the national budget in the name of defense. All available means must be channeled into the building of the national economy to prove the superiority of the Soviet system, although the way in which economic superiority can be converted into international gains appears to be less certain to the Soviet leaders. Nevertheless, demonstration of the "material and spiritual blessings" of the Soviet people is thought to be "a very strong means of agitating for Communism."[46]

While willing to accept economic competition as the principal form of struggle, Khrushchev made it abundantly clear that no accommodation can be expected on ideological questions. In October, 1959, he wrote in the American journal, *Foreign Affairs:*

> The principle of peaceful coexistence does not at all demand that one or another state abandon the system or ideology adopted by it. . . . The acceptance of this principle cannot lead to the immediate end of disputes and contradictions which are inevitable between countries adhering to different social systems.

Although peaceful coexistence calls for compromise and negotiations on some questions, compromise "must not be confused with concession on matters of principle, on matters that touch upon the very nature of our socialist system, our ideology."[47] In this area of conflict concessions would represent capitulation to the forces of aggression rather than peaceful coexistence. At the same time, however, ideological competition should not be permitted to preclude the attainment of important agreements, such as the nuclear test ban treaty of 1963, which are of mutual benefit to all sides. Some questions transcend the differences between the two systems and should always be open to negotiation.[48]

It should be emphasized that, in spite of the restrictions placed on concessions and the propagandistic overtones of the theme of coexistence, peaceful competition is considered more than a temporary policy or strategy. It is construed as a general line of historical development corresponding to the rise of the socialist system as a powerful factor in the international arena.[49] Peaceful coexistence is the only practical road to world socialism in the era of missiles and hydrogen bombs. The development is a new manifestation of the political, economic, and ideological competition between the socialist and capitalist countries.

The current ideological and theoretical situation in the Soviet Union contains both disturbing and encouraging features for the advocates of a pluralistic world. The ultimate goal of establishing some brand of Leninism throughout the globe, the emphasis on tactical flexibility encouraged by the concept of socialist morality, the continued commitment to the aim of remaking human nature, and the firm insistence on the organizational necessity of the vanguard party are all factors that help to create a picture alien to the eyes and ways of liberal man. Similarly, the concept of imperialism and the consequent view of a world divided into two camps, two socioeconomic systems, one pitted against the other in an inevitable struggle for total victory, provide little comfort to those who value the diversity permitted in free societies. Those who would see this planet as more than two systems locked in deadly combat over quasi-religious political ideologies could not but be disturbed by a seriously taken theory supporting that very struggle.

On the other hand, the Leninism of the post-Stalin period is not the Leninism of the early Bolsheviks who first ruled the Soviet state. While continuing to profess confidence in the eventual triumph of what they define as Communism, Stalin's heirs have modified the former emphasis on violence and insistence on complete conformity within the system of party-states. The renunciation of theory of inevitable war may ultimately have far-reaching consequences in terms of Soviet expectations and in the Kremlin's interpretations of the behavior of Western states. The transition to socialism and relations between capitalist and Communist states no longer involve the inevitable use of force. Also, other Communist countries and parties are now encouraged to work in harmony with the Soviet Republic while having greater freedom to interpret and apply the laws of Marxism-Leninism according to their respective national needs. Capitalism is no longer considered completely decadent, and it is now possible for the Russians to look openly toward the West for technological innovations and guides for industrial management. In short, the post-Stalin era has ushered in a period of rationalization that has, in relatively little time, had a discernible impact on both the cognitive and the normative theory of the Soviet system. Leninism has been redecorated to lend support and continuity to new policies stemming from the demands of modern civilization and of international politics.

To expect a renunciation of the core aspects of Leninism would be to expect too much at the present time. Ideology still provides, and will continue to do so for some time, an important instrument of control for the Kremlin elite, an important means of justifying their right to rule. But even the more conservative successors to Khrushchev appear to recognize that they cannot allow the system to evolve in a circular motion where the more it changes the more it remains the same.

PEACEFUL COEXISTENCE: THE MILITARY ASPECT

You cannot drive people to paradise with a club, or drive them to Communism by means of war. When people realize that Communism alone will give them a truly free and happy life, they will come running of their own free will.

—N. S. Khrushchev

THE REVOLUTION IN SOVIET MILITARY DOCTRINE

III

RETURNING TO the Soviet Union in 1959 from a trip that had taken him to such distant points as Washington and Peking, Premier Khrushchev remarked in Novosibirsk that peaceful co-existence is "an economic, political, and ideological struggle, but not a military one." If the power struggle between the United States and the Soviet Union is to continue unabated and if both sides are to go on spending billions of dollars on defense, as appears likely, then it is germane to inquire into the reasons why the Soviet leadership denies the need for war and to examine what strategic design forms the basis of Soviet military policy.

THE DEBATE OVER MILITARY STRATEGY

Under Stalin, postwar military thought in the Soviet Union remained singularly static, reflecting both the Russian geo-political tradition and Marxist-Leninist dogma. The decisive factor in any military conflict among states was deemed to be the social system of the nations involved. Hence, by virtue of the advanced position assigned to it by political doctrine, the Soviet armed forces held a decided advantage over others in military engagements. Once this interpretation was accepted, it was only logical that the Stalinist command should reject outright the possibly decisive importance of surprise attack and the concept of an "absolute weapon" such as the atomic or hydrogen bomb. If the decisive factor in war was the nation's political system, obviously any advantages an aggressor state might accrue from striking the initial blow would be only temporary, unless of course that state also had a superior ideology and social system. Likewise, emphasis on conventional forces, a factor that was traditional in both Russian and Marxist thought, led to the rejection of any strategy that made a particular weapon *the* decisive instrument in warfare. Stalin adhered rigidly to these basic concepts. While encouraging the development of atomic and nuclear weapons by Soviet scientists on the one hand, he so completely dominated the military that thoughtful officers could not challenge the validity of the dictator's "laws of military science" or the implications of the importance attached to the perfection of the new weapons.

The death of Stalin prompted an immediate re-evaluation of strategic concepts by the military and political hierarchies of the Soviet state. This re-evaluation has now gone through three general stages, all of which have been marked by an intricate interplay of political and military interests as well as by conflict among the ranking officers of the military establishment. The first stage lasted roughly from 1953 to 1955 and was resolved in favor of the advocates of a "new look" by the victory of Khrushchev over the Stalinist old guard. The second stage, from 1955 to the summer of 1960, was characterized by a supremely optimistic appraisal of Soviet power and further internal struggle between political and military groupings. The third stage has been marked by a more sober evaluation of Soviet strength and more serious consideration of the implications of nuclear weapons. It has also been marked by a division of opinion between traditionalist and modernist military officers. Common to all three periods has been the consideration of a broad range of alternatives in strategic designs. Furthermore, from the evidence of articles and letters in Soviet military journals and newspapers, the number of persons exposed to alternative approaches, unlike that of the Stalinist past, has grown to a large, though undetermined, total. The series of disputes embracing this struggle for a single strategic concept has been ably documented in the works of Herbert S. Dinerstein and Raymond L. Garthoff.[1]

During the initial period of adjustment, the struggle over succession resulting from the death of Stalin brought the military directly into the political arena for the first time in Soviet history. The army was employed as a counterweight to the secret police at the time of the first moves against Beria in the spring of 1953. On the removal of Beria from his party positions, Marshal Zhukov was brought up to fill the vacancy in the General Committee of the party. During the struggle between Khrushchev and Malenkov for dominance, Zhukov and the military threw their support to Khrushchev, who supported continued emphasis on heavy industry at the time. Malenkov's call for increased production of consumer goods at the expense of heavy industry foretold reductions in military expenditures and continued a threat to the interests of the military establishment. In 1955, Zhukov replaced Bulganin as Minister of Defense after the latter was elevated to Premier. The Marshal made a further advance in the party hierarchy when he was made a candidate member of the Presidium of the Central Committee during the 20th Party Congress in 1956. With the elevation of Zhukov to Defense Minister and to high party posts, the Soviet military began to assume a political significance that it had never previously experienced. Zhukov undertook with vigor and disregard for precedent to perform the tasks that he considered necessary to fulfill his obligation to the military establishment. In a sequence of moves, he laid the groundwork for reducing the role of political leaders in the armed forces. By the spring of 1957, Zhukov's insistence that political controls hampered the effectiveness of military machinery was rewarded by the issuance of an order by the Central Committee forbidding criticism of military leaders at party meetings in the armed forces.[2]

Marshal Zhukov's bargaining position was further enhanced by the attack levied on Khruschev in June, 1957. At that time a majority of the members of the Presidium, led by Molotov, Malenkov, and Kaganovich, joined in a verbal assault on Khrushchev's policies and called for his removal.[3] During the crisis, the Marshal apparently came to Khrushchev's rescue by ordering the Air Force to transport the members of the Central Committee to Moscow in order to ward off the attack on the First Secretary. As a reward, Zhukov was elevated to full membership in the Presidium, the first military officer ever to attain that status. However, a combination of factors, including his reduction of party influence in the armed forces and fear of the potential impact of his popularity with the masses, led Khrushchev to move to restrain any political ambitions that the Marshal might have had long before he was able to acquire truly independent power. In October, 1957, Zhukov was removed from his posts as Minister of Defense and member of the Presidium and the Central Committee. Zhukov's expulsion appears to have been abetted by rivalry among military officers, which Khrushchev fully exploited. Malinovskii and Konev voiced sharp criticisms of their former colleague and superior, and Konev published an article in *Pravda,* on November 3, 1957, that was particularly brutal in its attack on Zhukov. Malinovskii was rewarded with the post of Minister of Defense.

The experience of civil-military relations from 1955 to 1957 had thrust military officers into the cross currents of political controversy. The dispute that was waging within the armed services over strategic concepts had become a political dispute. While the threat of a single marshal to the political order had been eliminated, the interest of the military in political decisions had been sharpened by the experience of the preceding years.

The effect of technology on military science

The controversy over strategy grew out of the assessment of the impact of technology on contemporary military strategy. Evidence of serious re-evaluation of traditional strategic concepts was revealed by the reorganization of the Soviet Army in 1955-1956, the creation of the East European Defense Pact (the Warsaw Pact) in 1955, and the elevation of the Air Defense Command to a position of great strategic importance in the 1955-1956 period. Reductions of troops in the conventional forces were made in a sequence of moves between 1955 and 1958. Khrushchev later noted that in 1955 there were 5,763,000 men serving in the Soviet armed forces and that during the next three years the number had been cut to 3,623,000. These steps appear to have been taken for a combination of reasons, the most outstanding of which were attachment of greater importance to modern means of warfare and budgetary considerations.

The reductions were made possible by several factors. The Geneva Conference and the lessening of international tensions following the signing of the Austrian Peace Treaty appeared to reduce the likelihood of war. The rapprochement with Yugoslavia also contributed to the lessening of tensions. Furthermore, the development of nuclear weapons permitted the Soviet Union to continue to use western Europe as a "hostage" even more effectively than it had been able to do by relying on its huge conventional army. From Khrushchev's perspective no risk was taken in the substantial reductions of standing forces. Khrushchev may also have believed that a cutback in conventional forces might convince the United States that Soviet nuclear capabilities were greater than they actually were at that time.

Despite some moves toward a modernist approach, however, widespread disagreement within the ranks of both the military and the party prevented a single all-embracing strategic design from developing and replacing Stalinist doctrine. Questions evolving around the role of ground forces and surprise attack in future wars occupied the attention of the decision-making hierarchy. Marshal Rotmistrov, the head of the Tank Troops and an able military thinker, wrote in *Krasnaia zvezda*, on March 24, 1955, that although surprise attack with the use of atomic and hydrogen weapons "may appear to be one of the decisive conditions for the attainment of victory" in any future world war, "surprise cannot . . . yield a conclusive result, cannot bring victory, in a war with a serious and strong enemy." Premier Bulganin commented before the Geneva Conference in May, 1955, that "modern war is inconceivable without the deployment and concentration of large land, air, and naval forces."[4] Marshal Zhukov, while still occupying his posts as Minister of Defense and candidate member of the Presidium, noted that "air power and nuclear weapons by themselves cannot determine the outcome of an armed conflict."[5]

Only after the successful launching of its first intercontinental ballistic missile in August, 1957, and the spectacular success of Sputnik I in October of the same year did the Soviet high command openly begin to recognize the necessity of changing strategic concepts as a result of technological innovations in weapons development. The publication in 1958 of *Science and Technology in Contemporary War* by Major General G. I. Pokrovski stressed very strongly the relevance of physics and mechanics to military science and the need for military officers to acquire technical knowledge. This emphasis on modern weapons technology foretold the possible reduction of the role assigned to the conventional forces in future wars. It was to be expected, therefore, that the traditionalist advocates would press for important qualifications. Indicative of this was an article which appeared in *Kommunist* in 1958, declaring that "despite all the importance of technological material in a future war, the decisive role in achieving victory over an enemy belongs to people possessing high morale and combat qualities, capable of enduring the burdens of war for the sake of great aims and able to make skillful use of their weapons and materiel."[6] This conflict over the relative importance of missiles and men in modern warfare pitted modernists against traditionalists, and although arguments were often veiled in ideological terminology, it should be underscored that both sides to the controversy had very practical reasons for taking the positions that they took.

Having consolidated his position after the crisis of 1957, but still lacking the extensive dictatorial authority that belonged to Stalin, Khrushchev cautiously moved in 1960 to bring an end to the controversy. He did so by setting the guidelines to be used in developing a comprehensive military strategy in an address to the Supreme Soviet on January 14, 1960. Departing radically from the traditional Soviet emphasis on balance among the military services, the Premier declared that in the future the nation's armed power and general strategy would be based on missiles as the principal instrument of war and the nation's defense would be based on the principle of nuclear deterrence. The justification for this change was, he noted, acceptance of the theory that war would both "begin differently" and "develop differently" from past wars owing to the use of missiles carrying nuclear warheads. On these grounds Khrushchev insisted that conventional forces could no longer be considered the determining factor in the outcome of a war; rather, the "total firepower and means of delivery" had come to constitute the most decisive determinant of the results of modern warfare.

Intercontinental ballistic missiles thus became the basis of the Soviet Union's defense and general military strategy. Noting the existence of American bases ringing the U.S.S.R., Khrushchev announced that "we are locating our rockets in such a way as to insure double and triple protection; we can disperse rocket installations and camouflage them well." The Premier went on to ask

> If the possibility is not excluded that some capitalist countries will draw level with us in the field of modern armaments, will they not possibly act treacherously and attack us first, in order to make use of the factor of surprise, with such formidable weapons as rocket atomic weapons, and thus have an advantage for gaining victory? No. Modern means of waging war do not give any country such advantages.[7]

This statement was tantamount to saying that the Soviet Union had no need to fear a surprise attack or to plan its strategy around the possibility of launching a pre-emptive attack. The nuclear deterrent was to be the basis of Soviet defense. So confident was Khrushchev that this was the correct course that he announced the creation of a new arm of the military services—the Strategic Rocket Corps—and proposed the further reduction of the army by one-third, from 3,623,000 to 2,400,000 men, including a reduction of 250,000 officers by the beginning of 1962.

The removal of Marshal V. D. Sokolovskii from his posts of Chief of the General Staff of the Soviet Army and Navy and First Deputy Minister of Defense in 1960 suggests that there was disagreement among the officers over the propriety of the Prime Minister's course. However, important figures lent their support to the new moves during the remainder of 1960. Kuusinen endorsed reliance on a missile-based strategy in an article in *Krasnaia zvezda* on April 2. The U-2 incident and its aftermath, however, undoubtedly caused great alarm in military circles over real Soviet strength during the summer of 1960, and provoked renewed discussion of the strategy announced by Khrushchev on January 14. Nevertheless, the November 1960 issue of *International Affairs* contained an article by Deputy Defense Minister Andrei Yeremenko that went so far as to claim that the stockpile of Soviet missiles and their high degree of accuracy had made overseas military bases entirely obsolete, thus indicating that the modernist position had not been completely reversed.

Subsequently, however, it became apparent that Khrushchev had not had his way entirely. Reports leaked to the West by Colonel Oleg V. Penkovski indicated that the Kremlin had not pursued the 1957 success with the ballistic missile and, contrary to public claims, had allowed the U.S.S.R. to fall behind the United States in long-range missile development.[8] Considering Khrushchev's boasting about Soviet rocket superiority between 1957 and 1961, the reason for Moscow's failure to take real advantage of its initial lead is not clear. Evidence suggests only that it was a deliberate governmental decision, probably stemming from a combination of problems which included cost, operational difficulties, and differences of opinion in both the military and civilian elites over the priority of defense allocations. The differences of opinion on the latter question were manifest throughout 1961 by a continuing "debate" in the military press in which *Kommunist vooruzhennykh sil* represented the modernist pro-Khrushchev faction while *Voenno-istoricheskii zhurnal* and *Krasnaia zvezda* represented the voice of the traditionalists.[9]

By the time of the 22nd Party Congress in October, 1961, the changes that had been taking place in Soviet weapon development and military strategy and the dispute over them became more "open secrets" than theretofore. Defense Minister Malinovskii's report to the Communist conclave revealed further shifts in the thinking of the Kremlin strategists, shifts resulting from the strength of the traditionalists in high political as well as military circles. On the questions of surprise attack and the initial stages of war, Malinovskii reiterated the substance of Khrushchev's speech of the preceding year. Similarly, he noted the need to trim and reorganize the armed forces in order "to integrate nuclear weapons as instruments of Soviet policy." But on several key points he differed with his Premier's earlier declarations. Without explicitly saying so, the Defense Minister inferred that Soviet defense policy was being geared to the ability of the military to launch a pre-emptive attack against a country planning a preventive war on the U.S.S.R. This was implied by the stress given the preparations judged to be requisite to "repulse effectively any sudden attack and to rout the criminal plans of the imperialists." In order to accomplish this, "constant readiness" was demanded. While this view had not been explicitly denied in Khrushchev's address to the Supreme Soviet, the Premier had then indicated reliance on the deterrent value of overall Soviet strength. Another noteworthy difference was Malinovskii's recognition of all parts of the military services, including "large armies," as important forces in future wars. On the other hand, his report included two radical departures from earlier Soviet military doctrine that, in effect, bolstered Khrushchev's position: he clearly distinguished between primary and secondary arms by assigning greater importance to strategic missile units and he discarded the old theory that only military bases should be the object of attack, by declaring that the need had arisen to attack the industrial and transportation centers of the enemy in future warfare. While Malinovskii's speech reaffirmed the substance of Khrushchev's previous report, it is noteworthy that modifications of the Premier's assessment of the power distribution in the world could be forced on him.

Significant changes in the representation of the military in the higher party organs during and after the 22nd Party Congress bolstered Khrushchev's position to some degree. The new Central Committee of the C.P.S.U. contained fourteen full members and seventeen candidate members from the ranks of professional military officers. This compared with six full members and twelve candidate members in the Central Committee elected at the 20th Party Congress in 1956. The increase in the total number of military officers is probably not as meaningful as the distribution among the services. Formerly, only commanders-in-chief of the Navy and Air Force had been even candidate members. The new listing of full members was composed of seven army officers with four air force and three naval officers joining them. All twenty-five of the newly designated military members of the Central Committee came from the technical wings of their services. This factor suggests that the party elite may have moved not only to strengthen the representation of the military in the party hierarchy but to recognize and give support to the increasing significance of technology in the consideration of strategic plans. Then, as though to offset any potential rise in military influence in the party, F. I. Golikov, an erstwhile professional soldier, was replaced as head of the Central Political Department of the Soviet armed services by A. A. Yepishev, more noted as a party stalwart than as a military man. Furthermore, Marshal Sokolovskii re-entered the picture after being designated chairman of a committee to produce an authoritative statement on Soviet strategic concepts in the nuclear and missile age. Before turning our attention to the product of the Sokolovskii committee, we should consider the different views of the enemy among the members of the Soviet elite, the political allies of the traditionalist military officers, and the involvement of military circles in the formation of the Soviet budget.

The different outlooks of the modernists and the traditionalists

Differing interpretations of the intentions and capabilities of the "imperialist enemy" have been at the core of much of the dispute over Soviet military policy. Khrushchev, having been exposed to many leaders of Western states in his travels abroad and having a semipragmatic approach by nature, was careful to distinguish between different elements in Western decision-making elites. He categorized the principal elements as consisting of those who were reasonable and "realistic" and those who were aggressive and behaved like "lunatics."[10] In his letter to the Italian Communists in the spring of 1964, the Premier demonstrated his awareness of differences among the politicians of individual Western states by noting the positive role of "realistic" leaders and the possibilities of improving relations between states. He contended that it was possible to reach "agreements with the capitalist countries on the basis of constructive proposals" and that "personal contacts" between the leaders of the Communist system of states and the reasonable statesmen of the West could serve to reduce tensions between countries and promote international understanding.[11] Khrushchev, therefore, did not place all "imperialists" in a single category but saw them as having different qualities and posing different types of problems to the Soviet Union. In particular, the position of the Prime Minister and the modernists appeared to be that so long as "realists" were in control of the government of the United States, the Soviet Union would not be taking undue risk by devoting a smaller portion of its resources to defense.

In contrast, the traditionalists did not see fit to draw such fine distinctions. They chose instead to place all "imperialists" in one category whether or not they happened to be actual participants in the decision-making processes of a nation's government. In 1962, the Ministry of Defense published a book on N.A.T.O. that was indicative of this viewpoint. The publication strongly underscored both the capabilities and the aggressive aspirations of the members of the North Atlantic Treaty Organization, concluding that Soviet defense had to be prepared to meet any challenge that "aggressive imperialists" were capable of instigating.[12] As preparations were being laid for negotiations on the test-ban agreement, the conservatives only thinly concealed their opposition to dealing with imperialists and "warmongers." Typical of the traditionalists' references to Western leaders was Malinovskii's assertion in May, 1963, that "the reactionary circles of the USA and its allies are conducting a provocational policy. . . . Time has apparently not taught the imperialists anything."[13] Even after the signing of the test ban treaty, *Krasnaia zvezda*, on September 19, 1963, sharply attacked the "world consortium" of the imperialists.

Khrushchev, however, showed no indication of bowing to the traditionalists on this point. During his visit to Hungary in April, 1964, the Prime Minister appeared quite deliberately to raise the issue of differentiating between elements in Western states. "Even the representatives of the biggest imperialist state —the United States of America . . . are not devoid of common sense when it comes to the question of life and death for their own state. . . ."[14] Proceeding to praise the speech of President John Kennedy at the American University in June, 1963, Khrushchev commented, "I was criticized for having praised this speech of Kennedy." This remark suggested that controversy over the estimation of Western intentions still divided his colleagues. He went on to warn that "we must not think ourselves clever and all our opponents fools," and broadened his praise of Kennedy to include President Lyndon Johnson, Secretary of State Dean Rusk, and Senator William Fulbright. It was not sympathy for socialism, Khrushchev declared, that had brought forth moderate statements and policies from these men. "These were manifestations of a realistic approach, an acknowledgement that we do exist, develop, and possess an enormous might."

The differences between the interpretations of Khrushchev and Malinovskii, who often spoke for the traditionalists, appeared to stem primarily from their different starting points. Khrushchev built his case on the assumption that the *intentions* of the leaders of the Western alliance were moderate in aim and that responsible, not reckless, methods were used by the realists to advance those aims. On the other hand, Malinovskii based his argument on the *capabilities* of the West and added support to his contention by citing the orthodox Leninist interpretation of imperialism. Khrushchev and his supporters used their assessment of Western intentions in behalf of their efforts to effect a substantial cutback in the Soviet defense program, while Malinovskii and his supporters contended that the defense effort should have the goal of at least achieving a parity with the military capabilities of the "imperialists."

The political allies of the traditionalists

After eliminating his principal opposition in 1957, it initially appeared that Khrushchev had emerged as unquestioned dictator of the Soviet nation. If this was ever actually the case, it was not so for long. While Khrushchev had secured himself in a position of being "more equal" than other high party officials, he was still unable to dictate policy without considering the opinions of others and winning the support of key figures in the party Presidium. The restrictions on Khrushchev's freedom of choice emanated largely from competing demands placed on the budget. There were natural limits on the budget, which could not be divided in such a way as to satisfy all sections of the social structure. Some interests would inevitably lose out in their demands for the further development of their particular sectors. The selection of priorities, therefore, became the center of political controversies that involved both economic and military questions.

In January, 1960, when addressing the Supreme Soviet, Khrushchev appeared to be in rather complete charge. Shortly thereafter, however, a series of events resulted in a setback for whatever independence he had actually attained. The U-2 incident, followed by the sharpening of international tensions after the collapse of the Paris Summit, the announced increase in the defense expenditures of the United States under the new Kennedy administration, and technical and operational problems involving the development of intercontinental ballistic missiles forced Khrushchev to make certain accommodations with the traditionalists. The period from May, 1960, to the conclusion of the Cuban crisis late in 1962 was, therefore, a period of conservative ascendancy. This was indicated by the increased involvement of the Soviet Union in crisis situations and by Khrushchev's shift in emphasis away from dependence on one weapon as a means of defense toward acceptance of the need for diversified capabilities. Furthermore, there is no indication that the proposed reduction in the number of men in the armed forces planned for 1960-1961 was ever realized, particularly in regard to the elimination of 250,000 officers. The impunity with which Malinovskii added qualifications to Khrushchev's comments on defense before the 22nd Party Congress further attests to the strength of the Prime Minister's conservative opposition.

Considering the strong party controls over the armed forces, it is highly doubtful that Malinovskii or any other officer would have had sufficient strength to challenge openly parts of Khrushchev's program without support from high-ranking members of the party elite. Evidence, although sometimes fragmentary, suggests that the conservative military officers found powerful allies in members of the higher party organs, particularly within the Presidium, who had a more traditional orientation than that of Khrushchev. During 1962 and until his retirement in the spring of 1963, Frol Kozlov, once considered Khrushchev's heir apparent, appears to have taken the viewpoint of the traditionalists on the question of resource allocation and the assignment of highest priority to heavy industry. Rumors, which may have been deliberately planted, spread that Kozlov had been a friend and associate of Oleg Penkovski, the man who had just been arrested for treason. Furthermore, Kozlov's retirement as a result of ill health came at the height of a sharp controversy over resource allocations and priorities in the new budget. Following the decline of Kozlov, still another former trusted associate of Khrushchev, Nikolai V. Podgorny, appeared to assume the mantle of leadership for the conservative faction in the party, although the evidence of Podgorny's defection to the traditionalists is more tenuously documented than that of Kozlov.[15]

Khrushchev himself indirectly acknowledged numerous differences in the Soviet elite. *The New York Times* reported that in commenting on the November 1962 session of the Central Committee, "Mr. Khrushchev is said to have told Western diplomats after the meeting that he had wanted to propose further liberalization measures. He has been quoted as having added that 'people' felt, however, that the Soviet Union would get indigestion if it went too far."[16] The precise alignments of individuals are difficult to ascertain but circumstantial and indirect evidence points to continuing controversy between factions since 1960. Several of the points of contention, especially those over resource allocations and defense policy, are revealed most persistently in the consideration of the budget and the adoption of economic plans.

The Soviet budget and expenditures for defense

Estimates of the percentage of the gross national product of the Soviet Union devoted to defense expenditures vary from 10 to 25 per cent, compared with approximately 10 per cent in the United States. Morris Bornstein sets the percentage of the 1955 GNP of the U.S.S.R. at 11.2 per cent at established prices and 13 per cent at adjusted prices, compared with 9.7 per cent at established prices and 10.2 per cent at adjusted prices in the United States.[17] Abram Bergson and Simon Kuznets contend that general administration and defense accounted for 15.2 per cent of the GNP in 1955, compared with 17.2 per cent in 1950. Considering the growth of the Soviet economy during this interval, this estimate meant that defense expeditures had increased at the rate of 3.2 per cent per year.[18] This suggests that the Soviet Union has been devoting from 40 to 60 per cent more of its GNP for defense than the United States. Since the GNP of the U.S.S.R. is less than that of the United States, the estimates also suggest that the Soviet Union has been spending on defense only from 65 to 85 per cent as much as the United States. Considering the general reliance on nuclear deterrence and the absence of overseas bases, it is quite likely that Moscow is able to operate its defense system at a lower cost than the United States, where the counter-force strategy and the maintenance of a vast network of overseas bases create a demand for larger defense allocations. Nevertheless, the demand placed by defense on the Soviet economy must be significantly greater than that placed on the more broadly based American economy. It is, therefore, not surprising that the military section of the national budget has been the focus of political controversy.[19]

Khrushchev's own position on the priorities of budget allocations gradually shifted after he had disposed of Malenkov and his chief bureaucratic supporters in 1957. Khrushchev and Malenkov had disagreed earlier over the appropriate balance between the development of heavy and light industry. By 1960, the Premier had borrowed some of his former opponent's interest in less developed industrial areas of the Soviet Union. However, Khrushchev's emphasis was less on a clear-cut division of heavy versus light industry than on a reduction in that area of heavy industry which primarily served military needs and resulted in a drain on the more useful productive capacities of the nation. As we have noted, the Premier called for additional cutbacks in the number of men in military service and advocated reliance on the nuclear deterrence for defensive purposes. The rise in international tensions during 1960-1962 worked against Khrushchev's proposals, and he found it necessary to recognize the need for large conventional forces as well as for modern weapons. Not until 1963 did Khrushchev find himself in a position to push his program further. It was a year of domestic economic problems and an acute crisis in agriculture, and in international affairs it was a period of relative calm marked by an improvement in American-Soviet relations and the signing of the test-ban treaty.

The 1964 budget was to be presented to the Central Committee and the Supreme Soviet in December, 1963. Months before, evidence began to appear that indicated the sharp cleavage in the Soviet hierarchy over the question of allocations for defense. What must have been a very intense debate between the modernists and the traditionalists became apparent in comments found in the press. *Izvestiia*, edited by Khrushchev's son-in-law Adzhubei, reported developments from the modernist standpoint, while both *Pravda* and *Krasnaia zvezda* edited Tass reports and made editorial comments that were representative of the thought of the traditionalists.

During the preparation of the budget, *Krasnaia zvezda* emphasized the military capabilities of the United States. On August 8, 1963, the military newspaper took note of American plans for space weapons, strongly suggesting that the U.S.S.R. should devote more attention to the development of similar plans. On September 19, *Krasnaia zvezda* editorialized in boldface type that "until disarmament has been brought about, the socialist commonwealth is always obligated to maintain superiority over the imperialists in a military sense." In October, the campaign to call attention to the dangers of Western strength was intensified. Articles in the issues of October 3, October 22, October 25, October 30, and November 1, contained the comments of military spokesmen, including Malinovskii, who pointed out the aggressiveness of "American imperialism" and warned that preparations should be made to meet any challenge from "atomic lunatics."

Particularly telling was the editing of the report of Togliatti's comments on the nuclear test-ban treaty found in *Pravda* on August 27, 1963. *Izvestiia*, on the same date, printed the Tass release in full. *Pravda* omitted references to the cost of nuclear armaments and the "heavy burden that it represents for any economic system." Togliatti contended that while the Soviet Union may have been compelled to develop nuclear arms to protect "its very existence," the military burden "imposed and imposes great sacrifices and self-denial, the violation of proper economic development, as a result of which, naturally, the entire socialist system suffers."[20] Such views were hardly welcomed by the advocates of a hard-line military and foreign policy.

The modernist press, without ever openly recognizing the division of opinion in the Soviet elite, printed rebuttals to the fears and charges of the old guard. While recognizing the need for the maintenance of balanced forces, *Izvestiia* stressed the importance of the technical wings of the military services, thereby playing down the traditionalists' demand for more aircraft and ground forces.[21] Perhaps the strongest statement in behalf of the modernists came in an interview with Foreign Minister Andrei Gromyko, who, Khrushchev publicly boasted, says only what he is told to say. Among the highest priorities in Soviet foreign policy Gromyko mentioned disarmament and reduction of military expenditures, a nonaggression treaty between the members of N.A.T.O. and the Warsaw Pact, peace treaties with the two Germanies, agreement to prevent surprise attack, and the reduction of foreign troops in Europe.[22] This could hardly have been satisfying to the traditionalists, and Gromyko certainly would not have made such a bold statement without the support of the Prime Minister.

The budget finally presented to the Supreme Soviet on December 16, 1963 was essentially a compromise, for it did not represent a decisive victory for either the modernists or the traditionalists. Military expenditures were cut by a modest 4 per cent and the remainder of the document indicated no dramatic shift from the previous ratio of heavy and light industry. Consequently, neither faction was satisfied with the outcome. The dissatisfaction of the traditionalists was suggested by Malinovskii's attack on the Soviet film industry for not displaying the proper respect for the armed forces in *Krasnaia zvezda* on February 9, 1964. In unusual comments for what purported to be criticism of recent motion pictures, the Defense Minister lauded all the branches of the armed forces and insisted that "each type is important in its own place." He further warned that if the imperialists launch a war then victory "can be attained only as a result of the joint effort of all types of the armed forces." These remarks appeared only in *Krasnaia zvezda.*

The modernists were hard pressed to justify the disappointingly small cuts in defense expenditures. Air Marshal Sudets provided a partial explanation by noting in *Izvestiia,* on January 5, 1964, that Pentagon officials "are not sparing any funds on designing and creating a modern air defense system." The minor, but annoying, interference with Western access to Berlin may also have been prompted by a need to justify the continuation of a high military budget. Khrushchev himself, however, appeared to be less concerned with rationalizing the contents of the budget than with clarifying his position. Replying to Togliatti's message to the Soviet people the previous August, Khrushchev wrote:

> People also ask whether the need to maintain Soviet defenses at the current level slows down the growth of the living standards of the people. I will reply with all frankness that it does. Rockets and guns are not butter, milk, meat, bread or porridge. Were it not for the need to build up increasingly the might of the Soviet armed forces, we could have sharply improved the living standards of our people and could have made them the highest in the world in the near future.[23]

This comment suggests that Khrushchev had concluded that military expenditures not only constituted a drain on the national economy but were preventing the fulfillment of his ambitious plans to make the Soviet standard of living compare more favorably with that of the United States.

At the celebration of his seventieth birthday on April 17,

1964, the Soviet Premier noted that the defense of the country was not kept strong "in order to sound the trumpet and set out on campaigns. No, we do not want to sound the trumpet, and we are plotting no campaigns."[24] Such remarks further indicated Khrushchev's displeasure with the failure to reduce military expenditures in 1963 and the token reduction approved for 1964. Preferring to place the burden of competition with the Western nations on economic productivity, he found himself in opposition to a coalition of old-guard party leaders and the traditionalist military officers. The necessity for compromise and accommodations in Soviet defense plans was the principal reason for the irregular development of a unified strategic concept as well as for shifts in foreign policy between moderation and hostility in relations with Western states.

The removal of Khrushchev in October, 1964, appeared to stem in large part from the opposition of the Soviet conservatives—both the military traditionalists and the old-guard politicians. Malinovskii reportedly appeared before the session of the Presidium that was engineering Khrushchev's downfall. Moreover, it was significant that Brezhnev, a specialist in civil-military relations, was selected to replace him as First Secretary (General Secretary as of April, 1966). Evidence currently available on the removal of Khrushchev suggests, however, that the military as a group played a lesser role in the leadership crisis of 1964 than had been the case in either 1953 or 1957.

AN ATTEMPT TO FORMULATE A STRATEGIC CONCEPT

The confusion resulting from widespread disagreement in both military and civilian circles over the appropriate defense policy for the Soviet Union to pursue in the nuclear age led to the creation of a committee consisting of both modernists and traditionalists to draft an authoritative and acceptable statement of military strategy. Marshal V. D. Sokolovskii, former Chief of the General Staff, was made the chairman. The product of this group's labor was published by the Soviet press in 1962 under the title *Voennaia strategiia*.[25] As the first major work on military strategy produced in the U.S.S.R. since 1926, the book was received with great interest and subjected to much analysis in the Western world. Since this product of Marshal Sokolovskii's committee is the most authoritative Soviet statement on the strategic concepts of the Soviet Union, its content and implications deserve special treatment here. It is also noteworthy because the commission appears to have had the assignment of drafting such a persuasive statement of strategy as to lay the controversy over weapons and plans to rest. For the purpose of this study, the general concepts, the evaluation of Western military strategy, and the projected image of the nature of future war are the most pertinent topics for consideration.

General concepts of Soviet military strategy

The authors begin by examining certain features of past wars and evaluating their relationship to modern weapon development. First, there is the question of a state's *potential* capabilities and reserve forces. The emphasis placed on these principles stemmed primarily from the protracted length of recent major wars. This made a nation's potential especially important since initial weaknesses or deficiencies could be remedied in the course of the hostilities. Reliance on conventional forces required the replacement of men lost in combat or the reinforcement of segments of a battle line by moving fresh forces into the key positions. In the second place, there is the question of concentration of forces. Again, the use of conventional military strength gave the strategic advantage to "the most favorable concentration of forces and weapons in a military theater of operation. . . ." (p. 76). And, third, the principle of partial victory was accepted as a reasonable strategy on the battlefield. It was possible to push back the enemy without destroying him, to wear him down without seeking to annihilate him. These three laws of military science in recent wars were all predicated on the assumption that conventional forces—large ground units supported by air and naval power—were the decisive components of military strength. This was the view most strongly supported by Marxist theory and tsarist and Stalinist practice.

According to Marshal Sokolovskii, the new Soviet strategy rejects all three of these principles born in past wars. Missile and nuclear warfare has made the very outcome of future world war depend "largely on the extent and the effectiveness of the application of force at the very beginning of the war. . . ." Therefore, it is not logical "to count upon the state's potential capabilities and to reserve a large number of forces for conducting military operations later in the war" (p. 94). In short, the possible brevity of another war and the likely decisiveness of its early stages make a gamble on the opportunity to exploit "potential" strength irrational and unacceptable. Readiness to utilize the full military power of the nation at the beginning of conflict has assumed crucial importance.

The principle of concentration of forces in a strategic area has likewise been discarded. "Perfection of the delivery vehicles for nuclear weapons and their increased range and ability to retarget the nuclear attack rapidly have altered the previous concept of strategic maneuver" (p. 96). The vulnerability of communications systems to nuclear strikes and the greatly reduced amount of time available for regrouping of forces will make the maneuvers of conventional forces "difficult to execute and, in a number of cases, ineffective." In future war the essence of maneuver will move from the ability to mass great armies to "shifting and concentrating nuclear strikes."

Finally, the principle of partial victory inherited from earlier military doctrine has been replaced. No longer will it be necessary to rely so heavily on tactical and field forces in close-quarters combat. Modern weapons will make it possible "to achieve decisive results in winning victory in war sometimes" even without calling up field divisions at all. Armaments technology, therefore, makes "successes of a general strategic nature" real alternatives to reliance on "partial successes" (p. 94).

In discarding the old and laying the groundwork for the new, the Soviet source book sets forth the fundamental general concept of contemporary military strategy.

> In modern warfare, military strategy has become the strategy of missile and nuclear strikes in depth along with the simultaneous use of all branches of the armed forces in order to achieve complete defeat of the enemy and the destruction of his economic potential and armed forces throughout his entire territory; such war aims are to be accomplished within a short period of time [p. 93].

While paying homage to the historic significance of the older military services, the strategic concept accords the new weaponry its greatest recognition to date in the country where Marxist men are supposed to be superior to the state's machines.

Military strategy of capitalist states

The committee of high-ranking military officers characterized American and N.A.T.O. military policy between 1953 and 1960 as a strategy of "massive response" or "massive retaliation." Quoting Secretary of State Dulles, the Soviet report interpreted this as primary dependence "upon a great capacity to retaliate, instantly, by means and at places of our own choosing" (p. 152). This strategy was based on the supposition that the United States had "overwhelming superiority," both quantitative and qualitative, in nuclear weapons and strategic aircraft. By threatening to employ its military strength, the government in Washington could attain its political and military goals, since the inferiority of the nuclear forces of the Soviet Union would not allow her leaders to risk a general war. During this period American military technology was devoted to the development of strategic and tactical nuclear weapons, while conventional weapons and the strength of the ground forces were relegated to secondary importance. This strategy of "massive retaliation" failed and was rejected in the last year of the Eisenhower administration, when officials became convinced that there had been an overestimation of American strength and an "underestimation of the economic, technical, scientific and military capabilities of the Soviet Union." Balance in strategic weapons possessed by the two countries and the superiority of Soviet conventional forces compelled the United States to discard the Dulles policy and reassess the official attitude toward future world war.

It is most significant that at this point Sokolovskii's report does not boast of Soviet superiority and treats the ideas of "nuclear stalemate" and "mutual deterrence" in a sympathetic fashion.

> They [the United States] understand that when both sides possess very large stockpiles of nuclear weapons and various means of delivering them to targets, primarily strategic means, a general war holds great risks of complete mutual annihilation. Consequently, the greater the stockpiling of weapons of mass destruction, the greater becomes the conviction that it is impossible to use them. Thus the growth of nuclear-missile power is inversely proportional to the possibility of its use [p. 156].

On the other hand, the Soviet strategists expressed dismay at the "incredible danger" involved in this approach, thus recalling Khrushchev's oft-spoken fear that a miscalculation by some "American officer" might result in setting off a global nuclear war.

Less sympathy is given to General Maxwell Taylor's theory of "flexible response." The basic principles of this alternative to massive retaliation were set forth in Taylor's book, *The Uncertain Trumpet,* which has been translated into Russian, and are listed by the Soviet analysts as these:

> (a) The creation of an invulnerable strategic missile force, capable of delivering a crippling blow to the enemy "even after absorbing a surprise nuclear attack."
> (b) The formation of adequate and properly equipped mobile forces for limited wars, "i.e., armed conflicts short of general atomic war between the two nuclear power blocs."
> (c) The formation of an effective system of military alliances.
> (d) The assurance of the most favorable use of resources allocated to the military program.[26]

This strategy was considered the basis of the Kennedy-Johnson administration's military policy.

Marshal Sokolovskii's committee expressed alarm over statements contained in President Kennedy's message to Congress in March, 1961. In that address, the President stressed the importance of the second-strike capability of the United States as a deterrent to enemy attack and the necessity of responding "swiftly and effectively" to any action undertaken by the enemy. The latter phrase, plus the allocations devoted to further weapons development, evoked the fear of the Soviet officers that "a very real threat of a preventive war being unleashed by the American imperialists against the Soviet Union" exists (p. 162). The fear of surprise attack does not appear to be lessened by the concentration of the American defense apparatus on solid-fuel ballistic missiles and underground and mobile launchers, in spite of the fact that these techniques are geared to second-strike capability. Whether this fear is genuine or whether its expression merely provides a pretext for other policies, such as those affecting budget allocations, cannot be accurately ascertained.

Although Marshal Sokolovskii's committee makes full use

of the clichés of Lenin's theory of imperialism and the dependence of capitalist economies on armaments, there is ample evidence in its work of serious and detailed consideration of American studies on the deployment of nuclear weapons in any future wars. While its interpretation is by no means free of the common Communist stereotypes of the West, the open attention devoted to weapons technology, weapons priority, and the strategic concepts of the United States indicate a further move away from Stalinism. The most striking gap in its consideration of Western military thought lies in the failure, or refusal, to evaluate the possibility and character of limited wars. On this score, the Soviet officers follow Khrushchev's dictum that of the three types of war—world, local, and national-liberation wars—only the last can be considered just, and any limited war involving nuclear powers will escalate into a global thermonuclear conflagration.

The nature of modern war

In reviewing several of the fundamental tenets of Marxist-Leninist doctrine, the Soviet report stresses the economic and political bases of war. The pattern of a state's economic structure is held to contain certain features that may lead that country into war with another state or create the conditions that may give rise to civil war within it. However, political conditions and political goals are accorded at least equal importance to economic relationships as determinants of declarations of war and the conduct of wars. A combination of factors is thought to be at work within any state—"ideological, political, economic, and others." The strong implication is that when the political forces within a nation or among various nations fail to channel the diverse forms of struggle and conflict, then war is likely to result. War is the continuation of politics by other means, namely "violent means." On this basis, war is defined as "armed violence: organized armed conflict between different social classes, states, groups of states and nations, in order to achieve definite political goals" (p. 271).

Of particular interest is the stress placed on the variety of factors which produce conflicts. The formation of the world socialist system has effected "radical changes" in international political struggle. Similarly, modern technology has brought dramatic new variables into world conflict, even to the extent of making "the complete disruption of the enemy's economy and the demoralization of his population" political aims of future war, rather than merely the defeat of opposing armies as in the past. Nevertheless, "even though hundreds of millions of people are drawn into it, war is only one aspect of political life, one particular form of political and class struggle" (p. 273). Class and national forces and social trends in general are deemed to be "much more inclusive phenomena" than can be contained in any war, even if it is characterized as a global or total war. The class struggle continues with or without war and is more fundamental and far broader in scope than military action can be. "Thus it is improper to confuse and identify two such social phenomena as war and class struggle or war and politics" (p. 273). War can be but one aspect of either. Such views are food for Chinese thought and have contributed to the ideological and policy disputes within what was once thought to be the "monolithic bloc."

Sokolovskii repeats Khrushchev's threefold classification of wars. Only wars of national liberation and revolutionary wars are inevitable so long as imperialism and colonialism are in existence. Limited wars in which the nuclear powers have a high stake will not be possible in the future. If such a local war begins, it will develop into a war of major proportions. Recognition is also given by the military committee to Khrushchev's pronouncement that wars between capitalist and Communist states are no longer inevitable. However, today "Soviet military strategy must consider it possible that the imperialist aggressors will unleash new *wars of conquest* at the most diverse points on the globe" (p. 280). Presumably this statement refers to new colonial wars and wars among capitalist states.

There is still danger to the Communist states, the report warns, in spite of the strength of the Communist system as a whole. Since the economic basis for war exists while capitalism still exists, Soviet military strategy "must accept the fact that there is still danger of the imperialists initiating new predatory wars and attacking the socialist countries, particularly the Soviet Union, despite the growing influence of factors ensuring the preservation of peace" (p. 285). The threat and possibility of military aggression against the Soviet Union, probably in the form of a surprise attack, is therefore "by no means eliminated." In addition to the initiation of war by a surprise attack on the U.S.S.R., world war can develop out of an "aggressive local war against one of the socialist states" (pp. 286-287). In either case the resulting conflict will be a nuclear war of world coalitions into which an "overwhelming majority of the countries of the world would be drawn." In such a world struggle the belligerents will have to aim at "conclusive political and military decisions." The use of hydrogen bombs and missiles with nuclear warheads will make another war one of mass destruction and annihilation. The Soviet armed forces must be conditioned for a "severe, strenuous, and exceptionally violent war." Under present circumstances, Marshal Sokolovskii declares that "the struggle for peace and the fight to gain time depend above all on an unremitting increase in Soviet military power and that of the entire socialist camp" (p. 285).

Modern weapon technology is distinguished by the development of "*qualitatively new types of weapons and military equipment* and their rapid and massive introduction into the armed forces" (p. 295). The appearance of this feature in military techniques and armaments has produced a revolution in the art of war and strategy. Since modern weapons can be employed for strategic, operational, and tactical purposes, the combat capabilities of the army, navy, and air force have increased radically. In turn, this vast augmentation of power has necessitated sharp changes in the organization of the armed forces and in strategic planning.

The most significant weapon yet produced in this technological revolution is the missile. The potential range, speed, and accuracy of intercontinental and medium-range ballistic missiles and their practical invulnerability to defense give missiles "extremely advantageous characteristics." They lend themselves to use in surprise attack and can be deployed against any target in either the front or the rear of the enemy with devastating quickness and reliability. Since effective antimissile defense systems have not been perfected, ballistic missiles are given "first place among all other instruments of war" (p. 298). According to the Sokolovskii report, current Soviet military science operates on the assumption that in any future world war nuclear weapons "will be the chief instrument of destruction, and missiles the basic vehicle for their delivery to target" (p. 299). The principal means of destruction in the last world war—artillery and the bomber—will be used *to support* the primary means of attack rather than *as* the primary means of attack.

This question of the relative importance of missile forces and thermonuclear bombs, on the one hand, and conventional forces, on the other, apparently still troubles the Soviet strategists. Though clearly giving the greater stress to modern weapons as Khrushchev had long demanded should be done, *Voennaia strategiia* carefully and repeatedly notes the lasting significance of older techniques of conducting warfare. "Final victory" will require the extensive use of conventional means of war, for the aim will not only be the destruction of the nuclear capacity of the enemy but the conquest of his armed forces and military bases and the occupation of strategic regions of his territory. Therefore, despite the new general strategy, massive armed forces will be needed in a future war. This shared responsibility is essential to complete the main strategic goal of war, which is to stage in a single, continuous movement "the annihilation of the opponent's armed forces, the destruction of targets deep in his territory, and the disorganization of the country."

> All this shows that the relationship between the role and importance of armed combat, on the one hand, waged by forces in direct contact with the enemy in the zone of military operations and employing tactical and operational weapons of destruction, and of armed combat, on the other hand, waged beyond this zone by strategic weapons of destruction has changed sharply in the direction of increasing the role and importance of the latter [pp. 305-306].

On these grounds, troops in direct contact with the enemy have been superseded in strategic importance by modern weapons.

This basic modification of Soviet strategic doctrine has obviously necessitated the reorganization and reorientation of Soviet conventional services. As one outgrowth of the change in doctrine the submarine fleet is in process of becoming the major wing of the Soviet Navy. The construction of nuclear submarines was given priority over surface vessels in future construction. The role of bombers was subjected to serious reevaluation in the Air Force, and the increased reliance of the ground forces on tanks and missile weapons was also an offshoot of the new-look program as it applied to the Soviet Army. As evidence of this, the ratio of engineering and technical personnel to command personnel in the Air Foıce shifted from 1 to 4.2 in 1941 to 1 to 1.5 in 1962, and in the ground forces from 1 to 5.7 to 1 to 3. An effort to improve the mobility of all services had apparently resulted in further reorganization of the basic units of the military to a greater extent than had been revealed in the statements of Khrushchev and Malinovskii in 1960 and 1961. General Yepishev noted in *Krasnaia zvezda* in the spring of 1963 that "in accordance with the requirements of modern warfare, the whole organization of the army and navy has been altered as well as their training."[27]

That these new approaches had come over strong opposition is revealed by the Sokolovskii report. The document avers that "every country has adherents of the old and battle-proven methods of combat." Furthermore, not only is "every country" faced with such conservatives but the generals and officers of "many countries prepared to wage war with the methods of the previous one" (p. 399). The authors of a Soviet military report published in 1960 under the title *O sovetskoi voennoi nauke* are taken to task for believing that the situation had not changed sufficiently to alter the offensive-defensive concepts of World War II (p. 401). Emphasis on frontal offensives by ground troops and the penetration of enemy lines as the major concerns of modern commanders is openly derided and labeled as "incorrect" for "mechanically applying" past experiences to the present. Overall, the work therefore places itself on the side of the new look by its endorsement of the superiority of missile armaments and by occasionally issuing mild reprimands to those officers who cling to the concepts of the old school.

Having begun to show particular concern over the rising significance of surprise attack and the early period of large-scale nuclear war, the Soviet commanders displayed evidence of having followed through with serious consideration of the possibly decisive character of the first phase of future wars. Their study proclaims that in order to accomplish the desired results, the military units of the entire Communist bloc "will have to employ their main military forces from the very outset of the war, literally during the first hours and minutes" (p. 308). This is required as a result of the heavy losses that could be inflicted on the military and civilian populations, which, in turn, could create "an extremely difficult situation." The armed services and the entire nation must, therefore, maintain a "high degree of combat readiness." The attacking nation can be expected to hurl all of its missile and aircraft power to devastate the strategic military and economic installations throughout the victim's territory. The struggle can be expected to be fierce and highly destructive. War begun with such momentous intensity and conducted with such weapons attests to the fundamental importance which the new strategy assigns to the initial stage of the war. The new concept, therefore, affirms that "the initial period of a modern missile war will obviously be the main and decisive period and will predetermine the development and outcome of the entire war" (p. 308).

Patent contradictions are contained in the report's consideration of Western intentions in regard to a surprise attack on the Communist camp. On the one hand, the Soviet strategists claim that N.A.T.O. has been developing methods for the "secret, rapid, final mobilization" of forces so that troops and weapons will be deployed before hostilities begin. The aim will be to achieve full mobilization without the knowledge of the Soviet command. From this posture a surprise attack can be launched. On the other hand, the United States is declared to be "afraid to take the initiative in unleashing a nuclear war, since this would be disadvantageous from a political standpoint and extremely dangerous from a military standpoint" (p. 396). According to the Soviet officers, either strategy would be ineffective, for they expect to be able to detect the moves necessary to prepare for a surprise attack and insist that the United States will not be able to restrict the scope and weapons in the latter case.

With respect to the scope of future war between nations armed with nuclear weapons, the Soviet report contends that it will involve "*an enormous geopolitical expanse*" and will include the massive use of modern weapons. The aim of each side will be for "conclusive results." Strategic missile units have become "the basic troops of modern massive armed forces." Their purpose will be to accomplish the "conclusive" aims by destroying the strategic and operational weapons of the enemy wherever they are located, by devastating the opponent's economy, and by disrupting communications and civilian and military leadership. In short, the scope of future war will encompass nearly every aspect of life in the modern nation-state.

Defense of military forces in the course of nuclear war and defense of the homeland have received increasing attention from Soviet officials in recent years. Marshal Sokolovskii's report reveals the many uncertainties in this area due to the vast array of imponderables that, doubtless, perplex many persons in both East and West. Troop defense will, according to present plans, be based on a high degree of mobility. That this technique may be insufficient is accepted with the comment that "the present instrumentalities of nuclear attack are undoubtedly superior to the instrumentalities of defense against them" (p. 307). In part, the defense of both the military and the home fronts can be accomplished by breaking up "the opponent's aggressive plans by dealing him in good time a crushing blow. . . ." The vagueness of this statement may be interpreted as an effort to conceal plans to rely on the "cheap" defense of pre-emptive war. However, even if this appraisal is accurate, concern for the defense of the nation as a whole has led to the devotion of much energy and time (expense is an unknown factor) to civilian defense measures. But again, the best defense of the home front is held to be "destroying the enemy's nuclear weapons where they are based" (p. 417).

In addition, claims are made that Soviet science and technology have perfected an antimissile missile, thereby solving the problem of destroying missiles in flight.[28] This assertion was in all probability an exaggeration of Soviet accomplishments at the time the report was written. In listing methods of conducting air defense operations, antimissile missiles are noted only after other methods of defense—including "distant fighter interception of aircraft and air-breathing missiles . . . [and] destruction of aircraft before they are close enough to launch missiles" (p. 420). It is, therefore, hardly likely that Soviet military strategy had really come to rely on such a missile for defense. In essence, the Soviet elite has discovered that in a war of world coalitions fought primarily with missiles and nuclear weapons it will indeed be difficult to provide an adequate defense.

Whatever the difficulties of defense, however, the attitude of the Russian people and the outcome of a future war are deemed to be certain. Paying respect to their Leninist heritage, Marshal Sokolovskii's committee declared that the Soviet armed forces "united around the Communist Party" are prepared "to endure any privations and make any sacrifices" to protect the socialist motherland from aggression. Despite the possible costs, war will "*inevitably end with the victory of the progressive, Communist social and economic system over the reactionary, capitalist social and economic system, which is historically doomed to destruction.*" But a final word of caution is given against this very historical inevitability. "Victory in a future war will not come of itself. It must be thoroughly prepared for and secured in advance" (pp. 312-313).

MOTIVATIONS OF CHANGING STRATEGIC CONCEPTS

The striking changes in Soviet military doctrine are more than amply demonstrated by the policies of the Khrushchev regime and by statements contained in *Voennaia strategiia* and in the publications of the armed services of the U.S.S.R. The *Istoriia voennogo iskusstva* published in 1963 reaffirmed most of the general conclusions of the Sokolovskii report, although slightly more emphasis was placed on conventional forces. The profound impact of technology on the conduct of war was recognized as a "natural law in the development of military art." "The continuous growth of the percussive power of weapons determines the successive dispersion of battle formations as a fundamental tendency of development."[29] Although modern weapons technology and traditional military concepts have occasionally been in conflict, producing some ambivalence in Soviet strategic concepts, there has been basic recognition of the necessity to make changes on technological grounds. Those changes have been molded by increasingly pluralistic demands within the social framework of the Soviet state. The party, the government bureaucracy, and the military bureaucracies all play prominent and by no means unanimous roles in the decision-making process. In their introduction to *Soviet Military Strategy,* the American editors note that:

> Doctrine, strategy, forces, technical and economic realities react on each other, and various pragmatic considerations intrude. The result more often than not seems to be the less-than-perfect answer, the necessity to live with a series of adjustments and compromise solutions.[30]

The forces at work within the maturing Soviet system prevent the adherence of the elite to singular, static designs, particularly in preparations for long-term situations. Analysts of the politics and behavior of the U.S.S.R. who have not reappraised their interpretations of the Soviet state since 1953, much less since 1940, are bound to draw inaccurate and often highly misleading conclusions. While the consideration of recent developments and apparent trends does not, of course, assure accuracy, it at least lessens the errors implicit in static views of a changing world.

The ideological style of contemporary politics has engendered a process of rationalization that facilitates the practical tasks of decision-makers. This process permits exceptions to be taken to the cognitive, and sometimes the normative, theory but does not always identify the actual motivating factors behind particular decisions. Since 1953 there has been a rising stream of evidence in the military sphere of tension between dogmatic precepts and strategic necessities and, from this, competing interpretations of those necessities. Commitment to an ideological spectrum of the world requires the rationalization of forces at work in the world. For example, one of the ostensible reasons for the dismissal of Malenkov as Premier in 1955 was his suggestion that a world war fought with thermonuclear weapons could possibly be disastrous for both sides, including the Soviet Union. In this setting Mikoyan engaged in an inevitable battle of semantics before the 20th Party Congress in attempting to explain why capitalist nations may not be willing to launch at attack on the Soviet Union in the future and why, therefore, war need no longer be considered inevitable. In the past, he claimed, American monopolists had known only gigantic profits from war, not destruction. Hence they had not been averse to "plotting a war." However, since the Soviet Union and its allies had become so powerful, "this time war will definitely not be a source of enrichment for them; it can only bring destruction and annihilation." Furthermore, Mikoyan declared, war cannot destroy civilization even though the use of hydrogen weapons can result in vast devastation for the whole world. In the event of a thermonuclear conflict, only "that obsolete and pernicious system, capitalism, in its imperialist stage" will be destroyed. Knowing this, the capitalists are not likely to begin a predatory war against the socialist commonwealth. By this circuitous reasoning, Mikoyan credits some circles in "imperialist" states with a realistic awareness of the dangers of nuclear war, without explicitly admitting that the Soviet leadership had become aware of precisely the same dangers.

Within the Communist system ideological questions reflect the power distribution among the component national parties. The so-called "left-Communists" or dogmatic Leninists have demanded satisfactory explanations for the revised theory of inevitable war and the accompanying changes in military strategy. One of the most complete discussions of the reasons behind these new approaches appeared in *Pravda* on August 12, 1960. It was clearly designed to answer the questions posed by the leftists. The article explained that although past wars had often created revolutionary situations, war has never been, is not, and will never be "a mandatory condition for the development of revolution." Communist ideology is assumed to be "so omnipotent" that war is totally unnecessary to advance its aims. As a consequence, to oppose war in no way diminishes the revolutionary potential available to the movement and cannot be construed as being un-Communist.

However, confidence in the military and economic power of the Soviet Union and in the ultimate victory of Communism cannot reasonably be considered the fundamental motive for the revised theory of war and the revolutionary adjustments in Soviet strategic concepts. Realization of the destructive power of thermonuclear weapons, beyond all question, has been at the root of the ideological revisionism of Kremlin's rulers. While this awareness has been partially veiled by insistence that in the event of nuclear conflagration the capitalist countries will suffer the greatest degree of devastation, neither the words nor the actions of Soviet leaders bear out that conviction.

Despite the mental gymnastics of Comrades Khrushchev and Mikoyan during the 20th and 21st Party Congresses, rationalizations in the name of dogma cannot forever conceal the true objectives, and often not the true motivations, of a state's leaders. The re-evaluation of defense policies and subsequent statements of the Prime Minister and other high-ranking officials confirm the belief that the Soviet hierarchy is not nearly so convinced that the U.S.S.R. cannot be devastated as the earlier pronouncements asserted. Speaking to an assembly of workers in Dnepropetrovsk, the Prime Minister commented that in the event of world war, "great damage will be inflicted on us too, and we too shall have to bear great sacrifices. War bodes no one any good."[31] Even in his rather belligerent address before the assembly of party workers at the Marx-Engels-Lenin Institute in January, 1961, Khrushchev publicly revealed that his confidence in the survival of Communist Russia was tempered by an awareness of the possible cost.

> We know that if the imperialists unleash a world war, capitalism will be swept away and destroyed by the people. We have decided against war first of all because we think of the fate of mankind, its present and its future. We know that in case of war first and foremost the toilers and their vanguard—the working class—will suffer.[32]

The most revealing public expression to date of the fear of another major war came in Khrushchev's speech before the Sixth Congress of the East German Communist Party in January, 1963. Marxist-Leninists, he declared, "cannot propose to establish a Communist civilization on the ruins of centers of world culture, on land laid waste and contaminated by nuclear fallout."[33] This was one of the few occasions on which a prominent Soviet spokesman openly expressed the view that something could prevent the "historically inevitable" triumph of Communism. The dominant element in the Soviet elite had concluded that the risk had become too great to accept the inevitability of war between the opposing systems even in theoretical terms.

Putting his summation of the present international scene in more positive terms before the celebration of the tenth anniversary of the Chinese People's Republic in Peking in 1959, Khrushchev appealed to growing circles of Chinese critics of his policies in these words:

> But we must be realistic in our thinking and understand the contemporary situation. Of course, this does not in any way mean that if we are so strong, we should test the stability of the capitalist system by force. This would be wrong. The peoples would not understand and would never support those who took it into their heads to act in such a way. We have

> always been against predatory wars. Marxists have recognized and still do recognize only wars of liberation, wars that are just, and have condemned and still do condemn wars that are predatory and imperialistic.[34]

Had these statements been spoken to a Western audience, or perhaps even to a Russian one, they might be overlooked as mere propaganda. Considering to whom they were spoken and the events that have since occurred in Moscow-Peking relations, they appear to have more substantive significance insofar as they chart the new course in Soviet policy and make clear Soviet insistence on following it.

Khrushchev's interpretation of current international trends also reflected a fear similar to that which pervaded the first years of the Soviet state and which indeed can be attributed in large measure to the impact of Leninist theory on contemporary Soviet ideology. Recognizing the intense hatred many capitalists hold for Communism, the Soviet Premier contended that as a result of this hate and fear, the Western powers try to dampen the difference among themselves. "In these circumstances the most likely wars are not between capitalist, imperialist countries. . . ." Instead, the war preparations of the Western alliance are intended for use against the countries of socialism and, first of all, against the Soviet Union. The task of the U.S.S.R. is, therefore, to create such insurmountable obstacles that even the imperialists will be "forced to ponder over what the consequences will be."[35] But for the present, Khrushchev confessed, "we still cannot completely prevent the possibility of wars. . . ." The inevitability, not the possibility, of war has been removed. Only by a greater strengthening of the forces of the Communist system and the Zone of Peace is it judged possible that war can be prevented and peaceful coexistence ensured indefinitely.

The interpretations the Kremlin elite apply to the prospects of war and peace and to international trends in general are clothed in the terms of Marxist-Leninist ideology. The strategic concepts of the reorganized armed forces are also supported by appeals to doctrinal statements. The element of fear that is always implicit in Soviet considerations of the policy objectives of Western states may have its initial basis in the tenets of Leninism, or at least it finds support in ideological and theoretical precepts. Yet current Soviet military thought and recent innovations in the doctrine of war give evidence of being based on the consideration of a widening spectrum of alternative policies that are viewed from a relatively pragmatic approach. These alternatives are different designs for the promotion of the best interests of the Soviet Republic and the choices made increasingly come in the shape of compromises resulting from competing interests within the social framework.

The interests concerned with military strategy have generally divided the officer corps into modernist and traditionalist groups, each receiving support from powerful political factions in the party hierarchy and the state bureaucracy. Budgetary considerations have been at the core of the disputes, since limitations on financial and resource allocations make it necessary either to choose between the demands of the groups or to apportion the allocations in such a way as to strike a balance between them. In either case, some members of one or both factions are likely to be discontented with the decision and to strive to obtain what they consider fairer recognition of their particular interests in future plans. Khrushchev's sympathy appeared to rest with the modernist group after 1955, although he made accommodations with the traditionalists during the period of conservative ascendancy in 1960-1962. The Prime Minister often found himself in the position of wanting to reduce military demands on the budget without losing his allies among the modernist faction of the armed services. This inclination was reflected in his attempts to cut the size and cost of conventional forces and to bolster the position of the technologically oriented officers in the armed services in the Central Committee of the Communist Party. But Khrushchev rarely had his own way with the traditionalists during their ascendancy. The conservatives appeared to be able to force their views concerning the defense strategy of the U.S.S.R. on the Khrushchev regime from 1960 through most of 1962. However, neither side succeeded in controlling the other during 1963-1964; the consequent stalemate required each faction to bargain and encouraged each group to try to outmaneuver the other. The result was a series of compromises over strategic designs and military allocations. Nevertheless, the position of the traditionalists, even when they lost a skirmish, was usually strong.

It is important to recognize that Khrushchev's shifts in policy on military matters appear to have been more the result of such disputes and compromises than of some peculiar quirk of the Soviet leader's personality. The recognition and influence which the modernists temporarily acquired came only after a great deal of infighting, including setbacks as well as successes. Khrushchev appeared to be generally sympathetic with them, but as Prime Minister he was also compelled to support policy decisions that had been initiated and advocated by the conservative opposition. As he grew older, Khrushchev seemed to feel more secure and consequently grew less cautious in waging budgetary and policy battles against the old guard. Once a master of Kremlin-style politics, he became overconfident and less willing to make concessions to powerful factions that had serious doubts about some of his policies and grave reservations about his personal political style. This loss of caution in dealing with potential adversaries contributed to his dismissal from both his party and government posts.

MILITARY ENGAGEMENT AND DISARMAMENT IN SOVIET FOREIGN POLICY

IV

Having examined the development of Soviet military thought in the post-Stalin period, we must now consider the role of military policy in the conduct of Soviet foreign affairs. The policies pursued in times of international crisis and the professed interest of Soviet policy-makers in disarmament demonstrate the relationship of military strength and strategic concepts to foreign policy decisions in given situations. In the first case, the role of Soviet military capabilities as a support for foreign policy objectives will be considered by analyzing the risk-taking propensity of the U.S.S.R. during times of crisis. In contrast, the second case involves the reasons for the Kremlin's interest in disarmament and the effects of this interest on disarmament negotiations with Western countries. This problem provides an opportunity to examine the intent and motivation of Soviet policy in the area of nonbelligerent military relations with other nations. Although the two cases are at opposite ends of the continuum of military policy, both risk-taking and disarmament illustrate particular aspects of the policy of coexistence and demonstrate the relationship between strategic concepts developed by the civil and military authorities of the Soviet Union and the nation's foreign policy.

RISK-TAKING IN SOVIET FOREIGN POLICY FROM 1955 TO 1966

The willingness of Soviet decision-makers to take risks in the conduct of their foreign policy has been the subject of much discussion in Western circles ever since the Bolsheviks established the Soviet regime in 1917. A popular assumption among the general public has been that the Soviet Union has been more prepared to take risks and to provoke international tension than most other nation-states. Our purpose is to provide a framework for evaluating the level of Soviet risk-taking in crisis situations, to examine Soviet policies in the principal crises of the 1955-1966 period, and to draw some general conclusions about risk-taking in recent Soviet foreign policy.

In the formulation of the foreign policy of any nation, the decision-makers must take into consideration the possible responses of the state or states affected by their policy. This assumes that the decision-makers behave rationally in their perceptions and assessments of events and in their consideration of alternative policies. An assessment by the policy-makers of the reaction of other parties enables them to categorize the possible and likely responses as certain, uncertain, or containing a definite risk to their own nation. If the reaction of others or their available choices of action are clearly calculable and are acceptable to the Soviet decision-makers, then their assessment of the other party's move is *certain*. If the other parties' reaction or choices of action are unclear but the contemplated Soviet action is not likely, in the view of Soviet policy-makers, to lead to a significant amount of tension, then the assessment is *uncertain*. If, on the other hand, the members of the Soviet elite are aware that the initiation of a policy may evoke a physical response or the threat of a physical response that may directly involve the vital interests, prestige, or security of their nation, then the assessment indicates that *risk* is involved in pursuing

TABLE I

Indicators of Soviet Risk-Taking in Crisis Situations

TYPE OF ACTION UNDERTAKEN	SITUATION										
	Suez Crisis (1956)	*Poland (1956)*	*Hungary (1956)*	*Middle East (1958)*	*Algeria (1960-61)*	*Laos (1960-61)*	*Congo (1960-61)*	*Vietnam (1965-66)*	*Berlin (1958)*	*Berlin (1961)*	*Cuba (1962)*
A. Verbal and/or written criticism, threat, or provocation	+	—	—	+	+	+	+	+	+	+	—
B. Provision of non-military aid during time of crisis	+	—	—	+	+	+	+	+			
BC. Physical, but nonviolent, provocation such as closing a border, economic sanctions, recall of diplomatic personnel									+	+	—
C. Provision of military aid during time of crisis	+	—	—	—[a]	—	+	+[b]	+			
D. Full or partial mobilization of Soviet armed forces	—	+	+	+	—	—	—	—	—	+	+
E. Deployment of Soviet forces and weapons outside the U.S.S.R.	—	+	+	—	—	—	—	—	—	—	+
F. Actual use of Soviet military force	—	—	+	—	—	—	—	—	—	—	—
	A,B,C	D,E	D,E,F	A,B,D	A,B	A,B,C	A,B,C	A,B,C	A,BC	A,BC,D	DE_2[c]

a. Economic and military aid was not offered to Iraq until after the crisis had subsided in November, 1958.
b. Soviet planes transported Ghanian troops to the Congo and small quantities of Soviet arms are known to have been used by the rebel forces.
c. E is converted to E_2 in order to recognize the proximity factor as a matter affecting the level of risk.

that policy. A decision to adopt a policy of risk is predicated on both the willingness and, in the decision-makers' estimation, the ability of the Soviet Union to accept the consequences.

A policy involving risk may be either a response to the action of another party or an initial move on the part of the Soviet Union. Such a policy may also be employed either to make gains or to prevent another party from making gains. The kinds of actions that may be adopted range from verbal threats to the deployment and actual use of Soviet armed forces. This range is illustrated in Table I, which identifies the possible gradations of Soviet willingness to engage in risky actions. The scale of intensity of this willingness is based on observations of Soviet behavior in eleven crisis situations in the post-Stalin period.

Official verbal and written criticism, challenges, or threats occurred in eight of the eleven situations. There was a wide range of intensity in their use. For example, in the Vietnam crisis of 1964, resulting from the attack on North Vietnamese torpedo boats by an American destroyer, the Soviet response was comparatively mild. It consisted, first, of reporting President Johnson's message in factual terms, then, of criticism of the American retaliation on North Vietnamese harbors, and, finally, of urging a prompt and peaceful settlement. Only after the crisis had ebbed did the Soviet Union declare its intention to defend all Communist states against attack. This occurred before the activation of American troops in the ground fighting and the extension of bombing raids on North Vietnam.

In the Suez crisis, while the controversy over Egypt's right to nationalize the canal was still raging and before the Israeli attack on Egypt began, Radio Moscow warned against "acts of aggression" in violation of the security interests of the Soviet Union, threatened to destroy Western properties in Arab countries, and declared the Kremlin's intention of bringing "irreparable damage" to Great Britain and France if they interfered with the nationalization of the canel. Before hostilities began, Khrushchev promised to aid Egypt by sending "volunteers" and implied that additional forms of support would be given the U.A.R. On November 10, Khrushchev repeated his threat to send volunteers, but by that date the peak of the crisis had passed.

In the Middle East crisis of 1958, the Soviet Union protested the sending of American and British troops into Lebanon and Jordan by officially notifying Washington that the U.S.S.R. reserved "the right to take necessary measures" against "threats" to any area close to its frontiers. On July 20, Khrushchev sent a note to Eisenhower, urging an immediate summit conference and reminding the President that the Soviet Union had an arsenal of nuclear bombs and ICBM's. Khrushchev also pledged to send Soviet "volunteers" should the Arab countries need them. In the Congo situation, the Soviet press denounced American and Belgian activities, and Khrushchev threatened to send "the necessary help" to assure victory for the "progressive forces." The verbal support issued in behalf of the rebels in Algeria was comparatively mild, probably because the Soviet government wanted to conclude a favorable trade agreement with France and did not want to push France into closer alliance with the United States and Great Britain.

In all of these situations the Soviet assertion of its interest in the crisis was a response to unfolding developments and resulted in increasing tension, but could not be considered responsible for causing it in the first place.

In the two crisis situations involving Berlin, Soviet announcements were responsible for instigating the rise in international tensions. In a speech on November 10, 1958, and in an official note to the parties occupying West Germany on November 28, Khrushchev set a six-month deadline for signing a peace treaty recognizing two independent German states, requiring the removal of all troops from Berlin, and making the Western sector of Berlin into a demilitarized "free city." In the Berlin crisis of 1961, a similar declaration was issued with the notation that failure of other states to participate in a peace conference "will not stop us." None of the crises involving member states of the Communist system, including the Cuban crisis of 1962, were marked by the open use of demands, threats, or criticism in the initial stages of crisis.

The provision of Soviet nonmilitary assistance occurred in six crises and the provision of military aid in four. The Soviet Union continued to fulfill its obligations to Egypt under economic and military aid agreements approved in 1955 after the Suez crisis had erupted, although no steps were actually taken to enlarge the Soviet commitment after Israel began its attack on Egypt.[1] In the Middle East crisis of 1958, also, the Soviet Union already had an economic aid agreement with Egypt and Syria, and the agreement to provide economic and military assistance to the new Iraqi government was not consummated until several months after the crisis had subsided.[2]

The situation in Laos was more complicated. The U.S.S.R. had a formal and legal role to play because of its membership in the International Control Commission (ICC) established by the Geneva Convention of 1954. When it appeared that the Pathet Lao might win the civil war in the late autumn of 1960, the Soviet Union established diplomatic relations with Loas and offered economic aid to the rebel government, which was then in charge of the capital. However, only after the Pathet Lao suffered serious military setbacks and it appeared that the rebels might lose the war did Moscow openly begin to send military assistance. Following the rather steady loss of territory by the Pathet Lao in 1961, Soviet aid diminished (it is not clear at what point it stopped altogether), and the U.S.S.R. once again began to stress its role as mediator through the ICC.

During the revolution in Algeria, *Pravda* announced on September 22, 1960, that agricultural and medical equipment was being sent to the Algerian rebels. Similarly, during the Congo crisis Moscow provided small amounts of economic and medical assistance to the supporters of Lumumba and Gizenga. Soviet IL-18's were also used to transport Ghanian troops to the Congo and some Soviet arms were acquired from those troops. The staff of the Soviet Embassy was ordered to leave the Congo "temporarily" as a rebuff to the "imperialist agents" who were blamed for causing disorders. In the Vietnamese crisis, the Soviet Union cautiously provided military assistance to North Vietnam while avoiding a direct commitment to the Viet Cong.

In all six of these situations, with the possible exception of Vietnam, the volume of Soviet economic and military aid during the periods of crisis was so limited as to cast serious doubts on its real importance in affecting the outcome.

Both situations involving Berlin, in 1958 and 1961, were marked by physical but nonviolent provocations. These consisted of border incidents and efforts to force Western military personnel to deal with East German officials. The 1958 incident did not progress beyond this point, while the 1961 crisis was heightened by the building of the wall around West Berlin. Although the construction of the wall provoked indignation and strong condemnation by the Western powers, it was more a defensive device designed to reduce the loss of East German manpower than an act of aggression against West Berlin. Its construction could not be considered offensive in a military sense. The Cuban crisis was not marked by such incidents of nonmilitary provocation.

In five of the eleven crises partial or full mobilization of the armed forces of the Soviet Union occurred. In both of the situations involving eastern European states there were movements of Soviet troops along the western borders of the U.S.S.R. In addition, Soviet troops were alerted in the Transcaucasus region during the Middle East crisis of 1958. The troop movements in 1956 were primarily in the western reaches of Russia; hence it is assumed that the mobilization of troops was in response to events in Poland and Hungary rather than to the Israeli-British-French invasion of Egypt.

The Berlin crisis of 1961 also involved a sharp increase in Soviet defense expeditures and the movement of Soviet troops inside Russia in response to the efforts of the United States to test Soviet intentions by sending troops into West Berlin along established routes. In the case of Cuba, the mobilization of Soviet military divisions inside the U.S.S.R. was apparently not initiated until after the United States had exposed the secret moves of the Soviet Union on the Caribbean island. This suggests that the Soviet policy-makers either did not anticipate the hostile reaction from the United States to their effort to implant medium-range missiles in Cuba or that they were prepared to withdraw in the event of a strong response from the Kennedy administration.

The actual deployment of Soviet troops or weapons took place in three of the crises, all of them involving members of the party-state system. In two of these cases Soviet troops were directly involved, while in the third case Soviet weapons under Soviet control constituted the principal issue. During the leadership crisis in Poland in October, 1956, Khrushchev, Mikoyan, Molotov, and Kaganovich unexpectedly visited Warsaw to assure that the resolution of the conflict between old-guard and reformist party leaders would be acceptable to the Soviet leadership. While they were en route, Soviet tanks and troops were moved to the outskirts of Warsaw.[3] The troops began withdrawing the day after the confrontation of Polish and Russian party officials, but new maneuvers occurred two days later near Lodz, Lublin, and Warsaw, and were not called off until Gomulka conferred with Khrushchev on October 23. Considering the close proximity of Poland to the U.S.S.R., it is doubtful that the deployment of Soviet armed strength involved any risk of retaliation from a powerful third party. However, the reluctance of the Soviet leaders to do more than demonstrate the presence of their army suggests that they were anxious to avoid any overt show of force, even in an area where they could claim that their country had legitimate vital interests.

The Hungarian leaders were unable to control the development of events as successfully as the Polish party leaders, with the result that the Hungarian revolution moved much more swiftly toward fomenting a clear break between Hungary and the Soviet Union. As the pressure for liberalization increased, the Hungarian government called for Soviet assistance in order to suppress rioting in the streets of Budapest. The U.S.S.R. acted with dispatch and stationed her forces at several key points throughout Hungary, while pledging that no action against the local populace would be ordered "unless attacked." Mikoyan and Suslov were sent to investigate the situation in the Hungarian capital, while the Soviet delegate to the United Nations insisted that all actions had been justified under the terms of the Warsaw Treaty. Soviet forces began to pull back on October 31 as the reformists attempted to secure their control of the government. It is not known to what extent radio broadcasts from Western Europe before and during this period might have influenced Soviet policy, but it is well established that the appeals for revolt and the promise of assistance were taken quite literally by many of the young revolutionaries. The possibility of American intervention appears to have been considered by the Soviet policy-makers. Ferenc Vali places the date of the decision to intervene a second time with greater force on November 1, which was the day Mikoyan and Suslov returned from their mission to Budapest.[4] It was also the day after President Eisenhower announced the reluctance of the United States to become involved in the Suez crisis and expressed a cautious wait-and-see attitude in regard to developments in eastern Europe. The Soviet assessment indicated that the risk could be taken and that the Hungarian revolution had progressed beyond limits acceptable to Moscow even before the decision to withdraw from the Warsaw Pact was publicly announced by Imre Nagy. It is not known whether or not Nagy informed the visiting Soviet statesmen of this possibility. In any event, the second Russian intervention was conducted with great swiftness and force, leaving little time for a third party to send military assistance to the rebels. This episode is the only instance in the 1954-1966 period in which the Soviet Union employed its own armed forces in direct combat.

The third situation in which the deployment of Soviet troops and weapons was involved was the Cuban crisis of 1962, the only serious risk undertaken by Moscow in the post-Stalin period. This episode deserves special consideration.

Soviet behavior during the Cuban missile crisis

International politics since World War II has been fraught with crises but none has been more dramatic than the direct confrontation of the United States and the Soviet Union over Cuba in October, 1962. The crisis arose as the result of the installation by the U.S.S.R. of medium-range missiles equipped with nuclear warheads on the Caribbean island. Khrushchev's government was thereby making its boldest move far from the Soviet power base. The action was, in effect, a direct challenge to the supremacy of the United States in the western hemisphere. The interplay of forces resulting from the Soviet action provides the best available study of the military capabilities and intentions of the Kremlin.

The background to the case was one of deliberate deception. While the Russian missiles were being unloaded and assembled, the Soviet press was waging an intense propaganda campaign against an allegedly imminent invasion of Cuba under the auspices of the United States. Foreign Minister Andrei Gromyko assured President Kennedy in a personal meeting that all of his country's military assistance to Cuba was of a strictly defensive nature. Apparently the Kremlin strategists believed that their provocative action could go undetected until the Soviet military position on Cuba was firmly established. However, films taken by American reconnaissance planes uncovered the real mission of Russian military technicians on the island.

Without prior notification to the Soviet Union, President Kennedy seized the initiative by addressing the nation on October 22, informing the public of the U.S.S.R.'s military venture, and issuing in clear terms an ultimatum to the Soviet Union. The President announced that a naval quarantine was being placed around Cuba, that no further shipments of "offensive" weapons and supplies would be permitted to pass through, that the missiles already on location must be removed, and that the Soviet Union would be held responsible for any military action against the United States stemming from Cuba. The burden of initiating hostilities was thereby placed on the Kremlin. For the first time in the crisis situations of the post-Stalin period Moscow found itself on the defensive.

The immediate Soviet reaction was hostile, as expected. The government's official protest charged the United States with violating the United Nations Charter, declared that the Russian weapons in Cuba were aimed "only at enhancing the defense potential of Cuba," and noted that the United States maintained military bases around the world. The Ministry of Defense announced a postponement in the demobilization of rocket and antiaircraft troops, halted all furloughs, and issued an alert to all combat forces. On October 24, *Pravda* printed an editorial scathingly denouncing "imperialist action," and declaring that "if the aggressors unleash a war, the Soviet Union will strike a mighty retaliatory blow."

As the United States proceeded to mobilize land and naval forces to implement the quarantine, the Kremlin quickly moderated its position. *Izvestiia,* on October 25, somberly declared that "a militaristic frenzy is descending over Washington like a noxious fog." The same day, however, Khrushchev sent a letter to Lord Russell, indicating his concern over the military dangers evoked by the crisis and intimating that he would be receptive to the convocation of a summit conference to avert nuclear war. When the United States reacted unfavorably to the idea of a summit meeting, Khrushchev quickly accepted Secretary-General U Thant's proposal that the American government suspend the quarantine and the Soviet government suspend military shipments pending negotiations.

The most decisive negotiations leading to the resolution of the conflict were the direct exchange of communications between President Kennedy and Prime Minister Khrushchev and between the Soviet embassy in Washington and the White House, with an American newsman acting as intermediary. On October 26, a senior officer of the intelligence staff of the Soviet embassy met with the newsman, asking him to inform the President of his country's interest in averting a war. Daily contact was made between the two men during the crisis. The Embassy officer declared his government's willingness to withdraw the missiles and bombers if the President would pledge that there would be no invasion of Cuba. On October 27, Prime Minister Khrushchev sent a formal note to the President, agreeing to remove "those weapons from Cuba which you regard as offensive," provided the United States would remove weapons from Turkey which the U.S.S.R. regarded as offensive. In the same message Khrushchev asked the American government to respect the "integrity" of Cuba and pledge not to invade or give aid to an invasion again. However, the President rejected the Prime Minister's attempt to bargain over the removal of bases and notified the Soviet government that the United States was prepared to accept the terms offered by the official of the Embassy. President Kennedy's official response made no reference to the informal communiqué but merely affirmed agreement to lift the quarantine and to guarantee that no invasion of Cuba would be staged if the U.S.S.R. promptly removed the missile bases and permitted inspection to verify their removal. The American response, in short, offered the Soviet Union a dignified line of retreat.

Khrushchev's response to the President's offer gave no indication of the military considerations that had prompted his government to take such a grave risk. Instead, it indicated that he was most concerned with securing a noninvasion pledge from the United States, although he also used the occasion to call for a test-ban agreement and to protest air violations of Soviet territory by American planes. Significantly, during the exchange of these messages, the Prime Minister helped ease the tense atmosphere by ordering Russian ships destined for Cuba to alter course rather than test the earnestness of the quarantine maintained by the U.S. Navy. Finally, on October 29, Khrushchev sent a message to Kennedy formally stating that Soviet missiles would be dismantled and returned to the U.S.S.R. Although some issues remained—the question of inspection and the number of Soviet troops and technicians in Cuba—the outstanding problems responsible for sparking the crisis were resolved by December.

While many Western leaders and most of the Western press were hailing Khrushchev's offer to withdraw the bases as a great victory for the United States, the Russians attempted to portray their retreat as a demonstration of the policy of peaceful coexistence. *Pravda* claimed that the decision to withdraw the missile bases was based on "positions of reason and good will" rather than on "positions of strength." *Izvestiia* declared that the decision saved Cuba from certain nuclear destruction. It was also emphasized that the decision to halt the missile buildup was made solely because of the President's no-invasion pledge. This argument can hardly be accepted as the primary reason for the Soviet withdrawal.[5] At most the pledge was a face-saving device for the Soviet Union. The *post-factum* statements coming from Moscow were largely efforts to salvage some propaganda and prestige advantage from the policy failure.

Mirovaia ekonomika i mezhdunarodnye otnosheniia gave a most interesting account of the crisis. Ignoring the importance to Soviet military strategy of having missiles on Cuba, the journal followed the official line by contending that the aim of Soviet policy was "only the defense of Cuba."[6] "If there had not been the threat of invasion, if the U.S.A. had given a pledge earlier that it would not invade or unleash its allies for an invasion . . . then the necessity for placing Soviet rockets on Cuba would not have arisen." However, instead of placing the blame for the alleged threat directly on President Kennedy, the authors went out of their way to absolve him of personal responsibility and to place the blame on "adventurous elements of the Pentagon and extreme rightists . . . who accused President Kennedy of unwarranted softness." While repeating the official claim that the pledge of no invasion was a great compromise and that the outcome of the crisis had proved that "the right to revolution and to social progress does not depend on the sanctions of American imperialism," the authors also emphasized the fearful consequences of nuclear war on "the whole world." The crisis "made still more obvious the objective necessity of adjusting to peaceful coexistence" and "to bring to an end the breeding grounds of 'cold war' " in order to avoid thermonuclear catastrophe. The article suggests that in the months following the crisis, the Kremlin appeared unusually anxious to establish improved relations with the United States and appeared to have found a new respect for the Kennedy administration. After what must have been very tense moments in Moscow during the crisis, the tone of the article indicates that Khrushchev and his associates were not anxious to offend the President and were prepared to seek new ways to reduce the chances of nuclear war.

Although Russia has historically demonstrated a compulsion

to expand its territory and influence and the Soviet government professes an undying commitment to extend its system to other countries, the missile buildup in Cuba appears to have been based very largely on strategic considerations. In the course of 1963 it had become clear that the United States had been able to maintain superiority in missile development and nuclear capacity, contrary to Moscow's claims. Secretary of Defense McNamara had gone so far as to declare in Ann Arbor, Michigan, that American supremacy was so great that Washington was in a position to dictate the kind of strategy—as to both scale and target—in any military engagement.[7] The persuasiveness of his argument, coupled with the knowledge that certain secrets of Soviet military preparedness had been leaked to Great Britain and the United States, could hardly have set well with the men in the Kremlin. By geography and intention Moscow found itself bound by a highly inflexible strategy. To make matters worse for them, the Western powers had uncovered their predicament. The Soviet missiles in Cuba would have given military strategists in the U.S.S.R. greater flexibility by reducing the choices available to the United States and providing themselves with more alternatives. The risk of being caught before they had consolidated their position had to be taken.

A subsidiary motivation may have been to gain prestige by scoring a psychological victory over the United States. Yet when the Soviet decision-makers were confronted by the threat of nuclear war for an action so far from their own base of power and fraught with so much danger for their country as well as for others, they were willing to risk their own prestige by yielding to American pressure. In so doing, of course, the U.S.S.R. was able to retain the foothold of the Communist system in the western hemisphere, but in spite of that factor the point had been clearly made—limits existed even on Communist willpower and reason could be valued and could prevail in Moscow, even under intense pressure.

Soviet behavior in crisis situations: summary

Despite the lack of caution in the decision to plant missiles in Cuba, the Soviet Union has for the most part carefully avoided taking steps that might lead to the eventual use of force. Reliance on verbal admonitions and warnings was particularly pronounced in crisis situations located outside the Communist states. In these circumstances Moscow was prepared to offer modest quantities of economic and military aid but demonstrated no willingness to finance large-scale and prolonged military campaigns. The Soviet decision-makers took care not to commit themselves very deeply in terms of action, although they were willing to commit themselves verbally in all of the crisis situations outside the party-states. Only in one instance did Moscow order the deployment of Soviet military forces to an area of great strategic concern to the United States, and in no instance were Soviet troops and weapons deployed outside the Communist system of states. Indeed, the Kremlin demonstrated considerable restraint in the use of force within the system, for as distasteful as the suppression of the Hungarian revolution was to most Americans, the Soviet Union did not act abruptly in that situation and ordered the second intervention only after a period of vacillation and the consideration of alternatives and consequences. It should not be surprising that Moscow was prepared to take a calculated risk in order to prevent the disintegration of the party-state system.

The emplacement of missiles in Cuba appears to have been primarily a strategic move, in which Kremlin leaders were willing to assume a risk in order to increase the range of flexibility in Soviet defense strategy. With a far-reaching system of bases around the globe and the elevation of hard-based missiles to a high place in strategic plans, American defense efforts sharply curtailed the range of Soviet defense plans. The Soviet Union's inability to exercise much choice in its own strategic designs must have seemed highly unsatisfactory in Moscow. Even the possibility that the United States might be strong enough to dictate both the scope and the target area of a future war might have led the Soviet policy-makers to deviate from their usual unwillingness to avoid major risks. When the United States reacted strongly, the Kremlin was prepared to make concessions in order to avoid the greater risk of having the bases in Cuba attacked by the United States and of having to face the possible consequences of such a venture.

It is noteworthy that in the three situations marked by the actual deployment of Soviet forces and weapons or the use of armed force, there were neither verbal threats nor offers of tangible forms of assistance. Such silence has been common in regard to problems within the Communist system of states, for Moscow has rarely called attention to difficulties among the states governed by "fraternal parties." In Cuba, the silence was, of course, a strategic necessity, for the success of the venture depended on completing the installation of the missiles before they were discovered. In all other situations, there were strongly worded verbal and written protests or threats as the Soviet Union began her initial moves in the crisis areas. In none of these cases did the degree of risk-taking by the U.S.S.R. reach the point of deploying Soviet armed forces, although in at least five instances partial mobilization of the military was ordered. In the two crises in the Middle East and in Laos, the Soviet threats were later used by Moscow to support the claim that the Soviet Union had been responsible for compelling the other parties to reach a peaceful solution. In the same three crises, the Soviet Union used her "peace-keeping" role to encourage the neutral nations of Asia to endorse the Soviet position.[8] In the Berlin situations the Soviet decision-makers appeared to be more confident that they could better control events, thus preventing the risk from increasing any more than they wanted it to. The position of Berlin enabled the Kremlin to initiate and to end the crises pretty much at will.

The most extensive analysis of Soviet risk-taking was undertaken by the Stanford Studies of the Communist System under the direction of Jan F. Triska. After careful examination of the variables involved in crisis situations occurring between 1945 and 1963, this study sets forth conclusions which are largely in accord with the propositions made in this chapter. Triska states that "Soviet crisis behavior was found to be conservative rather than radical, cautious rather than aggressive, deliberate rather than impulsive, and rational (not willing to lose) rather than non-rational."[9] The project also concludes that "emotional investment in objectives" by the Soviet leaders is less important than "perceived material *capability*." The implication of this conclusion is that ideological motivations appear to play a minimal role in the formulation of policy in the situations examined.

The Triska study further makes the important point that perception of risk on the part of the Soviet policy elite is closely related to Soviet military capability in any given situation. "The greater the Soviet weapons-military parity with the West, the lower the Soviet perception of risk in actual East-West conflicts." Therefore, even though the Western leaders may view a particular action in terms of risk, the Soviet elite may not perceive the same action to be a risk-taking venture. In general, the Stanford project concludes that "the stronger the other party in crisis, the greater the geographical distance from the U.S.S.R., and the greater the stakes involved, the more cautious the Soviet crisis response." Perceived military capability of the Soviet Union and of the responding party may, therefore, be considered a major determinant of Soviet behavior in crisis situations.

The Soviet leadership has been more inclined to use verbal and written ultimatums and warnings than to take a high level of risk in actual policy commitment. Skillful use of words has been a weapon to enlarge the sense of risk in other parties, thereby increasing their caution in situations where the U.S.S.R. itself has been reluctant to take more than token action. Risk-taking in terms of action has been low in recent Soviet foreign policy, while word-making has served as a less costly and more frequently used substitute.

DISARMAMENT: PROGRAM OR PROPAGANDA?

Another area where Soviet military strategy and the program of peaceful coexistence can be evaluated is disarmament. In 1961, Khrushchev elevated the goal of disarmament to the top of the agenda of the struggle for peaceful coexistence. Labeling disarmament the most important factor in the effort to prevent war, he also interpreted the Soviet peace campaign as an effective instrument in the struggle for Communism. As a major aspect of Khrushchev's foreign policy, Soviet proposals in the area of disarmament reflect rather clearly the contradictory motivations that prompt the Kremlin's decision-makers to approach the subject with varying degrees of seriousness.

Victor P. Karpov, the First Secretary of the Soviet Embassy in Washington, D.C., has noted that the Soviet Union draws a "clear-cut distinction" between disarmament and arms control. Arms control allows the object of control (armies and armaments) to continue to exist. Karpov explained that the Soviet government deems "the arms control method as an inadequate method for the solution of the most outstanding problem of our time—to get rid of the menace of nuclear holocaust."[10] The mere regulation of the size of armies and the level of armaments, Karpov contended, does not in fact do anything to eliminate the instruments of war which make resort to war possible. "Disarmament is no more a question of reduction of armaments, it is a question of complete destruction of all armaments."[11] Only through disarmament can "the very possibility of war be eliminated."

Soviet thought on disarmament underwent a significant evolution during the Khrushchev era, which appears to have continued under the Brezhnev-Kosygin leadership. First treating disarmament as a rigid tactical device designed purely to counter Western proposals, the Soviets lated shifted to a more subtle approach which often cleverly combined propaganda with a concern for reducing both the economic burden of the arms race and the likelihood of a nuclear holocaust. The new attitude appears to be grounded on a combination of complex factors that are difficult to untangle: Soviet appreciation of Russia's historical experiences in warfare—the continental nature of its geography and power and the consequent stress on the importance of ground forces; a growing awareness of the possible cost of thermonuclear war and of the military strength of the United States; a belief in the propaganda value disarmament has in Europe and many newly developing nations; and confidence in the ability of the Soviet Union to outproduce the United States in circumstances of peace and reduced military expenditures.[12]

The first real indication that the Soviet approach to disarmament was undergoing serious re-evaluation came in May, 1955, when Malik introduced a new resolution in the United Nations Subcommittee on Disarmament. In part, the resolution repeated previous Soviet proposals, demanding liquidation of all foreign military bases and withdrawal of all troops from Germany before further steps could be taken. However, the succeeding sections of the resolution were generally considered by the West to be more negotiable. The proposal called for a freeze in the size of armed forces, in conventional armaments, and in military expenditures. After this step had been taken by the major powers, a gradual reduction in the size of the armed forces would begin. Also, for the first time, the Soviet Union announced that it favored an agreement on the cessation of nuclear tests.

The Malik proposals indicated continuing acceptance of the traditional stress on the importance of ground forces, which was bolstered by Russian military history as well as by Marxist-Leninist thought. The control devices acceptable to the Soviet Union were all closely related to "conventional armaments, which are of decisive importance to the outcome of any major war. . . .[13] Concessions were made to previously stated positions of American negotiators, for Malik agreed that control posts to prevent a surprise attack should exist at all large ports, at railway junctions, on major motor highways, and at airports. "The task of these posts shall be to see to it that there is no dangerous concentration of military land forces or of air or naval forces."[14] On the other hand, effective control over fissionable material was considered impossible. Khrushchev referred to the control proposals of the West, in the absence of a reduction in standing armies and armaments, as "military reconnaissance" to gain information "for choosing the most convenient moment for sudden attack."[15]

The Soviet Union made a larger number of concessions to the Western position on disarmament than they had made before or than they made in the following decade. The Malik plan resulted in a fairly high level of consensus between the United States and the Soviet Union on three vital areas: control stations to check conventional forces, the priority given to conventional weapons and forces in the staging of disarmament, and the levels to which they would be reduced. These concessions suggest that the Kremlin was genuinely interested in achieving at least some type of limited disarmament agreement with the Western powers. They were made during a period of relative calm and goodwill as preparations for the Geneva Summit Conference were being made. It was, therefore, all the more surprising that the United States unexpectedly announced that a reservation was being attached to previous proposals and that it was reversing the position taken earlier on reduction levels. Thereafter, neither side appeared to be disposed to grant concessions and the negotiations of 1955 ended without material accomplishments.

During the remainder of 1955 and throughout 1956, the Soviet Union continued to view Western proposals for control of nuclear weapons as designs for espionage and continued to stress the importance of limitations on conventional armaments. Gromyko argued before the U.N. Subcommittee on Disarmament "that the cause of disarmament would be advanced if an initial agreement could be reached on conventional armaments."[16] Nevertheless, the Soviet Foreign Minister added that the U.S.S.R. was disposed

(1) to discontinue forthwith tests of thermonuclear weapons;
(2) to ensure that no atomic weapons were included in the armaments of troops in German territory;
(3) to reduce military budgets by up to 15 per cent during the coming year.[17]

The Soviet government was prepared to make a further concession to American proposals by accepting the concept of aerial inspection. By 1957, Soviet insistence on separating conventional from nuclear disarmament began to diminish. However, Moscow's intransigeance against the Western concept of effective control to ensure the implementation of nuclear disarmament did not abate. Soviet spokesmen repeatedly denied the possibility of effective controls over the production of nuclear devices. In spite of these periodic concessions and retractions on some issues and the refusal to compromise on others, the Malik and Gromyko proposals of 1955 and 1956 have continued to be the basis of Soviet propositions on disarmament.

General disarmament proposals

General disarmament has been both the most dramatic and the most persistently advocated proposal by Soviet representatives to disarmament conferences since 1957. Following the introduction of the Malik plan and the conclusion of the Geneva Conference of 1955, the Soviet Union showed reluctance to separate the consideration of conventional and nuclear armament problems. Although Gromyko had suggested a program dealing largely with the reduction of conventional forces during the London talks of 1956, the Soviet proposals of 1957 called for sweepingly comprehensive disarmament. Delegate Zorin demanded an immediate cessation of the production of atomic and hydrogen weapons, destruction of all stockpiles of such weapons, reduction of the size of standing armies, and the abolition of foreign bases.[18] Zorin further insisted that this plan was quite practical without provisions for regulation and inspection if concluded as a "solemn agreement" by the interested parties. On one issue the 1957 proposals represented another concession to Western demands, for Zorin acknowledged the willingness of his government to accept three stages in the implementation of a disarmament program. Staging had previously been a major point of contention. On the other hand, the Soviet Union retracted its offer to include aerial inspection in the initial phase and insisted that it be postponed until the second stage. In general, the Zorin proposal lacked specificity and its vagueness may be considered a retrogressive step from the Soviet propositions of 1955 and 1956.

The Soviet disarmament program of 1957 was noteworthy for a more important reason, however, than its stress on broad, uncontrolled disarmament. It revealed the great concern of the Kremlin for N.A.T.O. strategy and its implications for Soviet security in central Europe by emphasizing the need to create a 500-mile-wide aerial inspection zone on either side of the Iron

Curtain and by placing more rigorous demands on the size and nature of armaments in East and West Germany. This part of Zorin's program very likely stemmed from the decision made by the United States to press for broader West German rearmament and to offer nuclear weapons to the forces of N.A.T.O.

After the Western powers rejected the proposals offered by Zorin in 1957, the Soviet Union boycotted the meetings of the U.N. Subcommittee for two years. The boycott ended following Khrushchev's tour of the United States and his personal appearance before the General Assembly of the United Nations in September, 1959. Boldly calling for general and complete disarmament, Khrushchev offered the most sweeping Soviet proposal yet presented. He insisted that this approach, rather than that of partial disarmament, would "clear the way for the institution of universal and complete control."[19] The program he suggested was stated in broad terms and included the creation of a control and inspection zone, the reduction of foreign troops in Europe, an atom-free zone in central Europe, abolition of military bases on foreign territories, a nonaggression treaty between the members of N.A.T.O. and the Warsaw Pact, and an agreement on the prevention of surprise attack. These steps were to be implemented in three stages over a four-year period, ending with universal disarmament. The West objected strongly to both the timing and the staging contained in the Prime Minister's disarmament package.

Subsequently, Soviet delegates to disarmament conferences presented more detailed versions of Khrushchev's proposals. Stage one included the liquidation of all means of delivery of nuclear weapons and all foreign bases. "This would, in practice, neutralize the danger of an attack with nuclear weapons."[20] In addition, all nuclear weapons tests were to be banned, controls were to be placed on the launching of rockets for peaceful purposes, and steps would be taken to prevent the further spread of nuclear weapons and the use of space for military measures.

A 30 per cent reduction in the size of armed forces and conventional weapons and the withdrawal of all troops from foreign territories were part of the first stage. These steps were originally set for fifteen months but later the time was expanded to nineteen months. The second stage envisioned the further reduction of armed forces and conventional weapons by 35 per cent of the original level, a reduction in military expenditures, and the complete liquidation of "nuclear and other types of weapons of mass destruction." This stage was also to encompass nineteen months. The third stage, to be completed in twelve months, would consist of the complete elimination of armament industries and military institutions, and a complete ban on military expenditures. The United Nations would be responsible for establishing a police force that would operate under the joint command of "Western, Socialist, and Neutralist" states. Karpov declared that the Soviet Union "is ready to give serious consideration to all further reasonable proposals—so long as these proposals do not undermine disarmament itself."[21]

On first glance the Soviet proposal for abrupt elimination of all nuclear stockpiles, all missiles, and all armies, navies, and air forces strongly suggests that propaganda was the paramount motive in the proposals of the Soviet Premier. The propaganda motif was further underscored by his emphasis on the proposition that complete disarmament would also create completely new opportunities for the assistance of "states whose economies are at present still underdeveloped and stand in need of cooperation from more advanced countries. . . . This could literally usher in a new epoch in the economic development of Asia, Africa and Latin America."[22]

While there is no doubt that the Soviet Union has attempted to capitalize on the propaganda value of its disarmament schemes, it is most likely misleading to treat the Soviet emphasis on general disarmament as nothing but propaganda.[23] All governments try to realize the propaganda potential of their policies, but this does not eliminate the possibility of their real concern for the implementation of their programs. Several factors make it quite possible that the Soviet Union is genuinely interested in disarmament. In the first place, it is now well established that the U.S.S.R. has been prepared to make important concessions in the course of negotiations and that the causes of the difficulty in reaching agreement have not been nearly so one-sided as was once popularly assumed. In the second place, a partial disarmament plan involving an inspection system would probably reduce Soviet security rather than increase it, since the secrecy of the emplacement of Soviet missiles and bases has constituted one of the most important foundations of the nation's security system. And in the third place, the Soviet view of the economic structure of the world includes a supremely optimistic appraisal of national potential; disarmament would permit concentration on the exploitation of the natural resources of the U.S.S.R. which would eventually result in the economic superiority of the Soviet Union over the United States and western Europe, according to Soviet predictions.[24] The elimination of conventional arms would simultaneously weaken the position of China. While complete disarmament may appear utopian as a proposal, there are nonetheless some very practical reasons for the Soviet Union to have confidence that general disarmament would be an asset and not a hindrance to the fulfillment of its objectives.

Partial disarmament

Although principal interest has centered in universal disarmament proposals, the Kremlin began to consider the possibility of concluding partial disarmament agreements in 1956. The proposals initially put forward were aimed primarily at achieving a reduction of conventional forces. The Soviet recommendation specified a maximum military force of 1 to 1.5 million men for the United States, the U.S.S.R., and China, 650,000 men for

Great Britain and France, and 200,000 for all other countries. The controls suggested were similar to those of the Malik proposal of 1955—check posts at ports, railway junctions, highways, and airports. This was to be accomplished by the creation of a permanent international control organ with the power of inspection. Limitation and control of conventional forces were repeatedly stressed between March, 1956, and September, 1959, as the essential first step to any broader plan.

The reasons underlying this new-found concern for partial disarmament measures that separated conventional and nuclear forces appear to have been largely the result of three motivating factors. In the first place, the Kremlin had already made the decision to reduce the manned strength of its armed forces for economic and strategic reasons. After first making the proposal to the Western allies, Soviet authorities announced a unilateral reduction of 1,200,000 uniformed men. A corresponding reduction in the standing armies of the Western allies would simply have assured that the decision already made in Moscow would not have reduced the relative military strength of the nation. In the second place, the proposals came at a time when West German rearmament was making marked progress. The limitation of "all other nations" to 200,000 would clearly have nullified the existing and potential military strength of the Federal German Republic. And, in the third place, acceptance of the Soviet plan would have compelled the withdrawal of a substantial part of American troops in Europe across the Atlantic, thereby leaving the Soviet Army in a much improved position. If fighting should break out over control of Germany and if the use of nuclear weapons were forsworn, the French army would represent the only significant force on the continent, and its willingness and ability to challenge the U.S.S.R. in a show of strength were both open to question. The partial disarmament programs presented by the Soviet Union in the 1956-1959 period were, therefore, ill-concealed attempts to improve the strategic position of the U.S.S.R. over that of the United States in Europe.

One question that invariably asserts itself in Soviet negotiations for partial disarmament is that of West Germany. In fact, the only proposal for partial disarmament in a fixed geographical region in which the Kremlin has displayed keen and genuine interest has been the Rapacki plan. This proposal was submitted to the General Assembly of the United Nations by the Foreign Minister of Poland in October, 1957. At that particular moment in the history of the cold war, the leaders of the U.S.S.R. were especially concerned about two problems—regaining prestige lost as a result of the Hungarian revolution in the fall of 1956 and thwarting plans to strengthen West German military capabilities and provide the members of N.A.T.O. with nuclear power. Adam Rapacki's proposal offered the potential means with which to accomplish both purposes. The plan itself was brief and simple.

It called for an agreement among the major powers that no nuclear weapons would be stationed or manufactured in East and West Germany, Poland, and Czechoslovakia.[25] In addition, the nuclear powers would be required to forswear the use of thermonuclear weapons against these territories. The Soviet Union promptly endorsed the proposal and suggested that it might even be expanded to include more countries between Scandinavia and the Balkans. The Rapacki plan's content struck a responsive cord by appealing to many Europeans whose emotions had long been disturbed by the possibility of nuclear war and even greater devastation than had resulted from the second world war.

The Soviet propositions on partial disarmament and the endorsement of the Rapacki plan were closely related to impending West German elections and to the relationship the Kremlin saw between disarmament agreement with the West and the status of the two German governments. On September 5, 1957,

Zorin had bitterly assailed the "remilitarization" of West Germany and the stationing of atomic units and nuclear weapons on German territory. He held that these actions "reviving German militarism" constituted "irrefutable proof" that the United States and her N.A.T.O. allies did "not desire a relaxation of tension in Europe."[26] The Soviet delegates walked out of the disarmament conference during the negotiations of November 11, 1957, three weeks before the national elections in the Federal German Republic.[27] The timing of this action made it pointedly clear that the Soviet Union was using disarmament and the Rapacki plan to influence the German electorate against Chancellor Adenauer and the hard-line policy he followed toward the Communist states. The German voters were told that the choice was either Adenauer or reunification, not both. After this tactic failed to work, the Soviet government dispatched letters to all members of the United Nations in which the Rapacki plan was supported in a broadened form.[28] The letter was released on the eve of a conference of N.A.T.O. officers. It proposed that no nuclear weapons be either stationed or manufactured in East and West Germany, Poland, and Czechoslovakia. Also, the nuclear powers were asked to pledge not to use such weapons against these territories in the event of war and to renew efforts to accomplish the reduction of conventional forces in the four states. The recommendations were accompanied by a plea for a summit conference to consider the creation of a nuclear-free zone in central Europe.

It was in the context of these events that Premier Khrushchev himself issued a call for a summit meeting to negotiate on problems concerning disarmament as well as other points of difference between Moscow and the Western capitals. The heads of state conference, he suggested, should be preceded "by a meeting of representatives of the two strongest powers—"the U.S.A. and the U.S.S.R."[29] Washington promptly rejected the idea of a summit conference, but it was not until May 4, 1958, that the United States officially refused to use the Rapacki plan as the basis for new negotiations. In the meantime, the Soviet government, increasingly frustrated in its efforts to prevent German rearmament, unleashed a violent verbal attack on Bonn. Foreign Minister Gromyko, addressing the Supreme Soviet, declared:

> The implementation of the atomic armaments plans of the Federal Republic of Germany in the present circumstances means that its government is deliberately making German reunion impossible. All things considered, the West German Chancellor Adenauer and those at one with him are in a hurry to burn the bridges leading to closer contact and negotiations between both German states and thus block the only road still open to German unity via an agreement between the two German states—the German Democratic Republic and the Federal Republic of Germany. The decision to arm the Bundeswehr with atomic bombs and rockets tolls the knell for the unity of Germany, and that is what every German should know.[30]

This statement was clearly addressed to the people and rulers of West Germany. It was a warning that German involvement in N.A.T.O. and the execution of Bonn's plans for rearmament were emphatically unacceptable to the Soviet Union. One price of unity, for Gromyko did not say that it was the only price, was West German abstention from Western alliances and the reversal of the decision to rearm. Concern over the armaments buildup in the West appeared to have also been a major factor in the decision to halt nuclear tests. On April 1, 1958, the same day on which it reported Gromyko's warning to West Germany, *Izvestiia* announced the unilateral cessation of testing by the U.S.S.R. and called for other nations to follow suit. The propaganda value of this announcement in the less developed countries as well as in some circles of Europe was used to bring the pressure of world opinion to bear on American policy in central Europe by discouraging Washington from providing other states with either nuclear weapons or nuclear secrets.

The western powers, of course, could not accept the partial disarmament program embodied in the Rapacki plan and the threats concerning German reunification were largely ignored. Only unofficially did the United States halt nuclear testing with a self-imposed moratorium. The creation of a nuclear-free zone in central Europe without a corresponding reduction in the conventional forces of the U.S.S.R. would have left West Germany highly vulnerable to the numerical superiority of the Soviet Army. Just as the Western insistence on elaborate inspection systems left the Soviet Union with a sense of insecurity, Moscow's proposals left the members of N.A.T.O. with the conviction that the Kremlin would have the advantage. Furthermore, Khrushchev's recommendation that the proposals be considered in a summit conference was coldly received in Washington, where summit meetings had come to be looked on as propaganda devices which might redound to the credit of the U.S.S.R. This feeling was exacerbated by Khrushchev's suggestion that only representatives from "the two strongest powers" attend a pre-summit session. The exclusion of Britain and France would hardly have promoted unity in the Western alliance. Western leaders were, therefore, not hesitant to reject both the Rapacki plan and the summit proposal to consider it. In addition, measures were taken to strengthen the military position of West Germany although, contrary to Soviet statements, no serious consideration was given to providing the West German armed forces with nuclear weapons. All of the Soviet overtures and threats concerning the status of East and West Germany were thereby rejected.

It was in this context of events that the Berlin crisis of November, 1958, was sparked by Khrushchev's threat to conclude a peace treaty with East Germany within six months. The issues that the Soviet Union raised and the manner in which they were disposed of by the West in the months preceding the Prime Minister's ultimatum suggests a rather close relationship between the frustrations of the Soviet elite in attaining their policy objectives earlier in the year and the decision to remind the West that Moscow still held a high card by prokoving the crisis over West Berlin and German reunification. It is also striking that once the issue of West German rearmament had been resolved by the fact of its accomplishment, the Kremlin again reverted to its bold schemes of complete and universal disarmament.

The Soviet attitude toward disarmament has been characterized by demands for universal and complete disarmament, a willingness to compromise on the creation of a control system for conventional forces, but a staunch refusal to admit the possibility of effective control to prevent the development of nuclear power or of the necessity for controls to detect the testing of nuclear weapons. Furthermore, a persistent concern evident in virtually all the proposals has been over the nature of military establishments in central Europe and over the nature of the political solution to the question of a divided German nation.

Perhaps Khrushchev himself best summarized the Soviet attitude toward disarmament in his address to the East German Sixth Party Congress in January, 1963. He commented that the unsettled question of Germany had contributed greatly to the size of military expenditures in countries of both the East and the West. Until that problem is resolved, he claimed, the conditions necessary for successful disarmament negotiations yielding broad reductions in military power will not exist. On the other hand, he noted, limited steps had to be taken to ease tensions, to lessen the costs of security, and to reduce the chances of nuclear war.

The issue of inspection

The question that has sparked the greatest controversy, whether the immediate aim of negotiations has been complete or partial disarmament or the attainment of a test-ban agreement, has been the necessity of and authority required for an effective control system. The Kremlin has recognized the desirability of minimal control devices, such as inspection units at airports, railway and highway junctions, and ports, as a means of forestalling the secret mobilization of conventional armed forces and reducing the possibility of successful surprise attack. However, either the number of ground control posts or the regions suggested for aerial photography zones have been considered too limited by the West or the proposals themselves have been so tied to other demands, particularly to the reduction of foreign troops in Europe, as to make them totally unacceptable to the Western allies. But the essential difference between the two sides on the control issue has been the different priority each side has given to disarmament agreement and inspection. Summarizing the Soviet stance, Kuznetsov observed that:

> One does not have to be experienced in politics or military matters to see that, in view of the mistrust and suspicion among the Governments, the establishment of a control and inspection system, particularly only over the types of weapons the West is interested in, without the parallel application of disarmament measures, cannot be otherwise regarded than as an attempt to take advantage of the control for purposes of reconnaissance.[31]

Kuznetsov was expressing an interpretation that Soviet representatives have since repeated countless times—namely, that Western insistence on extensive control installations on Russian territory before disarmament measures have been carried out is a tactic designed to reduce the strategic Soviet advantage of secrecy while the United States still maintains its striking power.

The problem of inspection has, therefore, been closely associated with the particular staging proposals embodied in American plans. This was demonstrated most graphically in regard to the disarmament plan submitted by the United States to the eighteen-nation Disarmament Conference in April, 1962. The first stage proposed in the plan included reduction of American and Soviet armed forces to 2.1 million men, elimination of the means of delivering nuclear weapons, and controls over all air bases and industries engaged in the production of nuclear weapons and aircraft. The control system consisted primarily of regular inspection teams and aerial surveillance. The Soviet reaction to these propositions was expectedly unfavorable: "Not one of the measures of the first stage stipulated in the American document is it at all possible to call a measure of disarmament. As before, the facts of the U.S. plan do not strive for disarmament but for control over arms."[32] The Soviet interpretation asserted that the plan was "aimed at undermining the system of defense of the Soviet Union" without significantly affecting the strength of the United States. Foreign Minister Gromyko noted in his report to the Supreme Soviet that "the generals of the N.A.T.O. staff simply want to set up a kind of X-ray radioscope of all the territory of the Soviet Union."[33]

It is likely that these proposals would indeed have placed the Soviet Union at a disadvantage. While American bases ring the world often at points close to the U.S.S.R., the entire Soviet defense apparatus is confined to the territory of the Soviet Union and dependable members of the Communist system of states. Secrecy would be an advantage in any similar case. However, when coupled with the likelihood that Soviet defense expenditures during the 1960-1963 period were devoted largely to improving the conventional forces while missile development was given secondary priority, secrecy may have become a *crucial* advantage simply because there may have been comparatively little to inspect in the way of intercontinental missiles. Certainly, secrecy is far more important to a country with very limited assets than it is to one with great reserves capable of employing a flexible course in its policy. Confinement within a set geographical area combined with the decision not to press its initial advantage in missile development sharply restricted the flexibility of Soviet strategy and elevated the importance of secrecy to that strategy. The decision to take the risk of placing intermediate-range missiles on Cuba in 1962 appears to have been prompted primarily by this very need to increase flexibility. If such a grave risk as that was taken to enlarge the number of choices available to the Kremlin, a factor over which the Soviet elite has greater control, like that of internal secrecy, is not likely to be surrendered at a low price.

On the other hand, it should not be thought that the Soviet Union has not been prepared to strike some bargain on the question of inspection. Concessions were made in 1955 on control posts for conventional forces, and in 1956 the concept of aerial inspection was accepted. In 1960, the Soviet delegation at the ten-nation Disarmament Conference accepted the principle of on-site inspection by permanent control teams. The Soviet attitude on the possibility of placing effective controls over the production of nuclear weapons has been most unbending. In spite of the intransigent position taken on the latter issue, it is possible for a noted scholar of disarmament negotiations to state that "there has been virtually no basic issue of disarmament which has not seen some compromise from both sides."[34]

The test-ban treaty of 1963

Negotiations for a nuclear test-ban treaty followed a similar pattern to those for full and partial disarmament until the Kremlin altered its course in 1963. After first openly revealing interest in the prohibition of nuclear testing in May, 1955, the Soviet government has since found the test-ban issue a convenient weapon in its "peace campaign," as well as a desirable achievement for the very practical purposes of reducing military expenditures and lessening the danger of a highly destructive war. During the two-year period following the Geneva Summit

Conference, the Soviet Union repeatedly called for a moratorium on testing and insisted that inspection was not necessary. On June 14, 1957, Moscow surprised the West by offering to accept a two- to three-year agreement, including the stationing of control posts on Russian territory. The Eisenhower administration was basically unprepared to give serious consideration to this proposal, however, and insisted on the inclusion in the agreement of several features which were clearly unacceptable to the Soviet Union. In January, 1958, Eisenhower reversed the approach taken at London six months earlier by modifying the amendments previously demanded. This reversal was primarily the result of a rising world concern about the effects of radiation. A committee of experts from both major nuclear powers met to consider the technical problems involved and successfully reached agreement on the requirements for inspection. In the interim the Soviet Union hastily conducted a series of tests in March and announced that, on April 1, a self-imposed moratorium on nuclear explosions would begin for an indefinite period.[35] In the fall of 1958, the United States and Great Britain followed the example of the U.S.S.R. by suspending tests while the negotiations were in progress. The failure of the subsequent conference must be attributed largely to the United States for succumbing to the pressures of certain high-ranking military officers and members of the Atomic Energy Commission. The off-again-on-again discussion lasted until 1960, when the U-2 incident provoked the Soviet Prime Minister to demonstrate his own explosive powers. In 1961, testing was resumed.

In 1960-1961 Moscow once again followed a policy of unilateral cessation of testing. At an unexpected moment Khrushchev announced the resumption of testing on the ground that the United States had failed to comply with the Soviet request that other nations cease exploding nuclear weapons.[36] The announcement was made while a conference of neutral states was meeting in Belgrade. Considering the outspoken opposition of the leaders of most of those states to testing and the elaborate courtship of their favor by Moscow, the decision was probably reached on the basis of what the Russians deemed sheer military necessity. The failure of the U.S.S.R. to push as far ahead in long-range ballistic missiles as it had publicly claimed and the growing anxiety of certain military experts over lack of parity with comparable American weapons forced Khrushchev to take the risk of wrecking his vaunted "peace" campaign. The hostility of the Chinese to a pacific policy may also have encouraged the Kremlin to demonstrate its vast superiority over other members of the party-state system.

Negotiations were stalemated in 1962 as a result of Washington's reaction to the Soviet Union's resumption of testing and Moscow's uncertainty over finding the proper course to follow in relations with other members of the Communist system. The next series of abrupt starts and stops began in January, 1963, when Khrushchev, in a letter to President Kennedy,[37] suddenly agreed to make concessions on the question of inspection. The Soviet Premier tacitly consented to "two or three" inspections on Russian territory in the hope that a test-ban treaty could be concluded with the United States and Great Britain. For the first time the Soviet Union recognized the principle of control by inspection for underground testing. Even though the number of inspections was lower than the Western allies considered necessary and even though the concession was somewhat modified by Gromyko's insistence that de Gaulle's France be a party to any test-ban treaty, Western spokesmen viewed the changed Soviet attitude on inspection as the first substantial indication that a breakthrough was possible.

Other factors were then at work, however, of which London and Washington were not entirely aware. Khrushchev was facing domestic opposition from a segment of the military and from opponents of the deterioration in Moscow's relations with Communist China. Frol Kozlov, once considered the likely successor to Khrushchev, had taken up the battle in behalf of the traditionalists. He warned of the necessity of maintaining a high state of preparedness against imperialists and tangled with Khrushchev on the issue of resource allocations. Kozlov stressed the production of steel and heavy industry while the Prime Minister defended the growth of "general prosperity" as a better index of Soviet competition with the West.[38] Khrushchev apparently wanted to prove to his colleagues and critics that agreement was possible and to present them with tangible evidence of the correctness of his coexistence policy. He had limited room within which to bargain, so that his concession of three inspections was made as an all-or-nothing proposition. Furthermore, he had been led to believe by Allied representatives that they would accept three inspections rather than a larger number. When the United States insisted on twenty inspections, the Russian delegates marched out of the test-ban conference on February 1. The initial optimism proved itself short-lived.

In the spring of 1963, Khrushchev's public statements began once more to raise hopes that a test-ban agreement could be reached, at least to cover testing in the atmosphere, in outer space, and under water. After many preliminaries, Averell Harriman and Lord Hailsham met with Premier Khrushchev and Foreign Minister Gromyko in Moscow. Negotiations took place in a remarkably cordial atmosphere, particularly when compared with previous discussions in the cold war period. Agreeing to forgo the inclusion of underground testing until a later time, the delegates of the three nations quickly, though carefully, produced a five-article treaty declaring that no signatory of the document would explode any nuclear weapon in any environment "if such explosion causes radioactive fall-out outside the territorial limits of the state under whose jurisdiction or control such explosion is conducted." The Test-Ban Treaty was initialed by the representatives of the respective states on July 25, 1963. By October of that year it had been ratified by the original signatories and signed by representatives of the governments of over 100 nations.

The motives behind the Soviet desire to conclude the treaty were numerous, but two reasons stand out above all others. Economic productivity began to show a definite downward turn following 1961. Agriculture fell sharply behind goals and even, in the area of grain, behind immediate needs. The continuing devotion of huge sums to defense became increasingly difficult. There were simply no places in the budget where significant cuts could be made except in military expenditures. On the other hand, Khrushchev's supporters genuinely feared to reduce military outlays without some guarantee that the United States would not use the opportunity to build up even greater superiority. A treaty offered the best means of binding the United States as well as themselves and also helped to create a more relaxed atmosphere on the world scene. Under these circumstances further military cutbacks would become more plausible. In addition to these economic and military factors, political developments had made the treaty more possible from Khrushchev's point of view. The traditionalists' rally against the Prime Minister's course ended in a setback for their own cause after Kozlov became incapacitated by what was officially described as a stroke. Khrushchev seized on the opportunity to demonstrate his ability to improve relations with the United States.

Another factor encouraging the Soviet Union to seek more cordial relations with the West was the growing rift with China and problems within the Communist system. By the summer of 1963 a break between the two Red giants had become all but official. Whatever pressure Peking had previously been able to exert on Moscow was rapidly vanishing. Khrushchev no longer had to bargain and make concessions to appease his one-time "fraternal comrades" even though he still had to contend with the traditionalists in his own country. Significantly, however, the public statements issued by the Soviet government after the treaty had been signed were explicitly directed to Peking, reminding the Chinese that this could not be held to constitute "capitulation to imperialism."[39] One result of this conflict was that Khrushchev was freer to act in the summer of 1963 than he probably had ever been before. Although there were sharp economic pressures which might have caused political difficulties at a later date, the internal sympathizers with Mao and the influence of Kozlov and old-guard military strategists were temporarily on the downgrade. Khrushchev needed the treaty, limited though it had to be, and he got what he was after.

The more moderate section of the Soviet press used the occasion of the test-ban agreement to drive home one of Khrushchev's long-standing arguments—the differences among various "imperialist circles." President Kennedy's "realism" and his call for a "period of fruitful cooperation" before the General Assembly of the United Nations in September, 1963, were welcomed as evidence of a new tone coming from Washington. In addition to the quality of American leadership, "a new element was considered in the discussion of the Treaty in the Senate of the U.S.A. as wide sections of the people were drawn into the discussion of vital questions of international relations and the position of the popular masses brought pressure for the isolation and defeat of the 'lunatics'."[40] The twin factors of leadership and public opinion were cited as basic reasons for the conclusion of the treaty and the creation of "a new political climate, an atmosphere of hope." The treaty was held to show "in practice that the solution of vital international problems by means of negotiations between states belonging to different social-economic systems is a fully realistic prospect."[41] The moderates had won an important victory in the conduct of foreign policy. It did not necessarily follow, however, that the victory would also apply in the conflict over domestic economic policy.

An examination of Soviet behavior in crisis situations reveals that the Soviet Union, while attempting to improve its strategic position and to offset Western influence around the perimeter of the Communist states, was not given to a high degree of risk-taking in the decade beginning in 1955. In three of the eleven crisis situations considered (the two Berlin crises and Cuba), the Kremlin was clearly responsible for provoking international tensions, while in eight cases Soviet involvement came as a response to existing troubles. Five of the crises occurred between May, 1960, and November, 1962, the period in which the members of the old guard reasserted their influence in Moscow. Considering the fact that the Soviet leaders were largely responding to, rather than generating, difficulties in Poland and Hungary, it can be reasonably claimed that they took only modest risks in the 1955-1960 and 1963-1965 periods. Those risks involved areas of strategic interest to the Soviet Union in the Middle East and central Europe. Negotiations in disarmament and arms control conferences also reflected Moscow's concern for national security and protection of the vital interests of the U.S.S.R. as perceived by her leaders.

For those who place great emphasis on ideology as a determinant of Soviet behavior, the question of the relationship between recent Russian policy and the ideological explanations offered by Khrushchev assumes great significance. Evidence strongly indicates that the ideological precepts were altered because of Moscow's recognition of the fact that modern military technology was changing the very nature of war. Leninist doctrine was revised because in the Kremlin's eyes history itself had unfolded a major change. Although Marxism had never declared that war was a favored or necessary means of extending socialism, Leninism declared that a final violent clash between Communist and capitalist systems was inevitable. But technological developments now made it mandatory for Moscow to make clear to all Communists that hot war was to be avoided and military moves were to be made only with great deliberation. Policy requirements compelled a re-examination of doctrine. The announcements of formal modifications of Leninism came in 1955 and 1956—*after* policy had already begun to be revised. The expectations and confidence of the Kremlin's leaders were being shaken by technology. The struggle for world Communism would continue, but the techniques used in waging the struggle had to be subjected to a thorough re-evaluation.

In spite of some indications that ideology exerts a guiding influence on the policy-makers in the Soviet Union, recognition must be given to other factors that influence their decisions and behavior. While it can be contended that the constant probing of the Communists to gain a foothold in Latin America—whether Guatemala or Cuba—indicates an "ideological compulsion" to expand the Communist system and to weaken the capitalist enemy, the strategic consideration of countering Western military bases near the borders of the Soviet Union appears to have been a factor of greater importance. Soviet policy in the Berlin crises, the low degree of risk-taking where the center of action was outside the Communist system, and policy in negotiations over disarmament indicates an acute sensitivity of the Kremlin strategists to the relative power positions of the countries involved. Khrushchev adroitly pursued his policy of struggle through coexistence by shying away from situations where a confrontation with the Western powers might have threatened to trigger a major war. Miscalculations of the response of others, as in Cuba, have generally led to retractions of the policy. Soviet decision-makers must take account of the reactions of other nations as well as of the power available to the Soviet Union, and this places definite and recognized limitations on ideological commitments.

In addition to strategic considerations, relations among the members of the Communist system influence the policy lines followed by the Kremlin. The resumption of testing and the

Berlin crisis in 1958 followed the dissension between Moscow and Peking over the appropriate course of action in the Middle East crisis of that year. The resumption of a hard line in disarmament negotiations in 1960, the precipitation of the Berlin crisis of 1960-1961, and open support of the rebels in Laos, the Congo, and Algeria in 1960-1961 came after the U-2 incident. This was also the period in which the Soviet Union was attempting to smooth its relations with China, whose leaders wanted stronger action against the capitalist states.

But the outstanding Soviet concern in disarmament negotiations and in the Berlin crises has been the settlement of the German question. Moscow remains uneasy over the precarious position of East Germany. Although no proof is available, it is not unlikely that the arms buildup in Cuba was initiated with the primary intention of forcing the United States to negotiate on the status of West Berlin and East Germany. The Soviet policy-makers probably saw little immediate hope that Communist parties would attain power in free Europe, and decided instead to concentrate their efforts to expand their influence by wooing the less developed regions of the world. However, so long as there is nothing more than an uneasy truce in central Europe their whole system in East Europe remains insecure and the defense costs to protect it remain high and burdensome. The Soviet leaders have repeatedly attempted to force a settlement of the German issue in order to increase the security of the Communist system of states. They have also been pushed in this direction by the historic fear of a powerful Germany.

Concern for Soviet security in Europe, however, does not indicate the complete abandonment of the hope of a Communist world. It does not mean that ideology has become entirely irrelevant. Indeed, as long as ideological precepts serve to justify the existence of the Communist regime and as long as ideology provides the party with an important means of domestic control, Leninism will continue to play a vital role in the Soviet system. Nonetheless, this should not be allowed to obscure the fact that it is most difficult, if not impossible, to identify a single major conflict situation in the post-Stalin period in which ideological commitment has taken precedence over national security considerations. Technology has contributed to the exacerbation of this conflict of interests between doctrine and the nationalistic values of domestic progress and preservation of the state. As a result, the Kremlin elite has been able to consider policy alternatives in a more objective and less ideological framework.

Another element in Soviet policy has been a desire to add to the prestige of the Soviet state by exploiting propaganda techniques in the "peace" campaign. Most of the significant concessions made by the Kremlin in the area of disarmament and arms control have occurred during periods when the Soviet government was attempting to regain lost prestige, as after the suppression of the Hungarian revolt, or when a major peace offensive was under way, as in 1955, 1958, and 1963. The peace offensive corresponded to the concentration of energies on domestic economic construction while freeing the country from some of its international burdens. The unilateral cessation of testing in 1958 and again in 1959 and the utopian universal disarmament schemes sometimes presented by the Soviet Union have been repeatedly used by Moscow to demonstrate the peaceful nature of Communist countries, particularly to the nonaligned states. The same type of propaganda followed the Russian withdrawal from Cuba, when Moscow attempted to portray the removal of missiles as confirmation of the seriousness of the Soviet peace policy.

It becomes increasingly apparent that many factors enter into the motivation of Soviet international behavior. It is certainly more accurate to conclude that the theory of the noninevitability of war was designed to describe one aspect of the policy of coexistence than that Soviet policy was determined by this revised tenet of Leninism. Evidence indicates that fear of nuclear war and its consequences is the greatest limitation on pursuit of an activist military policy and requires the most extensive modification and rationalization of ideological concepts. The concern about the status of Germany, the cautious yet often earnest efforts to promote disarmament, and the speeches of Premier Khrushchev pointed to a genuine and profound fear of a thermonuclear war. Not only could such a war destroy the Soviet Union and the United States, but Peking might be left to carry its version of the revolutionary system around the world. Moreover, especially between 1957 and 1960, Khrushchev persistently claimed—whether or not he really believed—that the Communist cause could and would be victorious without resort to warfare. The logic of history, Soviet scholars have argued, shows that as technology makes military power increasingly difficult to use, so do Soviet technology and economic power enhance the capacity of Moscow to wage the economic and ideological struggle ever more intensely.

Purely strategic considerations, the desire for prestige, ideology, and domestic politics and economics all influence the formulation of Soviet policy involving the military aspect of peaceful coexistence. Furthermore, all of these elements are interrelated in the minds of Soviet officials, for the contemporary policy-makers, like Lenin and Stalin before them, find themselves involved in a struggle between Communism, in one of its varieties, and Russian nationalism. As Communists the Soviet leaders may have great confidence in the success of their long-range struggle against capitalism. But as national Communists they must protect their homeland and provide for the needs and aspirations of Soviet citizens in order to assure the existence of a powerful base for the international Communist movement. To do this, they cannot risk destruction by forgetting that they are Russians with national interests, customs, and values as well as Communists with international goals.

PEACEFUL COEXISTENCE: THE ECONOMIC, POLITICAL, AND IDEOLOGICAL ASPECTS

> The [foreign leaders] no longer doubt that the Soviet Union will overtake the United States. The question that worries them now is when. Here is what I replied: you can put this down in your note-book—we shall overtake you in industrial production per head of the population in 1970; we shall overtake you, and then go farther ahead.
>
> —N. S. Khrushchev

SOVIET ECONOMICS AND THE POLITICS OF FOREIGN AID AND TRADE

V

THE MODERNIZATION of Soviet strategic concepts, the pursuit of low-risk policies, and interest in disarmament, accompanied by modification of former theories of war and of the transition to socialism, became the foundation of the military aspect of the Soviet strategy of peaceful coexistence. The rationalization that supported these practices and explained the innovations in Leninist theory was the contention that the international class struggle can at present be waged most successfully in the form of economic competition between the capitalist and communist systems. This interpretation was justified on the ground that the growing strength of the Soviet Union and the other members of the system create the conditions necessary to make economic struggle rather than violent revolutionary struggle of decisive importance. New conditions would enable the U.S.S.R. to conduct an economic offensive against the Western allies that eventually would prove the superiority of the Soviet mode of production and distribution.

In challenging the Western states to economic competition, the Soviet leadership perhaps was reasserting the traditional Marxist emphasis on economics and expressing confidence in the superiority of the Soviet socialist system over that of contemporary capitalism. But, more important, the policy-makers were attempting to transfer the struggle between two systems from military to less dangerous methods of competition. The economic offensive associated with this analysis during the Khrushchev period is revealed in the domestic economic plans of the Soviet Union, including the politics of formulating those plans, in relations among members of the Communist system, and in the programs of foreign aid and expansion of foreign trade.

THE ECONOMIC FOUNDATIONS OF SOVIET FOREIGN POLICY

Although in earlier periods the Kremlin had frequently boasted of the successes of the Soviet economic system, the announcement of the Seven-Year Plan in 1958 introduced a new and broader drive in economic competition with the United States and her allies that rapidly climbed to a peak in 1961. Khrushchev told the 21st Party Congress that a new stage of the struggle against capitalism had been initiated. The aim of the Seven-Year Plan, the Prime Minister declared, was to direct the Soviet Union toward fulfillment of its principal economic task—"to overtake and surpass the most highly developed capitalist countries in production output per capita in the shortest possible historical period."[1] He asserted with evident satisfaction that in 1958 the U.S.S.R.'s industrial production exceeded that of France, Great Britain, and West Germany combined; having accomplished this, the Soviet Union "intends to surpass the United States . . . economically" in the stage of history just beginning to unfold.

In January, 1961, the *World Marxist Review* published a comprehensive report on the economic development of the U.S.S.R. and the other Communist-controlled states of eastern Europe.[2] The underlying assumption of the entire report was that material production had come to constitute the decisive sphere of competition between the socialist and capitalist systems. In accordance with this assumption, the Soviet economic planners have tended to give highest priority to expansion of those sectors of production that can best enhance the position of the U.S.S.R. in competing with other advanced states. Such fields as space technology, energy resources, and the traditional heavy industries have therefore been emphasized. The inclination to view policy as struggle and to associate domestic and foreign policy so closely strongly indicates the continuing intellectual commitment of the Soviet leaders to at least a part of the revolutionary code. Only the policies themselves, as finally accepted by the decision-makers, reveal the devolution of the Soviet revolutionary technique.

Statistically, the aim of the Seven-Year Plan was to increase the output of the means of production by 85 to 88 per cent and the output of consumer goods by 62 to 65 per cent over the 1958 figures.[3] These goals were to be attained by the end of 1965. This required an increase in the national income of a staggering 9 per cent every year. This optimistic aim was based on the annual increase achieved between 1955 and 1959. A further breakdown of the data attempts to demonstrate the humanitarian concern of the government by claiming that 75 per cent of the national income in 1960 was devoted to satisfying the "material and cultural needs" of the people, while only 25 per cent was used for expanding industry and for other governmental activities. The report also purported to show that the production goals could be met even while reducing the work day of the Soviet worker. Claiming that 16 million workers had already been placed on a seven- and six-hour day in April, 1960, the survey announced that a six- and five-hour day would be introduced by 1964. Stress was laid, therefore, not only on surpassing the United States in industrial output, but on presenting the world with an example of a system capable of producing the most favorable working conditions and the highest standard of living in a relatively short period of time.

After the inception of the plan, the overfulfillment of the goals invariably evoked great fanfare. Less than two years after the plan had been announced, *Izvestiia* proudly declared that the goals were being revised upward, since the 1959-1960 gross industrial output had increased 23 per cent instead of the anticipated 17 per cent.[4] The Chairman of the U.S.S.R. Economic Council announced in December, 1962, that industrial production had increased 45 per cent during the first four years of the Seven-Year Plan against the target figure of 39 per cent and that in accomplishing this there had been a 9 per cent expansion of industry.[5] The Central Statistical Board reported on January 25, 1963, that the 1962 plan for industry had been exceeded by 6 per cent and that the total industrial production equaled 63 per cent of the United States total compared with 47 per cent in 1957.[6] This report claimed that there had been a 10 per cent increase in the production of the means of production and a 9.5 per cent increase in total industrial output. The report on the 1963 plan indicated a smaller growth rate than in previous periods, but pointedly noted that in five years 37 billion rubles worth of industrial goods above the amount envisaged for that period in the 1958 projection had been produced.[7] As a result of the performance, the announcement stated that the targets for industrial output, including capital investments in light industry, had been raised for 1964.

Thus the Seven-Year Plan served the Soviet strategy of peaceful coexistence in two important ways. First, it gauged the pace of industrial and agricultural growth to the international struggle between two competing systems. The ability of the Kremlin to give certain sectors of the economy—such as the petroleum industry or the development of sputniks and other spacecraft—priority over others permits the U.S.S.R. to compete on favorable terms with the United States in certain highly selective areas. Second, the plan served as a convenient propaganda weapon by providing data, however exaggerated they might have been, to demonstrate the long-term welfare plans of the government and the general concern of the Soviet leaders for the living standards of their subjects.

The Seven-Year Plan was basically designed to lay the groundwork for implementation of the goals later expressed in the new Party Program. The Program itself provides only general guidelines for the Soviet economic planners, but it, too, stresses the importance of overtaking the United States in production. According to the new long-term goals, the Soviet planners expect to surpass the U.S.A. in per capita output by the close of the first ten-year period in 1970 while also instituting the world's shortest workday. By the end of the second ten-year period, the program promises an "abundance" of material and cultural benefits for all the people and the gradual application of the Communist principle of reward according to needs.[8] More specifically, the national income of the U.S.S.R. is expected to increase 400 per cent by 1980 and real per capita income to advance over 250 per cent.

In order to examine the plans and achievements of Soviet production in greater detail, one area that has been of particular concern in the West—the petroleum industry—will be reviewed. As recently as 1953, the Soviet Union imported part of its petroleum requirements. A decade later the U.S.S.R. stood as the second largest oil-producing nation in the world and crude oil and petroleum products had become its principal export commodities. The Seven-Year Plan called for a production goal of 48 million barrels daily by 1965, thereby allowing a surplus of one million barrels daily for the needs of other members of the Communist system (400,000 barrels) and for export (600,000).[9] This compares with 285,000 barrels daily for those purposes in 1959. In spite of setbacks in other areas of production, the plan was fulfilled in 1965. By March, 1963, the Soviet oil industry had increased production 262 per cent over 1953 and was producing 4.3 million barrels daily. This meant that Soviet petroleum production had risen from 18 per cent of the United States' output in 1953 to 58 per cent by the spring of 1963.

In addition to the projected production increase, at least eight new refineries were planned and 3 billion dollars were allocated to tripling pipeline miles by 1965. The specific projects included the completion in 1963 of three major trunk lines connecting the principal Soviet oil fields in the Urals-Volga region and Uzbekistan with outlets in Klaipeda, Lithuania, and Ventspils, Latvia on the Baltic and Schwedt, East Germany. Pipelines connecting the central line in the Soviet Union with outlets in Czechoslovakia and Hungary were also completed in 1963. The completion of these "Friendship Pipelines" combined with the expansion of oil and gas lines within the U.S.S.R. permitted the Soviet Union to transport over 78 per cent of its crude and processed oil by pipeline. These projects at first had to use imported steel pipe, but subsequently two new plants capable of producing 40-inch steel pipe were constructed.

Another important factor has been the development of advanced production techniques in the petroleum industry. For example, the first completely automated oil field in the world was constructed in Leninogorsk in the Volga region. All processes of extracting and transporting the product were automated. To give additional support to the Soviet oil industry, tanker fleets operating from the Black Sea and the Baltic have been steadily enlarged. Furthermore, 1963 witnessed the continuing development of offshore fields and the opening of the promising Markovo oil field on the Lena River in Siberia. The oil boom resulted in a shift in the types of fuel and power used in the Soviet Union and gave the U.S.S.R. a greater opportunity to participate in international commerce.

The successes in the petroleum industry and in spacecraft should not, however, be permitted to obscure the considerable difficulties experienced in other areas of the Soviet economy. In spite of the roseate reports and forecasts of the government, the

Kremlin demonstrated noticeable anxiety over agricultural productivity, the growing demands of consumers, and, most important, basic problems of resource allocations. The approaches of powerfully placed individuals and groups toward solutions to these issues were by no means harmonious during the Khrushchev period and are not likely to be much more so under his successors. The coalition that removed Khrushchev regarded some of his economic programs and his promise to overtake the United States by 1970 as "harebrained schemes." Economic problems have, therefore, often exacerbated dissension within the ranks of the party elite and the resulting controversies have often affected the composition of the leadership and the conduct of foreign policy.

The politics of economics

During 1956 and 1957 the question of the proper organization of the economy was one of the most divisive issues before the party and state leaders. Khrushchev's inclination toward utilitarian innovations first became manifest during this controversy over economic organization. Seven of the full members of the Party Presidium had devoted most of their careers to the state bureaucracy. These were Molotov, Kaganovich, Bulganin, Pervukhin, Saburov, Voroshilov, and Mikoyan. In addition, Malenkov had been divested of his influence in the Secretariat and now found his source of power solely in his position as Premier and head of the government. Only three of the members had primary associations with the party apparatus—Khrushchev, Kirichenko, and Suslov. Khrushchev's proposals for the decentralization of industrial management met with strong opposition from all of the members of the first group except Mikoyan. Fighting to retain their power, the bureaucrats struck at Khrushchev's weakened coalition in December, 1956, and pushed through resolutions strengthening the Council of Ministers and the State Economic Commission. At the same time Gosplan, in which Khrushchev found his strongest support among the organs of the state bureaucracy, was deprived of some of its power.[10] The additional power given to the State Economic Commission over the economic ministries and the reduced role of Gosplan suggested that Khrushchev's interference in economic matters was being rebuffed by the more conservative bureaucrats. The influence of the Molotov-Malenkov group was apparently heightened by the setback given Khrushchev's policies in eastern Europe by the difficulties in Poland and Hungary in the fall of 1956.[11]

Working through a core of solid supporters in the Central Committee, Khrushchev moved to reverse the decisions of the December Plenum. This core included Aristov, Beliaev, Brezhnev, Furtseva, Ignatov, Mukhitdinov, and Pospelov. By February, the innovationists were prepared to test their strength in another session of the Central Committee. *Pravda,* on February 15, 1957, merely announced that a decision had been made in the Plenum "to rearrange the work of the State Economic Commission," but subsequent events made it clear that the status of Gosplan was increased and that the trend toward decentralization had been officially endorsed. Khrushchev noted soon after the session of the Central Committee that "the need for Union and republic ministries in charge of industry and construction is past."[12] Subsequently, twenty-five Union and republic economic ministries were abolished. This was a blow at the heart of the strength of the state bureaucrats.

These moves against the well-entrenched bureaucrats led to their dramatic attempt to force Khrushchev's resignation in June, 1957. The alignment against the First Secretary included all of the members associated with the state bureaucracy except Mikoyan. His firm supporters consisted of Mikoyan and Kirichenko, while Suslov, a man of conservative inclinations who had spent his career in the party apparatus, wavered between the two principal groups. With the aid of Minister of Defense

Zhukov, the Khrushchev group was able to bring the Central Committee into session in time to halt the onslaught on the First Secretary. Malenkov, Molotov, and Kaganovich were immediately removed from their posts in the Presidium, as eventually were Bulganin, Pervukhin, Saburov, and Voroshilov. The new members of an enlarged Presidium included Zhukov and eight members from the party apparatus—Aristov, Beliaev, Brezhnev, Ignatov, Kozlov, Kuusinen, Furtseva, and Shvernik, thus sharply reversing the ratio of bureaucrats and apparatchiki in the party Presidium and at the same time rewarding most of those who had loyally served Khrushchev in the Central Committee. This victory of the Khrushchev faction initially appeared to place the First Secretary in a position of absolute dictatorship. Khrushchev's assumption of the post of Prime Minister in 1958 supported this contention.

However, the antagonists of Khrushchev in June, 1957, were not merely personalities who were in conflict with personalities. They were closely associated with developing economic interests that were by no means crushed with the elimination of Molotov, Malenkov, and Kaganovich, although they were set back for want of leadership. By 1960, they had once again found voices in the higher councils of the party. In that year the emergence of new conservative leadership under Frol Kozlov and setbacks for Khrushchev in foreign and defense policies resulted in the decline of several of the Premier's strongest supporters—Aristov, Beliaev, Furtseva, Ignatov, Kirichenko, Mukhitdinov, and Pospelov. Khrushchev himself was relatively secure in his dual role as head of party and head of state, but the price of that security consisted of bargaining and compromise and occasionally submission to the will of a hostile Presidium majority.

The issues which engendered conflict and made compromise necessary stemmed from three basic problems. In the first place, there were differences over resource allocations among heavy and light industry and the agricultural sectors. In the second place, there was controversy over the scope of decentralization and the principle of one-man management. And, in the third place, there was conflict over the economic functions of the intermediary and lower echelons of the party. Foreign and defense policies were particularly closely tied to the question of resource allocation, and all three issues were interwoven. It is probable that conflicts over these issues will continue in the higher party and state organs in the post-Khrushchev leadership.

After yielding to the conservative advocates of heavy industry, of a military establishment of powerful conventional forces, and of a more militant foreign policy in 1960, Khrushchev did not make another frontal assault on his critics until November, 1962. His attack came shortly after the Cuban crisis had encouraged the Soviet elite to reappraise foreign policy tactics and objectives. In November, the Plenum of the Central Committee ordered the drastic reorganization of the Communist party, dividing the intermediary organs into industrial and agricultural divisions. Voicing his support of the reorganization, Khrushchev violently assailed the "duplication and unjustified diversity of types" in production and demanded the consolidation of research efforts and the pursuit of a "single technical policy." He also attacked the lack of coordination in small industrial regions and chastised the "old school" for failing to deemphasize steel production in favor of less costly synthetics. Problems in planning were blamed on "insufficient economic substantiation" in the formulation of economic plans. Khrushchev contended that this difficulty would persist as long as plans were "not always based on the careful work of economic teams and investigations."

The reorganization of the party, therefore, had a multiple purpose. Khrushchev intended to increase the functional economic responsibilities of the party members while reducing their propaganda duties. At the same time the measure would enlarge the role of the party in intermediary and lower units of the economic system at the expense of the bureaucracy. In addition, Khrushchev apparently hoped that the decentralization of planning would reduce the effectiveness of the champions of heavy industry and make it easier to veer away from concentration on steel and other heavy industrial output. The importance that Khrushchev attached to decentralization and to more responsible economic planning was further demonstrated by his admonition to the Council of Ministers shortly after the November Plenum to take "into account the need to endow the economic councils with broader rights and safeguard them against petty tutelage."[13] In short, he attacked the inclination of old-guard bureaucrats to issue too many directives from above, thereby preventing managers and regional coordinators from exercising independent judgment.

Comments in the Soviet press suggested that the conservatives were not prepared to accept Khrushchev's bold new moves toward decentralization and increased party responsibility without a struggle. *Pravda* assailed the "dogmatists" who challenged the bifurcation of the party on the grounds that it would lead to antagonism between urban and rural areas.[14] *Izvestiia* indicated that some party members feared that the decision would result in the "depolitization of the party."[15] Brezhnev defended the decision and sharply criticized "conservatism" among certain unnamed party members.[16] The spokesmen for the conservatives were silent except for Kozlov, who defended "one-man management" in industrial enterprises as sound Leninism and chose to ignore the recent far-reaching decisions of the Central Committee in a major address before the Italian party Congress.[17]

In March, 1963, the conservatives acted to prevent Khrushchev's second major attempt to reduce their effectiveness. In an unusual joint session of the party Presidium and the All-Union Council of Ministers, the decision was made to retard the trend toward decentralization by establishing the U.S.S.R.

Supreme Economic Council as the "highest state agency for the leadership of industry and construction" with the power to make decisions "binding on all state agencies regardless of their subordination." The purpose of this Supreme Economic Council, if the decree was to be taken literally, was to supervise the activities of all economic organs on both the national and the republic level. The effect of its power would be to circumscribe the independence of the regional sovnarkhozy created by Khrushchev's original decentralization proposal in 1957. Khrushchev himself explicitly made this charge on April 24, 1963, by declaring that "leaders of state committees" who thought themselves capable of making all economic decisions would "drag us backward."[18]

Although Khrushchev agreed with the conservatives that poor coordination existed and sometimes caused "colossal damage to the state," he was not willing to accept the authority of the Supreme Economic Council without a fight.[19] His apparent victory was indicated by the failure of the Council to play a recognized role in the plans for the 1964-1965 budget, for the representatives of Gosplan were given preference in the deliberations of June and December, 1963. Despite their seeming failure to make the Supreme Economic Council dominant, the conservatives were still sufficiently strong to achieve a stalemate on the question of budgetary allocations. The military was required to take only a modest cut, and Khrushchev's victory in winning endorsement of a vast new chemical program was tempered by the decision to devote about half of the new investment in chemical industries to military and heavy industrial segments of the economy. Agriculture and light industry would divide the remaining investment. Nevertheless, the budget report of the Supreme Soviet could legitimately be considered an opening for further shifts in resource allocation. For years agriculture had been the "forgotten child" of the Soviet system and had been required to bear a disproportionate share of the cost of industrialization. For the first time in Soviet history, industry was called on to pay the cost of improving agricultural production of fertilizers and the general improvement of farm output. Khrushchev also asked for improved wage incentives for workers on farms and sharply criticized Stalin's policies on agricultural wages and prices of agricultural commodities. As these events were unfolding, Western observers were clearly seeing for the first time in recent years that the Soviet decision-makers were not nearly so free to assign economic and military priorities without considering the overall needs of the national economy as had often been presumed.

Further indication that Khrushchev's faction was not fully satisfied by the prescribed distribution of the investment in the chemical industry came with the publication of the February 1964 issue of *Mirovaia ekonomika i mezhdunarodnye otnosheniia*. The lead article noted that while the chemical industry would be of benefit to heavy industry, agriculture, and light industry (in that order), "the proportion of chemical materials in raw materials for light industry will gradually increase."[20] The authors contended that the chemical industry would show "a revolutionary influence on all aspects of the economy." It was also suggested that "the increased scale of net profit received in agriculture, in our view, can be used as an important source of new capital accumulation that will create a realistic economic base for the reduction of future prices of food and consumer goods. . . ." The same article lectured the conservatives by declaring that Soviet successes "are explained in large part by the progress of Soviet science and technology." This progress was made possible because "the party freed the development of science from harmful dogmatic canons, connected with the cult of the personality of Stalin. . . ." These comments suggested that Khrushchev's coalition of party functionaries and technocrats was preparing to press the conservatives for additional concessions on the issue of resource allocation and to insist on sufficient decentralization to draw scientists and technicians into the planning process.

In 1964, further indications suggested that Khrushchev had won a tactical victory over the conservatives on decentralized planning and industrial management. A series of articles in *Sovetskoe gosudarstvo i pravo* pointedly singled out the decisions of the November 1962 Plenum for praise. Particular stress was placed on the importance of collegial leadership and the participation of the people from factory committees on up the scale in planning and coordinating economic activity. One author quoted Khrushchev as having remarked that:

> In the direction of enterprises we have the principle of one-man management. And this is right. But several comrades have a one-sided view of the principle of one-man management as administering, commanding, directing production without the active participation of workers, specialists, and professional employees. These comrades forget the Leninist instructions about properly combining the principle of one-man leadership with broad participation of the masses. . . .[21]

He went on to remark that such "one-sided" persons forget that there are "scientific-technical" and "operational-organizational" functions of economic enterprises and that both of these often involve "questions of technical politics."[22] These questions are held to demand collective decisions in which those with technical knowledge and practical experience inform and advise the general manager. The Supreme Economic Council had been construed as a potential impediment to such procedures by the innovationists. It is significant that the Council was listed after the sovnarkhozy and state committees as playing a leading role in the "centralized organization of planning"; but it was noted that recent "measures broaden the rights of the union republics and local organs, extending the creative initiatives of a wide section of the workers in the formulation . . . of the plans."[23] The 1964-1965 plans were worked out, it was claimed, under "a new order of formulating plans" that consisted of participation of party, Soviet economic, trade union, and Komsomol organizations as well as workers, engineers, and scholars.[24]

This trend toward a more pragmatic, utilitarian approach to economic issues among the modernists was given additional support in a *Pravda* article on August 18, 1964, by Viktor Trapeznikov, who declared, "it is time to abandon the obsolete methods of management of economy founded on decreed norms and go over to the simpler, cheaper and more effective economic regulation of the work of enterprises." This could be accomplished, Trapeznikov suggested, by introducing a new system of incentives, by improving technology, and by permitting factories to increase their profits. Khrushchev and his supporters appeared to be paving the way for additional innovations in the Soviet system that hardly emanated from orthodox Marxist economics.

The experiments in techniques of economic planning and in the decentralization of industrial management were accompanied by Khrushchev's program of reorientation of party work. After the intermediary organs of the party were split into agricultural and industrial sectors, party workers were instructed to perform functional economic tasks and to concentrate less on the dissemination of propaganda. There were some indications that a number of party members were displeased with their new economic assignments, for the party press devoted an unusual amount of space to stressing the importance of "party guidance" of the economy and emphasizing that "production is the focus of party and ideological work."[25] This development in party work orientation, if continued, could be expected to increase the technocratic complexion of the C.P.S.U. particularly in the intermediary party organs, and eventually to alter significantly the manner in which the political decisions of the regime are made and the political responsibilities are carried out. This possibility had been made all the more likely by the decisions of the 1962

Central Committee Plenum, in which Khrushchev, in effect, deepened the utilitarian-traditionalist conflict by forcing it into the middle and lower units of the party. Some members of the coalition that forced Khrushchev from power had not concealed their opposition to this restructuring of the organization and purposes of the party. In fact, one of the first Khrushchev programs repudiated by the Brezhnev-Kosygin leadership was the decision to bifurcate the party organizations. This step alone, however, could not assure an end to the problem of conflicting role functions among party members even though the traditionalists had clearly won the battle.

Despite the restoration of conservative influence after the fall of Khrushchev, the new leadership slowly unfolded economic reform programs of its own. Brezhnev assumed leadership in the agricultural sector and announced plans to pursue the expansion of fertilizer industries as a means of increasing output per acre. Kosygin's leadership in the industrial sector was marked by plans to enlarge the roles played by profit and market demands in the determination of general policy and resource allocation. A modest increase in the production of consumer goods was counterbalanced in the 1965-1966 period by a slight increase in military expenditures. The principal difference between the programs of Khrushchev and his successors appeared to be the more cautious, reflective approach of Brezhnev and Kosygin.

Although the most basic part of the strategy of peaceful coexistence is the drive to equal and surpass the United States in economic productivity, the decisions on resource allocation, decentralization of most of the economic ministries, and the role of the party all engendered conflict among powerfully located group interests and prevented a consistent, unified plan of domestic economic construction from being approved and implemented. The assumption that the decision-makers are free to assign priorities at will or that the elite members of the C.P.S.U.

are fully committed to achieving the same goals by the same tactics simply cannot be substantiated. They must face up to the needs of various, and often competing, sectors of the national economy. Economics means politics in the Soviet Union. Hence it should not be surprising that international economics has a similar meaning.

The role of the east European states in Soviet economic plans

Just as plans for internal economic development frequently met with alterations or reversals of policy, plans for coordination of the economic development of the entire Communist system of states (more particularly, the east European party-states) were subject to even greater twists and turns. Here the number of variables naturally increased, for not only different factions but different governments and competing national interests had to be considered. Moreover, the strategic value of the east European states to the Soviet Union made stability in those countries a primary goal of the Kremlin's policy. Therefore, while the Soviet leaders were anxious to establish stable regimes and stable interrelationships among those regimes, the situation was actually becoming increasingly fluid. Khrushchev and his supporters had the responsibility of working out these competing and potentially destructive tendencies in eastern Europe.

The Khrushchev era witnessed a profound transformation of relations among the states of the Communist system, due in large part to the renewed emphasis on economic cooperation. Although the Council on Mutual Economic Assistance (Comecon) had been founded under Stalin in 1949, most agreements during the early period were bilateral arrangements with the U.S.S.R. as the dominant party. Rigid controls were maintained in the satellites by the Soviet Union, much of the productivity of the countries was pre-empted by Moscow through joint stock companies, and demands were levied for the development of heavy industry with little regard for the resources available in the individual countries. Under Khrushchev there was a gradual evolution from bilateral to multilateral agreements and from the latter to large-scale coordination of national economic plans and specialization in production according to available resources and skills. The accent on specialization and economic interdependence sharpened, particularly after the events of 1956 in Poland and Hungary, and has since constituted the principal means by which the Kremlin has fostered unity within the Communist system of states.

Moscow conceives of Comecon as having two primary functions. In the first place, it is responsible for the "organization of the economic and scientific-technical collaboration of the member states in the direction of more rational use of their natural resources and the accelerated development of their productive strength."[26] In the second place, the Council has the responsibility of "preparing recommendations on the most important questions of economic union," with the aim of coordinating the various national economic plans. In order to accomplish these functions, Comecon calls on each member to contribute its part in five general areas: (1) the development of industry and agriculture on the basis of consistent implementation of the international socialist division of labor, specialization, and coordinated production; (2) the development of transportation with the purpose of assuring the prompt shipment of all exports and imports; (3) the most effective use of capital investment in the construction of objectives following the principle of joint participation; (4) the development of commodity circulation and exchange among the member states; (5) the exchange of scientific-technical achievements and advanced productive experiments in order to minimize duplication of effort.[27] These measures were designed to assure the economic integration of the east European states with the Soviet Union, partly for reasons of security and partly to make it easier to draw on the talent and natural resources of the European members of the Communist system.

The coordination of national economic plans began with the Berlin conference of the members of Comecon in 1956 as a step in "concerting economic development and planning."[28] The introduction of the Soviet Union's Seven-Year Plan was construed as "the basis for the rapid development of the entire socialist camp" and, consequently, prompted the drafting of new long-term plans for all Comecon members.[29] Meeting in Budapest in the summer of 1960, the delegates to the Council not only worked on drawing the national plans of their respective countries into line with the Soviet plan but began drafting a program to coordinate the economic development of the member-states through 1980.

In the hope that the states in the Communist system would yield over one-half of world industrial production by 1965, the Soviet Union extended to members of Comecon over 30,000 million rubles in credits and loans to assist them in economic development. By 1961, the peak year of the outwardly directed economic program, the U.S.S.R. was providing economic and technical aid to the east European states in the construction of 226 large enterprises and 110 factory shops and installations—most of them thermal and hydroelectric plants, steel plants, and coal mines. These enterprises were distributed as follows:[30]

Country	*Industries*	*Other Installations*
Poland	68	6
Czechoslovakia	8	8
Hungary	27	4
Romania	60	23
Bulgaria	45	25
Albania	58	23

The assistance to the east European states was further augmented by supplying patents of Soviet processes and machinery. These coordinated development programs gave particular attention to the expansion of fuel and chemical industries in eastern Europe and greater exchange of scientific and technical information and personnel.[31]

The Council on Mutual Economic Assistance released an authoritative statement on cooperation among east European members of the Communist system in June, 1962. The grand object of the international division of labor, according to the report, is the elimination of different levels of development among socialist countries by paving the way for their "more or less simultaneous transition to communism within a single historical epoch."[32] While approving the coordination of national plans and the threefold increase in trade among the member-states between 1950 and 1960, the Council's statement called for more specialization in production and the cooperative building of fuel and chemical projects. It envisioned coordinated power development and eventual conversion to integrated power systems and the joint development of chemical industries. In implementing these goals, the Council cautioned that historical traditions must not be overestimated since "the tasks of socialist and Communist construction" require the creation of new conditions. In July, 1962, the Executive Committee of Comecon ratified a long-range plan incorporating the ideas of the June conference.

Before the 22nd Congress of the C.P.S.U., Khrushchev claimed that the joint endeavors of the socialist countries had resulted in increasing their share in world industrial output from 27 per cent in 1955 to 36 per cent in 1960. In comparison with capitalist countries, which had increased industrial production only 2.5 times the 1937 figure, according to Khrushchev's data, the socialist states in 1960 produced 6.8 times their output of 1937. The actual growth rate and rise of the standards of living of the east European states, however, has been disappointingly low to the Kremlin. Growth rates in these countries in 1962 were 7 per cent in Romania, 6 per cent in Bulgaria, and 5 per cent in Hungary, compared to 13, 14, and 9 per cent planned, respectively. The rate of growth in East Germany and Poland was less than 3 per cent compared to 6 per cent planned, while the growth of Czechoslovakia barely exceeded that of the preceding year.[33] While publicly stating his satisfaction with the advances of the members of Comecon, Khrushchev also displayed great concern for these disappointing economic conditions within the Communist system.[34] In order to spur coordinated economic activity, the Prime Minister asked the members of the Council to lead their states in striving for a 50 per cent increase in machine and equipment production and a 45 per cent increase in mutual deliveries in 1960-1965. These stepped-up demands and the distribution of productive goals among the states produced rumblings of dissatisfaction among some of the members of Comecon, indicating that the integration of the economies of the participating states was meeting opposition from formerly subservient satellites.

Although there may have been disagreement among the members of the Council previously, the strongest indications of dissension began with the effort to establish broad-scale coordination of the separate national economic plans in 1962. At that time the Soviet Union appeared to be discouraging the development of heavy industry in most of the countries and encouraging investment in chemical and light industries that would be of greater utility to the Soviet economy. It was noted in an official journal that "presently, when almost all the fraternal socialist countries have become industrialized," attention should be devoted to raising the productivity of labor and other industrial efforts.[35] This suggestion that most of the members of Comecon had already completed the industrialization of their economies was most unusual.

Subsequent Soviet comments referred to problems within the Council and attempted to assuage fears of Soviet dictation. *Mirovaia ekonomika i mezhdunarodnye otnosheniia* declared that "it is impossible to manage [effective coordination] without two-sided cooperation" and that "the most important questions of the development of economic relations between states of the world socialist system are decided by collective means."[36] The authors of the article dwelt on the rights of members in the decision-making processes of the Council, insisting that the equality of all members "is assured since all recommendations and decisions are made by the Council only with the agreement of the interested members of the organization." Equality was held to be further guaranteed by rules providing that decisions "in which a country is not interested are not binding on it." Similar assurances were followed by detailed statements purporting to prove the advantages of mutual cooperation and joint planning, but the advent of the open schism in the international Communist movement appeared only to exacerbate the inclinations of some east European leaders to go their own ways. Romania, a state that had often been considered the most amenable to the ways of Moscow, declined to send delegates to meetings called by the Kremlin, and openly courted trade agreements with the United States and France. The Soviet Union expended its ill-concealed anger on the Chinese for promoting the "obstructionist and dogmatic theory of economic autarky." To substantiate this criticism, it was asserted that the growth rates of China and Albania had declined since they had rejected "economic cooperation with the Soviet Union and set out on a path of autarky."[37] The same source included a long quotation from an earlier speech of Gheorgiu-dej, party leader of Romania, on socialist internationalism and the importance of cooperation among socialist states. The Sino-Soviet rift had found its way into the bowels of Comecon and was producing various kinds of discomforts. By the summer of 1964 Moscow had made polite overtures in meetings with various leaders of the Council states, suggesting that a revision of plans for the coordination of economic policies of the members was in the process of formulation.

Khrushchev demonstrated a disposition to negotiate with the leaders of the east European states and attempted to avoid outright dictation, in the interests of achieving greater economic integration of the European sector of the Communist system. There appeared to have been three basic reasons for the Kremlin's emphasis on this approach. First, Moscow sought to lift some of the rigid Stalinist controls in favor of reliance on ideological unity founded on a highly integrated economic system. The maintenance of the system by sheer brute strength had proved to be too costly, particularly in situations where manpower and resources were scarce. The utility of the scheme was probably a factor also, for coordinated development plans required recognition of available skills and resources. Second, Khrushchev still viewed the world as consisting primarily of two camps. It was, therefore, to the interest of all members of the Communist system to prove the economic success of the system, for both domestic and international reasons. Coordination of plans and cooperation of effort were expected to facilitate economic growth and thereby to demonstrate the superiority of the Communist system over those of other countries. Third, the effect of the split between Moscow and Peking on relations among the members of the Communist system was as yet unclear to the Soviet elite. Measures to assure the continued ties of the members of Comecon to Moscow would be welcomed as means to prevent the further intrusion of Peking into European Communist politics. Hence the Soviet Union was prepared to appease the discontented members of the Council.

The economic plans for domestic construction and for the coordinated development of the members of Comecon were devised with the intention of giving support to the foreign policy aspirations of the Soviet Union, as well as with the aim of increasing the well-being of Soviet citizens. The struggle over the formulation of economic policy both within the Soviet Union and among the east European states has given evidence of disagreement over priorities in domestic economic development and over methods and objectives of foreign policy. The emergence of two fairly clear-cut economic methods of foreign policy under the Khrushchev leadership did not eliminate the controversies over resource allocation, the organization of industrial management, the role of the party in the economy, and the integration of economic planning in the system of party-states. Indeed, in several respects the policies only exacerbated the conflicts. Nonetheless, it is important to consider the two most consistently developed manifestations of the policy of coexistence—the foreign aid program and the expansion of trade.

THE SOVIET FOREIGN AID PROGRAM

Although economic competition with capitalist states influences the production goals set by the Kremlin and by Comecon, the question remains as to what direct effect this has had on Russian foreign policy. Perhaps the clearest illustration of the Soviet "economic offensive" is the development of the foreign aid program, begun in 1954-1955. The program built up to a peak between 1958 and 1961 and began to experience a downward trend in 1962. Large new credit agreements were signed with India, Indonesia, Algeria, Somalia, and Egypt in 1963-1964, but these arrangements seemed to be designed to maintain the most successful ongoing aid programs rather than to launch a large-scale aid offensive comparable to the 1958-1961 period. The Brezhnev-Kosygin leadership followed this modified foreign aid plan, concentrating Soviet efforts on particular countries rather than spreading the program more thinly over a larger number. During the peak of the foreign assistance program the U.S.S.R. advanced 3.8 billion dollars in credits and grants to twenty states. The east European countries contributed 740 million dollars in similar programs. All but 800 million dollars of these credits was for economic assistance.[38] Although these figures represent formal paper commitments rather than actual expenditures, the sums involved indicate the seriousness with which the Kremlin approached the endeavor.

V. Rimalov, Soviet specialist on economic relations with less developed countries, asserts that the Russian foreign aid program assists new states in three principal ways.[39] First, it grants credits on favorable terms. Second, it provides them with "broad and varied scientific and technical assistance." And, third, the acceptance of goods (in many instances) as a form of payment encourages "the all-sided strengthening of fraternal cooperation in trade." Stripped of the Communist jargon, the comments of Rimalov are reasonably accurate. Industrial and technical assistance normally takes the form of credits extended to 2.5 to 3 per cent per annum for twelve years, with the payment period beginning after the last delivery of equipment or on completion of the project. The tendency has been for the U.S.S.R. to concentrate on major credit arrangements, those totaling 100 million dollars or more over a period of three to five years. In addition, the types of projects in which the Soviet Union has participated have followed a general pattern—the "big-package" deal. This kind of project involves the completion of some major undertaking—dams, industrial plants, schools, hospitals, stadiums—that will stand as a constant reminder to the native populace of the builder. Concentration of such projects maximizes the propaganda value of Soviet aid but often prevents the consideration of long-range economic development problems faced by the receiving states.

The most extensive Soviet credit arrangements have been made with India, the United Arab Republic, Indonesia, Algeria, Afghanistan, Iraq, Ghana, Guinea, and Ethiopia. India has received by far the largest loans. In addition to 132 million dollars provided for construction of the Bhilai steel plant, the U.S.S.R. lent 126 million dollars for the development of heavy industry under the second five-year plan and 375 million dollars under the third five-year plan. The latter arrangement was enlarged in 1964 as India experienced economic difficulties. Other credits extended after the Chinese attack on India brought the total amount of Soviets credits to over 1 billion dollars in 1964. Through the programs specified under these agreements, the Soviet Union has built or is building a steel plant, major machine-building factories, precision instrument plants, power stations with a capacity of 1.5 million kilowatts, coal processing plants, two oil refineries, and medical equipment factories, besides shipping electrical equipment.[40] Soviet authors have held that, under the conditions of an underdeveloped economy and traditional economic dependence on colonial powers, only the development of the government sector of the national economy can assure economic independence. Accordingly the Soviet Union, other members of Comecon, and Yugoslavia "have played a major role in the growth of the state sector of the Indian economy" by extending credits and providing technical assistance to help the government fulfill its five-year plans.[41] The Russians have probably been more cautious in their economic relations with India than with any other state. Soviet technicians keep largely to themselves, and no charges of espionage have marred their record. The principal complaints of the Indians have been of the high cost of parts required to replace worn-out pieces of Russian machinery.

Other Asian states to receive large credits have been Indonesia and Afghanistan. Khrushchev and Sukarno signed an agreement during the former's visit to Indonesia in 1960 for 250 million dollars in credit. The projects to be constructed included metallurgical plants, chemical plants, and textile mills. The construction of a giant stadium at Djakarta typified the effort of the Soviet aid administrators to build large projects capable of attracting public attention and admiration. The utility of the stadium for the Indonesian economy, however, is open to serious question. Following the anti-Communist rebellion and the loss of much of Sukarno's influence, Soviet aid declined significantly. Afghanistan signed three major credit agreements with U.S.S.R. between 1954 and 1962, totaling over 400 million dollars. Afghanistan shares a common border with the Soviet Union and has traditionally had close economic ties with her neighbor to the north. Burma, Ceylon, and Nepal have also received Soviet credits, but in much smaller sums than the three primary targets of the Soviet program in Asia.

In the Middle East, Soviet aid has gone primarily to the U.A.R. and Iraq. Nasser accepted over 800 million dollars in credits toward the building of over 100 industrial projects and also in military assistance between 1955 and 1964. Well over half of this total was devoted to the construction of the Aswan Dam.[42] It was estimated that the dam would cost close to 1 billion dollars by the time of completion. The dedication of the first stage of the project was the occasion for Khrushchev's three-week visit to Egypt in the spring of 1964. Kosygin made the same trip in the spring of 1966 to participate in the dedication of another stage. Egypt has also been the recipient of the Soviet Union's largest grants of military assistance to any non-Communist country. Elsewhere in the Middle East, a 137.5 million dollar credit agreement was signed with Iraq in March, 1959, apparently to compensate for serious Soviet setbacks in that area in 1958. However, after the Ba'athist coup d'etat in 1963, Moscow appeared to have retracted its aid commitments and withdrew its technicians from the country. Other aid agreements and grants in the Middle East were extended to Yemen and the Syrian sector of the U.A.R. before its withdrawal from the union with Egypt.

Ethiopia became the first African country below the Mediterranean area to receive Soviet aid. In 1959, an economic and cultural treaty provided for 100 million dollars in credit to be used for industrial and educational projects. Shortly thereafter the Soviet Union signed a 35 million dollar credit agreement with Guinea. An economic and technical cooperation agreement providing for a loan of 40 million dollars was reached with Ghana in 1960. The following spring the Republic of Mali received a similar loan. In 1962, the credits to all three of the latter countries were increased and; in 1963, the Republic of Algeria received a 100 million dollar long-term loan. Somalia, Nigeria, and Tunisia also began to participate in the Soviet foreign aid program in 1963. While permitting overall aid commitments to decline in 1962-1963, the Kremlin still persisted in bestowing much attention on the newly independent countries of Africa. The *Soviet Weekly* claimed that 750 million dollars had been lent to African states as of June, 1963, involving the construction of 200 industrial and agricultural projects, 20 communications centers, and 40 schools and colleges.[43] The heightened attention devoted to Africa was further indicated by the growing study of African culture and political development under the direction of the eminent Soviet scholar, Ivan Potekhin.

In addition to this general form of Soviet aid, the U.S.S.R. offered to provide "extensive aid" to nationalist forces in the Congo and in Algeria in 1960-1962. The government pledged to give the forces of Patrice Lumumba "extensive economic aid for purposes of creating in the republic normal conditions for its economic life." Medical assistance and a small number of conventional arms were supplied to the supporters of Lumumba. In so doing, the Soviet Union adamantly refused to recognize the legitimacy of United Nations action in the Congo and vigorously protested the arrest and execution of Lumumba.

Soviet behavior during the struggle of Algerian nationalists for independence was particularly interesting. In accordance with Communist precepts of aiding revolutionary nationalist forces, Moscow reported that Soviet societies (not the government) had sent agricultural and medical equipment to the Algerian rebels. On the other hand, the Kremlin appeared to be exceptionally careful not to arouse the antagonism of the

French government, with which the Soviet government was anxious to conclude trade and cultural exchange agreements. Khrushchev, while pointing out Soviet belief in the right of self-determination, strongly applauded the decision of the French government to negotiate with the Provisional Government of the Algerian Republic. The Soviet press claimed that independence was in the interest of both the French people and the Algerian nationalists. "Only the granting of freedom and independence to Algeria will lead to peace in this part of the world and will help to establish truly friendly and neighborly relations between France and Algeria." As the revolution was ending to the advantage of the nationalists, *Izvestiia* praised the cease-fire and called the prospective settlement of "mutual benefit" to both countries.[44] The revolutionary commitment of the Soviet elite was clearly muffled by the interest of the Soviet government in other matters. Ambivalence over commitment to international revolution and concern for protecting the special interests of the Soviet Union have marked relations with other states as well. In such cases no more than verbal support or, as in the case of Algeria, token physical support has been given to the anti-Western, if not pro-Soviet, forces of internally torn countries.

By the fall of 1963, the Soviet Union was providing foreign aid credits and sending Russian technicians to twenty nations—Indonesia, Cambodia, Burma, India, Nepal, Ceylon, Afghanistan, Yemen, Syria, Iraq, the U.A.R., Sudan, Algeria, Tunisia, Ethiopia, Somalia, Mali, Guinea, Ghana, and Nigeria. The aid to Syria and Iraq had gradually been terminated. The total sum actually expended from the beginning of the program to the end of 1963 was approximately 3 billion dollars.[45] Additional commitments were pledged to many of the recipient nations but the sums were generally small except for India, Algeria, Somalia, Indonesia, and Egypt.

The basic motive behind the foreign aid program was to

counter the influence of American aid. This fact was further demonstrated by the addition of a Peace Corps type of program to the Soviet technical assistance administration in 1964. American and Allied policies in the underdeveloped areas of the world have received great attention in Moscow. Soviet propaganda has blamed the great discrepancy between the per capita incomes of the peoples of North America and western Europe, on the one hand, and the peoples of Asia, Africa, and Latin America, on the other, on colonialism and the resulting exploitation of the natural resources of the underdeveloped countries. Western aid is purportedly designed for three purposes. First, it is used to keep former colonial countries "in the system of capitalist economy as agrarian-raw material sources of the industrialized powers."[46] Second, Western assistance is primarily military, designed to draw less powerful states into military blocs and unions with imperialist powers.[47] The volume of military commodities in American aid is held to demonstrate the disinterest of capitalist states in contributing to the welfare of the people. Third, Western aid programs are often disguises for the dissemination of anti-Communist propaganda among the peoples of less developed countries. Citing the construction of 500 industrial projects by the Soviet Union and over 400 by the east European states, Lavrechenko asserted that foreign aid from members of the Communist system helped the new states "establish independent economies with their own industrial sectors." The economic burdens placed on former colonial territories can be lifted only if the young governments "break all relations" with "foreign monopolistic capital, liquidate the colonial structures of their economies, and concentrate on the construction of varied national economies." The Soviet assistance program is administered with these aims in mind.

That the Soviet foreign aid program is primarily a response to the comparable American program is further indicated by the pledge of the Soviet government to work "against the organization of imperialist blocs and unions which constitute a foremost threat to the independence and security" of underdeveloped states."[48] Soviet ambitions appear to be particularly directed toward minimizing Western influence in areas of strategic concern to the U.S.S.R. Thus, *Mirovaia ekonomika i mezhdunarodnye otnosheniia* cited the principal overt threats from Western military aid and alliances in the preceding decade as the Suez crisis in 1956, the Middle East crisis of 1958, and the Cuban crisis of 1962.[49] No reference was made to the Laotian and Vietnamese problems of southeast Asia, suggesting that Moscow had focused its attention, first, on the Middle East and the Mediterranean, which are of continuing strategic interest to the Soviet Union, and, second, on areas of strategic interest to its principal opponents in the cold war. The stepped-up aid program to Indonesia after 1960 appears to have had its roots more in the Communist system than in basic controversies between Moscow and Washington, for the Kremlin hoped to discourage the powerful Indonesian Communist party from associating fully and openly with Peking. After the destruction of that party's leadership in the Indonesian revolution, Soviet interest in providing aid declined appreciably.

The general aim of the Kremlin in its aid program centers on weakening Western influence by promoting neutralism. In turn, the neutral states "contribute to the crisis of imperialist politics" by serving as counterweights to the policies of " 'positions of strength,' 'the cold war,' and balancing on the brink of war." Developing states can, therefore, play a major role in international relations, especially by cooperating with the Soviet Union, by supporting proposals on disarmament, and by persisting in strong anti-imperialist stands. Young states can pursue such policies because Soviet aid and influence are held to free them from the political and economic ties with "imperialist" countries.

The aid program of the Soviet Union was not adopted without internal conflict. Moreover, its continuation has not been unanimously endorsed by other Communist parties. The molding of the program in 1954-1955 required the repudiation of earlier policies toward the new governments. The "CPSU and the Soviet government have worked to correct and overcome these mistakes" of the Stalin period.[50] This repudiation of the Stalinist attitude through the economic and military assistance given to non-Communist states and the generally cordial approach to neutrals were major issues used by the Molotov faction against Khrushchev.[51] Having won the right to pursue his policies, Khrushchev discovered that victory over domestic opposition was followed by opposition from non-Soviet Communists. Soviet aid to non-Communist governments was criticized by national Communist leaders on the grounds that it was helping "bourgeois" rulers to entrench themselves in power, thus hindering the "ideological struggle." This criticism was especially sharp where aid was given to countries whose governments had outlawed national Communist parties and arrested their leaders. Nevertheless, the aid program continued with unfortunate effects on the revolutionary élan of the Communist movement. Foreign aid has been interpreted by numerous national Communists as a tacit withdrawal from them of Soviet support.

Khrushchev's answer to his Communist critics was that loans and trade with underdeveloped nations greatly enhance the prestige not only of the Soviet Union but of the whole Communist movement. The programs permit the U.S.S.R. to develop economic ties with other states and to set itself forth as the model for rapid industrialization. By setting an example of industrial progress and demonstrating concern for the welfare of impoverished peoples, Khrushchev claimed that the Soviet Union could encourage the acceptance of Communist ideals everywhere, but particularly in the new states.

> The spread of these ideas is the logical outcome of the times, the result of the long and bitter experience of peoples whom capitalism had nothing to offer beyond poverty and degradation. The American sociologist, Adam B. Ulam, an avowed

> anti-communist, has had to recognize the real reason for the attraction of communism for the people in the underdeveloped countries. 'Without having read a word of Marx or Lenin,' he writes in his book *The Unfinished Revolution*, 'an illiterate peasant who is being squeezed economically or forced to give up his land and work in a factory experiences almost instinctively the feelings that Marxism formulates in a theoretical language.' To such people, he goes on, communism is 'a systematic expression of their own feelings and reactions, something which again makes sense out of an apparently senseless world.[52]

For this reason Moscow ostensibly expects the backward countries to choose Communism and promises that their cooperation with the Soviet Union and other party-states will "ease the birth pangs of the new society" by allowing them to bypass the capitalist stage of economic development. Whatever the actual expectation, it should be noted that after a decade of existence, "ruble diplomacy" had produced no conspicuous successes. None of the recipient nations had joined the Communist system of states. At best, from Moscow's perspective, the program may have encouraged the continuing neutrality of the participating countries. At worst, the program engendered dissension within the international Communist movement.

THE POLITICS OF SOVIET FOREIGN TRADE

Trade with underdeveloped countries

The growth of Soviet and east European trade with the countries of Asia, Africa, and Latin America has primarily been the result of two factors—the willingness of the Communist states to accept commodities in payment of loans and to accept goods that have low value in international commerce. Demonstrating the Khrushchev regime's sensitivity to the problem of many of these countries in finding world markets for their limited produce, the members of Comecon by 1962 had more than tripled the 870 million dollar trade volume of 1954. The peak year in this trade offensive was 1961, when a concerted drive to conclude bilateral trade agreements resulted in 206 accords with 32 countries.[53] This expansion of trade with underdeveloped countries has been integrally linked with the Soviet foreign aid program.

From the modest short-term trade agreements sought in the mid-1950s, the members of Comecon have expanded their efforts to reach three- and five-year mutual trade arrangements with less developed states. Such long-term agreements have been made with India, Indonesia, the United Arab Republic, Guinea, Brazil, and Somalia. Typical of these is the 1959 agreement between the U.S.S.R. and Brazil. A mutual exchange of 25 million dollars in commodities in 1960, 37 million dollars in 1961, and 45 million dollars in 1962 was called for. In the spring of 1963, negotiations between the two governments were conducted to broaden their trade relations by concluding a similar accord for 1963-1966.[54] In this and other exchanges, the Soviet Union's exports consisted largely of petroleum and petroleum products, rolled steel, machinery and transport equipment, lumber, cement, and grains. Soviet imports consisted predominantly (70 per cent) of agricultural goods—natural rubber, cotton, wool, raw hides, coffee, cocoa beans, sugar, rice, and tea. By 1962, the pattern of bilateral agreements had been established, by which the Soviet Union traded machinery and manufactured goods for agricultural products and raw materials. This pattern held true for the lesser members of Comecon as well as for the U.S.S.R. Approximately one-half of these agreements set specific goals in terms of volume or value, while the remainder of the accords left negotiations for specific items open.[55] However, the volume specified in the general agreements was frequently not fulfilled in subsequent negotiations.

TABLE I
Soviet Trade in 1962 on a Commodity Basis
(in percentages)*

	Export	*Import*
Finished products	63.6	74.5
Machines	16.6	34.7
Metals and metal articles	9.5	6.5
Fuel	11.2	3.0
Food products	5.1	6.1
Industrial products for the people	2.6	17.8
Raw materials	36.4	25.5
Oil	5.2	0.1
Ores and concentrates	3.9	4.6
Grain and livestock	11.2	7.7
Grain for production of food goods	8.2	5.4

* This table is a translation of one presented in I. Diumulen, "Sovetskii Soiuz v sisteme mezhdunarodnykh ekonomicheskikh sviazei," *Mirovaia ekonomika i mezhdunarodnye otnosheniia,* No. 3, 1964, p. 82.

The Soviet Union, Czechoslovakia, and Poland made extensive use of trade fairs and exhibitions as means of encouraging expanded trade. In 1963, nearly thirty less developed countries scheduled exhibits in the Soviet Union alone, the Indian display being by far the largest and most publicized. Soviet trade fairs were also staged in Damascus and Tripoli in 1963. There the Kremlin hoped to repeat the 1962 success of the Soviet pavilion in Lagos, Nigeria, which led to the first Soviet-Nigerian trade accord the following year. Public radio and press pleas to specific governments for greater commodity exchange have also become common, although the impact of this approach, if any, cannot be accurately measured. This tactic was used to appeal to Brazil, Iran, Syria, Ceylon, and India before new trade agreements with those states were initialed.

In some cases price and domestic requirements appear to have had little to do with some of the Soviet trade with poorer countries. In four instances, the Soviet Union and other Comecon states clearly stepped in to relieve single-commodity nations of surplus produce—fish from Iceland, rice from Burma, wool from Uruguay, and cotton from Egypt.[56] Willingness to purchase goods for which they have little need has permitted the members of the Communist system of states to increase their share of the foreign trade of the U.A.R., Iceland, and Afghanistan beyond 25 per cent, and to make substantial inroads into the trade of Guinea and Uruguay. Although the program has not produced disproportionate increases in Soviet and east European trade in most cases, *New Times* happily predicted the acceleration of the trend discernible in trade with the U.A.R. and Afghanistan by noting that the U.S.S.R. and People's Democracies were prepared to fill the vacuum as new states learned that the West was far more interested in selling than buying.[57]

TABLE II

Total Soviet Trade with Selected Developing Countries (in millions of rubles)

(Exports refer to Soviet exports to the country noted; imports to Soviet imports)

Country	*1955*	*1958*	*1959*	*1960*	*1961*	*1962*	*1963*	*1964*
Afghanistan								
Exports	12.2	20.8	25.5	28.8	35.5	35.5	40.4	42.7
Imports	9.8	11.4	14.0	15.2	17.7	22.8	17.6	20.4
Burma								
Exports	0.2	2.3	1.4	1.6	3.5	5.3	6.0	5.9
Imports	15.1	0.0	3.6	4.5	2.2	11.1	12.4	18.3
India								
Exports	6.6	117.0	61.2	42.4	85.9	112.3	199.7	208.6
Imports	4.0	45.8	54.5	61.6	60.2	64.5	85.3	140.3
Indonesia								
Exports	0.1	24.5	14.2	14.6	28.2	52.7	44.9	42.0
Imports	3.3	10.4	9.9	28.3	30.5	34.8	26.8	23.2
Iraq								
Exports	0.0	0.0	21.0	18.2	33.6	46.8	39.1	28.2
Imports	0.3	0.0	2.1	3.1	4.2	3.4	4.7	2.2

TABLE II *(continued)*

Country	1955	1958	1959	1960	1961	1962	1963	1964
Iran								
Exports	20.2	24.7	16.2	16.2	16.3	14.5	21.4	19.6
Imports	17.2	23.8	16.9	17.1	16.5	14.8	16.0	18.9
Ceylon								
Exports	0.0	0.5	0.5	0.9	1.6	9.1	17.3	22.2
Imports	0.0	3.9	4.2	7.7	8.1	5.5	6.6	20.6
Syria								
Exports	0.3	13.7	13.6	9.9	15.3	4.7	11.8	11.0
Imports	0.0	21.0	5.5	7.0	3.9	6.2	12.8	16.0
U. A. R.								
Exports	9.9	78.9	79.2	62.8	97.8	93.0	121.7	140.1
Imports	13.8	96.4	83.4	109.2	86.6	65.7	111.2	111.2
Ghana								
Exports	0.0	0.0	0.0	5.0	13.9	8.9	15.0	17.6
Imports	10.4	2.4	7.4	19.5	6.1	15.0	19.4	18.7
Guinea								
Exports	0.0	0.0	0.8	5.2	24.5	18.0	12.7	8.3
Imports	0.0	0.0	0.7	2.0	3.8	2.4	2.1	2.0
Mali								
Exports	0.0	0.0	0.0	0.0	7.7	7.7	11.0	11.9
Imports	0.0	0.0	0.0	0.0	3.4	3.9	2.7	3.3
Argentina								
Exports	21.6	15.5	15.1	12.6	9.5	7.2	0.8	4.0
Imports	25.3	14.4	25.1	19.5	17.9	8.8	16.6	17.9
Brazil								
Exports	0.0	0.0	0.9	14.2	16.5	27.1	26.5	21.6
Imports	1.7	0.8	4.3	8.2	21.6	32.2	39.1	33.4
Cuba								
Exports	0.0	0.0	0.0	63.7	258.3	333.7	359.8	331.1
Imports	32.2	14.0	6.7	93.4	280.7	210.6	148.0	259.6
Uruguay								
Exports	0.3	5.0	8.4	1.2	0.5	0.2	0.2	0.2
Imports	9.0	22.3	13.6	1.2	3.7	13.8	4.7	0.9

Sources: *Vneshniaia Torgovlia SSSR za 1961 god, statisticheskii obzor*, Moskva: Vneshtorgizdat, 1962, pp. 8-12; *Vneshniaia Torgovlia Soiuza SSR za 1962 god, statisticheskii obzor*, Moskva: Vneshtorgizdat, 1963, pp. 10-14; *Vneshniaia Torgovlia Soiuza SSR za 1964 god, statisticheskii obzor*, Moskva: Vneshtorgizdat, 1965, pp. 11-15.

The Kremlin has also exploited the dissatisfaction of the leaders of less developed countries with the international market. The responsibility is held to rest with "exclusive trade groups" set up by Western nations.[58] For several sessions the Soviet delegate introduced resolutions in the General Assembly of the United Nations to hold an economic conference on trade and economic relations with less developed states. In proposing such a conference, the representative of the U.S.S.R. has invariably blamed the West, particularly the Common Market members, for levying undue hardships on poor nations. The proposed solution was an International Trade Organization which would pay no heed to political groupings of states in working out the rules for fair trade. In 1962, with the cosponsorship of thirty-four Asian, African, and Latin American nations (and Yugoslavia), the resolution was approved. Hardly had the United States agreed to participate in the conference before the Soviet Union insisted that the issue of East-West trade be included on the agenda. The propaganda purpose of this move was to give the new states the impression that the West alone was responsible for high tariffs, trade blocs, and other obstacles to the free flow of international commerce.

According to the Soviet conception, the International Trade Organization (I.T.O.) should study the ways and means of solving problems of international trade and recommend measures conducive to the expansion of trade among all countries regardless of their social and political systems. To fulfill these general aims, the I.T.O. should direct itself to the following tasks: (1) ascertainment of the correlation between world trade and economic development, (2) liquidation of all types of discrimination and obstacles in trade, (3) elimination of the "harmful influence of closed economic groups on the trade of third countries, especially on the trade and economies of less developed states," and (4) improvement of conditions of international trade with respect to the demands and needs of the developing countries and regions of the world.[59] The organization requires financial powers in order to assist in the provision of credit to the underdeveloped states. These proposals actually differed very little from propositions presented by advocates of free trade in Western countries. However, the exploitation of the trade proposals for propaganda purposes as part of the Soviet appeal to less developed nations created apprehension in many Western circles.

While such political exploits have sometimes been disconcerting, a more careful analysis reveals the very limited nature of the successes of Soviet trade efforts. Percentage gains alone are highly misleading, for the volume of trade with the U.S.S.R. in most instances was very small, or virtually nonexistent, to begin with. A percentage gain of several hundred points could still signify only a small fraction of the total volume of a nation's foreign trade. Furthermore, a significant portion of Soviet trade derives directly from the foreign aid program, which does not necessarily lead to a continuous pattern of trade development. (Note the sharp increases and declines in trade with foreign aid recipients in Table II.) Even the statistics printed in the 1962 *Annual of the Great Soviet Encyclopedia* make clear that the overall exchange percentages of Soviet and Comecon trade on a country-by-country basis usually constitute less than 10 per cent and often less than 5 per cent of the other state's foreign commerce.[60] In spite of the Kremlin's great efforts to woo India

TABLE III

Soviet Trade with Asia, Africa, and Latin America
(except Cuba)
(in millions of rubles)

	1955	1958	1962
Asia	122	459	636
Africa	40	189	265
Latin America	58	58	96
	220	706	997

Source: *Mirovaia ekonomika i mezhdunarodnye otnosheniia*, No. 3, 1964, p. 87.

and Indonesia, for example, the volume of trade with both of those states remained low. In the case of the latter country the Soviet report lamented that over 90 per cent of its foreign trade was still with the "capitalist bloc."

Soviet and Comecon trade with industrial countries

Although still small in total volume, Soviet trade with the advanced countries of western Europe and Japan showed a marked increase in the early 1960's. Trade agreements were made with all the major European powers and with Austria, Sweden, Belgium, and Denmark. Japan concluded a major trade accord with the Soviet Union in January, 1963. While the principal Soviet commodities exported were crude oil and petroleum products, the imports to the Soviet Union and the People's Democracies consisted of steel pipe, precision and automatic machine tools, electric power generators and transmissions, electronic equipment for communications, and complete petrochemical and synthetic plants.[61]

TABLE IV

Comecon Trade with Selected Western Countries*
(in millions of U.S. dollars)

	IMPORTS			EXPORTS		
Country	*1959*	*1960*	*1961*	*1959*	*1960*	*1961*
Italy	155.9	266.8	311.2	120.3	172.8	217.2
West Germany	323.2	280.5	392.0	314.2	440.3	476.3
Great Britain	325.6	389.3	436.4	170.1	214.0	294.2
France	160.4	154.4	166.4	158.3	220.5	234.9
Sweden	105.0	121.3	127.8	99.0	110.1	102.3

* Compiled from statistics in *The Soviet Economic Offensive in Western Europe*, U.S. House Report No. 32, Committee on Foreign Relations, 88th Congress, 1st Session, 1963.

The Soviet trade accords with France and Japan and the further expansion of reciprocal exchanges with Italy in 1963 illustrated the broadening interest of Moscow in trade with "imperialist" states. The Soviet-French agreement of 1960-1962 expired without prompt renewal as a result of the Kremlin's demand, on the basis of its most-favored-nation agreement with France, to be granted tariff rights equal with those of members of the Common Market. Finally relenting on this demand, Moscow concluded a trade accord with France in February, 1963, for 1963-1965. Under this new arrangement, France was scheduled to export equipment and machines for chemical, electronics, pulp and paper, and food industries in return for Soviet anthracite, crude oil and petroleum products, manganese, chromium, and lumber. The Soviet-Japanese agreement called for a similar three-year exchange of commodities. The Soviet exports included the same items as those in the French list supplemented by pig iron, coking coal, and machinery. The Soviet imports from Japan were oil tankers, pipe, electron microscopes, floating cranes, and other hoisting and transport instruments. The negotiations with Italy produced little that was different in terms of export-import commodities but did establish an Italian-Soviet Chamber of Commerce to promote further trade. Under the auspices of this organization Italy was authorized to stage a trade exhibition in the Soviet Union and Moscow was authorized to stage a giant industrial exhibit in Genoa in 1964.[62]

Although British-Soviet trade had been of very small volume, Great Britain showed signs of growing interest in the extension of trade relations with the U.S.S.R. in 1963. Facing reduced markets on the European continent as a result of the Common Market, Britain was compelled to search for new markets for its products. The President of the Board of Trade, Frederick Elliot, openly noted different attitudes toward trade with the Soviet Union on the part of his government and Washington. Experience has taught, he insisted, that Russia's record in the international market "is no worse than that of our closest friends."[63] Mr. Elliot pointed out that the fact that Comecon countries often settled the balance of their exchange with international currency reserves or gold indicated that they were not using trade purely for purposes of politics and economic warfare. The policy of his government, he announced, was to promote commerce between East and West without undermining the goodwill of states that had long provided the traditional sources of British trade. A meeting in Moscow of the head of the British Board of Trade and the Soviet Minister of Foreign Trade in 1963 resulted in plans for the two governments to conduct extensive negotiations in 1964 for the purpose of concluding a broadened, long-term trade agreement.[64] Although a trade treaty was not concluded, arrangements were worked out for long-term credit to the Soviet Union in order to facilitate the purchase of British chemical plants.

TABLE V
Soviet Trade with Industrialized States
(in millions of rubles)

Country	*1955*	*1958*	*1959*	*1960*	*1961*	*1962*	*1963*	*1964*
Great Britain								
Exports	152.2	131.0	149.1	173.2	204.1	191.8	193.5	214.7
Imports	64.0	65.6	81.8	97.3	115.4	104.8	116.9	92.9
Italy								
Exports	15.7	34.7	70.2	92.4	117.2	118.3	123.0	121.0
Imports	14.7	31.7	47.5	81.3	86.4	88.7	122.5	88.5
West Germany								
Exports	26.3	59.1	80.3	106.9	106.9	121.0	118.0	112.4
Imports	21.4	64.9	108.1	179.3	161.4	183.9	134.1	117.6
France								
Exports	53.7	78.4	79.0	66.4	71.5	76.9	93.2	95.3
Imports	32.5	72.5	90.4	116.9	108.4	137.7	63.8	62.3
Sweden								
Exports	25.7	27.2	39.4	48.1	46.3	47.8	57.9	49.5
Imports	15.3	25.3	37.5	41.5	46.6	68.8	62.5	79.3

TABLE V *(continued)*

Country	*1955*	*1958*	*1959*	*1960*	*1961*	*1962*	*1963*	*1964*
Japan								
Exports	2.0	17.9	30.0	68.5	101.7	101.7	111.5	148.2
Imports	1.6	16.0	21.1	55.4	59.9	131.2	148.9	173.9
Canada								
Exports	1.8	2.1	3.6	4.7	4.2	2.1	3.1	4.7
Imports	2.3	22.7	13.6	9.0	41.1	2.4	157.3	291.8
U.S.A.								
Exports	21.4	23.5	23.1	22.2	21.9	15.7	22.3	18.6
Imports	0.5	4.2	16.0	53.9	45.6	24.3	25.1	146.3

Sources: *Vneshniaia Torgovlia SSSR za 1961 god, statisticheskii obzor,* Moskva: Vneshtorgizdat, 1961, pp. 8-12; *Vneshniaia Torgovlia Soiuza SSR za 1962 god, statisticheskii obzor,* Moskva: Vneshtorgizdat, 1963, pp. 10-14; *Vneshniaia Torgovlia Soiuza SSR za 1964 god, statisticheskii obzor,* Moskva: Vneshtorgizdat, 1965, pp. 11-15.

The government of the United States has been more reluctant to encourage large-scale trade agreements between the Soviet Union and private American industries. Indeed, the already small volume of trade between the two nations was sharply reduced in 1962, primarily as a result of the Cuban crisis. American exports to the U.S.S.R. fell from 45 million rubles in 1961 to 24 million in 1962. Likewise, Soviet exports to the United States dropped from 22 million dollars in 1961 to 16 million dollars in 1962. Some of these losses were regained in 1963, but the total volume of trade between the two states remained small in all commodities except wheat. Government policy, while not officially opposing trade expansion in this area, maintained a rather broad list of excluded products on its list of "strategic goods." This factor, coupled with the inability or lack of desire of the Soviet Union to purchase available goods, has inhibited the growth of commodity exchange between the chief protagonists of the cold war. On the other hand, the willingness of Moscow to provide American steel manufacturers with a highly advanced steel processing formula and the gradual easing of cold war tensions in the summer of 1963 promoted interest in the United States in selling surplus agricultural commodities to the Soviet Union. After prolonged bargaining, the first agreement to sell surplus American wheat to the U.S.S.R. was reached in January, 1964. This may have opened the door to a more liberal trade policy.

The general trend after 1958 was, therefore, toward gradually increasing trade between the Soviet Union and advanced non-Communist countries, although the percentage of East-West trade remained a small part of the total trade volume of the countries concerned. There was a marked increase in Soviet exports of fuel and raw materials, particularly of chrome ore, and an equally sharp rise in Soviet imports of machinery and base metals. Domestic agricultural failures in 1962 and 1963 resulted in the importation of huge quantities of grains and the purchase of Western chemical industries by the Soviet Union. However, the development that attracted perhaps the greatest attention in the Western states was the growing importance of Soviet petroleum on the world market.

The role of petroleum in Soviet trade

As has been noted, the principal exports of the Soviet Union have been crude oil and petroleum products. Since 1959, Moscow has relied heavily on its ability to supply petroleum commodities to advanced industrial nations in order to import their products. By 1961, Neftexport, the international commercial arm of the Soviet oil industry, was supplying West Germany with 10.31 per cent of its petroleum requirements, Italy with 22.9 per cent, Greece with 37.9 per cent, Austria with 38 per cent, and Iceland with 93.1 per cent. The U.S. National Petroleum Council estimated that Soviet sales to the West would reach nearly 500 million tons in the mid-1960's compared to 30 million tons in 1961.[65]

In the advanced countries of the West, Soviet oil was made

particularly attractive by the increasing fuel needs of expanding industries and the cut-rate prices offered by Neftexport. The Ente Nationale Idrocarburi (ENI), the state petroleum company of Italy, met 72 per cent of its requirements in 1961 through Soviet imports, as opposed to 8 per cent in 1958. Neftexport sold crude oil to ENI at $.85 to $1.10 less per barrel than oil imported from the Persian Gulf. The Federal German Republic purchased Soviet crude oil for $12.64 per metric ton, compared with $17.93 for Western-produced oil. In addition, ENI constructed two refineries in southern Germany, a factor that portended the further introduction of Soviet petroleum to supply West German needs. Another interesting fact about the cost of Soviet oil was that Western purchasers could buy it cheaper than the People's Democracies. The per barrel price of crude oil in eastern Europe was $2.97 in 1961, while it was sold to Brazil for $1.65, Italy and the Federal German Republic for $1.39, and Egypt for $1.44.

The goods Moscow has sought from industrialized states have been large-diameter steel pipe, tankers, and equipment for petrochemical plants. Although West Germany terminated its shipment of pipe in November, 1962, before that time the Soviet Union had acquired an estimated 40 per cent of its requirements to complete the three pipelines to eastern Europe from the Federal German Republic, Italy, and Sweden. Oil tankers were also purchased from Italy, Denmark, and Japan. The ability of the Soviet Union and her Communist allies to export increasing quantities of petroleum was being enhanced by her trade commitments with industrial nations.

The expansion of Soviet oil markets, despite the opposition of the United States, introduced new friction into the cold war. In the fall of 1962, the United States successfully persuaded the North Atlantic Council to place steel pipe on the strategic goods list. The West German and Italian governments accepted the ruling over strong protests from domestic industrialists and

Japan later voluntarily acquiesced in barring such shipments. This was followed by a United Press International report in March, 1963, that there had been a sudden stoppage of oil deliveries from Soviet ports on the Black Sea. The report prompted a scathing rebuttal from Moscow. *Izvestiia,* on March 19, claimed that Washington was merely trying to frighten Soviet customers and insisted that "Soviet oil is exported on mutually acceptable conditions on a reliable long-term basis." Later in March an official protest was delivered to the American Embassy in Moscow complaining that Washington had pressured West Germany into discontinuing delivery of large-diameter steel pipe to the U.S.S.R. and was attempting to persuade other countries to do the same.[66] By early 1964, it had become clear that the ban on steel pipe shipments had only retarded, not prevented, the completion of the Soviet pipelines and that the primary result of the American action had been only to exacerbate tension. Russian petroleum exports continued to increase gradually, with no evidence of dumping.

While the Soviet Union was facing these obstacles with members of the Western alliance, however, it continued to effect a modest expansion of its petroleum market in less developed countries. There the issue was closely related to the foreign aid programs of the members of Comecon. After building refineries in Iraq, Egypt, Ethiopia, India, and Indonesia, the Soviet Union stepped up its campaign to provide the crude oil required for the operation of those refineries.[67] In the other hand, the U.S.S.R. provided assistance in prospecting for and extracting oil in those countries as well as in Burma, Syria, Argentina, and Ceylon. Furthermore, the response of less developed states to the offers of Neftexport was generally rather cautious, for they demonstrated reluctance to rely on any one country as the only source of supply of crucial products.

The economic aspect of peaceful coexistence reveals the decline of Communist revolutionary theory. It is predicated on the assumption that in a period when the use of military force to achieve political objectives has become extremely dangerous and threatens national survival the goals of the movement can be achieved through economic example. By surpassing the United States in productivity and giving the Russian people the highest standard of living in the world, the Soviet leaders contend that their socioeconomic system will draw the entire world into the Communist pattern. The scheme is based on two assumptions: first, that a high rate of growth in the U.S.S.R. will continue indefinitely while that of the United States and western Europe will gradually fall further and further behind; second, that the Soviet Union and the other members of the Communist system of states will be relatively unaffected by these developments—that is, their political and social values will not be altered by technological innovations and cultural change. Economic and sociological evidence and the continuing significance of nationalism and pluralism in the world belie both assumptions. Economic competition provides the Kremlin with goals and a yardstick for measuring domestic successes, but no program has been spelled out explaining precisely how productivity and national prestige will or can lead the Soviet Union to some kind of global victory. Furthermore, divergent opinions among the elite on economic questions and conflicts among domestic economic groups suggest that such a neatly devised program is unlikely to materialize.

When the foreign aid program was first launched, Khrushchev apparently sincerely believed that the Soviet Union would gain such prestige among the underdeveloped nations by a demonstration of the economic advantages of Communism that they would feel moved to imitate the Soviet system. By this method and by establishing close economic ties with the new states, the Kremlin hoped to draw them under its influence and control. Instead, the Kremlin has discovered that the governments of the new nations have been no more prepared to embrace Moscow without reservations than they have been willing to embrace

Washington. National Communists have fared badly from their own countries' governments—India, the U.A.R., and Algeria, for example, which have been principal recipients of Soviet aid. The program has not only failed to yield the desired results, but has become a financial burden on the economies of the Soviet Union and the states of eastern Europe. While Russian prestige has probably benefited, Moscow has had to learn that it is often difficult to translate prestige into tangible results and far from easy to acquire economic control of other states purely through economic means. The foreign aid program has thus far not contributed to proving the superiority of Communist theory and there are no indications that it will do so in the foreseeable future.

The Kremlin has confronted similar problems in the area of foreign trade. According to theory historically accepted by the Soviet Union, trade with non-Communist states is to be used for political purposes. To the orthodox Leninist the lessening of the new states' reliance on Western markets is an important step in eliminating the vestiges of "economic colonialism," whereby the imperialist nations have permitted formal political independence but have retained economic control over their former colonies. It is highly questionable that the Soviet Union meets many domestic economic requirements through much of its trade with the less developed countries. In regard to items such as coffee, cotton, rice, spices, and fish, there is evidence that the members of Comecon have resold substantial quantities at a loss on the world market after purchasing them from weak nations in economic difficulties. It is, therefore, only natural to assume that price-cutting, favorable trade terms, and the acceptance of commodities from underdeveloped nations that have trouble selling their produce in the international market indicate a political aim.

Commodity exchange agreements are also often linked with the Russian foreign aid program. By assisting these countries to develop industrial and transport systems, the Communist states can help accelerate their demand for fuel and other industrial goods. Practice leaves little doubt that the Soviet-built refineries and industrial plants are intended to process and use Russian oil. Such methods afford a welcome opportunity to the Kremlin to decrease the reliance of the developing world on the give-and-take of fluctuating international markets and on economic ties with "imperialist" nations.

Communist theory, however, should not be permitted to blind observers in the West to other factors implicit in the Soviet trade program. In their competition for prestige and allies, Washington and Moscow challenge one another's policies on terms far more practical than purely ideological considerations permit. From the standpoint of her own national interests, the U.S.S.R. could not permit the continuation of a Western trade monopoly with former colonial nations, particularly since so many of them are of strategic importance to the Soviet nation. The geographical proximity of many new states to countries in the Communist system was itself a factor that invited trade accords once the colonial powers had given up political control. The Kremlin's need for a program to counter the influence of commerce with Western nations and to supplement and help support Soviet foreign aid were likely reasons for the broadened view of trade. Furthermore, in view of the relatively small volume of trade that most of the new states conduct with the U.S.S.R., the cries of alarm appear out of proportion to actual developments. The fact remains that not one new state has been lured into the Communist orbit through either trade or aid politics.

While recognizing the possible motivations underlying Soviet commercial agreements with economically underdeveloped nations, the student of trade policies cannot ignore the more pronounced economic purposes behind Russian trade with the advanced countries of the West. Promotion of such trade is contrary to received theory, and Communists have as strong a traditional antipathy toward allowing their domestic economies to be drawn into the fluctuations of the international capitalist market as American strategists have toward permitting Communist governments to acquire major influence over the markets of the West. But, in the Kremlin's view, only after the production goals of the Communist states have been attained can the politics of trade assume paramount importance over the economics of trade. Only then can the strength of the Soviet economy and those of other Communist-governed states be sufficiently great to launch an all-out economic campaign against capitalist nations, for only then will the members of the Communist system be in a position to influence the world market drastically by offering whatever goods at whatever prices they wish and still be able to protect the domestic economies from external conditions.

Although it is necessary, of course, for lenders of the West to keep these long-term claims of Communist theory in mind, distant hopes and fears should not be allowed to obscure current and prospective facts. Evidence strongly indicates that Soviet trade with industrialized states is important to the Kremlin mainly for domestic economic reasons. The nature of the commodities most frequently sought in exchange—pipe, tankers, chemical plants, electronic instruments, grain—suggests that the Soviet planners opened trade with the West in 1958-1959 primarily to overcome difficulties in domestic production. Even though there has been much speculation that the Soviet petroleum exports at a time of oversupply on the international market were designed to wreck international petroleum companies operated by Westerners, the most likely reason for the introduction of petroleum on the market is the simple fact that the Russian oil industry attained maturity during that period. Crude oil and petroleum products offered Moscow its best opportunity to break into a well-established market by bartering those commodities at attractive prices. Moscow has been looking to the West more as a source of supply than as a market for surplus products. It could best acquire the goods it needed by selling those commodities that were in demand. The caution with which the Soviet officials moved in selling their petroleum and the lack of evidence of any deliberate attempt to flood the world market lend support to the contention that the Kremlin was treading lightly and was pursuing moderate policies for the purpose of economic gain.

In some respects the West has been guilty of bolstering the Soviet claim of the infallibility of Communist theory and the inevitability of Communist victory by focusing attention on the bold plans set forth in Soviet proclamations. Examination of behavior patterns and operational problems would provide a more meaningful understanding of Soviet policy. In reality, the apparent cohesiveness and effectiveness of Moscow's plans are deceptive. The creation of the abundance and self-sustaning autarky envisioned by theory is, at most, a very long-range aim. It should be remembered that trade is a two-way proposition, for it influences the exporter and importer alike. To concede that the Soviet Union can be immune to the influences of the world market as that country expands its activities in international commerce is to grant the Soviet economy peculiar immunity to the realities of economic life. As it seeks to influence, so can it be influenced.

The end of Soviet economic isolation and the policy of coexistence and competition may well prove to be of considerable importance to the gradual reduction of cold war tensions as trade becomes a more open channel of communication and exchange between East and West. Paraphrasing the old saying that a dog's bark is worse than his bite, the Communist theory of foreign trade is far more alarming than the reality of its practice.[68]

POLITICAL METHODS OF SOVIET POLICY

VI

As was seen in the economic aspect of the policy of coexistence, the Soviet elite makes little distinction between domestic and foreign policy. The aims of internal policy are related to international goals, while achievements and setbacks in the conduct of foreign affairs affect domestic politics and policy. Since the Soviet policy-makers had found it dangerous to rely on military means to advance either national or ideological aims, the Khrushchev coalition placed great reliance on other techniques for achieving the international objectives of the U.S.S.R. as determined by the ruling elite. While some of the harshness of Leninist theory was removed or modified in 1955-1956, the inclination to look on all policy in terms of struggle remained. Soviet foreign policy, according to Khrushchev, had to be formulated to continue the struggle with capitalist nations, but the tools for conducting that struggle had to be economic, political, and ideological in nature. Furthermore, these techniques had to be employed in such a manner that the military would not have to be called on to lend active support except in the most extreme and threatening circumstances.

The division of foreign policy techniques by Soviet spokesmen into economic, political, and ideological compartments is somewhat arbitrary. Certainly a strong thread of political methods and objectives is woven through Soviet economic policy and ideological programs. Indeed, many Communist references to the methods of struggle associated with the policy of peaceful coexistence omit the word "political" and refer only to economic and ideological means. Apparently the meaning that Prime Minister Khrushchev sought to convey by occasionally using the word "political" was to single out those policies which required neither economic nor military support. Negotiations with representatives of other states over political questions (disarmament, boundary controversies, personal diplomacy, and the general relaxation of international tension) and many of the activities of individual national Communist parties that are undertaken with the purpose of advancing the interests of the Soviet Union fall into this category. Ideology is often only a latent factor in these political moves, the general underlying objective being to strengthen the position of the U.S.S.R. vis-à-vis the leading countries in the West.

THE SOVIET CONCEPT OF DIPLOMACY AND THE POLITICS OF SUMMITRY

D. B. Levin, eminent Soviet authority on diplomacy, contends that the diplomatic method of the socialist states constitutes a new type of diplomacy, founded on the principle of proletarian internationalism and designed to assist the workers of the world irrespective of their nationality.[1] It can be considered "new," however, only to the extent that the use of the regular diplomatic corps for espionage and subversive purposes finds its rationalization and justification in the ideology of international class struggle. Furthermore, the fact that one of the most important methods of diplomacy is considered "the protection of the workers by guaranteeing world peace and security through the peaceful settlement of disputes" suggests that the Soviet concept of diplomacy has been somewhat revised to conform more closely to the policy of coexistence, thereby letting the professed commitment to proletarian internationalism take second place to the national policy objectives of the U.S.S.R.

According to Levin, Soviet diplomacy places great emphasis on high-level personal negotiations and meetings of national leaders, on international organizations, and on exploitation of contradictions between opponents. The Soviet government assumes that under "existing conditions of international life" conferences of national leaders "can, along with the activities of the United Nations, be a very important means paving the way toward the settlement of disputed questions, the liquidation of tensions in international relations, and the guarantee of peaceful coexistence of states with different social systems."[2] All "meetings and personal contacts between statesmen of different countries" are considered welcome techniques of conducting modern diplomacy. Levin also notes that "the socialist states lean upon the sympathy and support of the broad masses of the people of all the world." This indicates the reliance of the Kremlin on international organizations that serve as fronts to Communist and pro-Soviet movements as well as on Communist parties that are loyal to Moscow. One of the principal tasks of Soviet diplomacy is to "unmask the aggressive plans and activities of imperialists" in such organizations at N.A.T.O. and S.E.A.T.O. Another aspect of diplomacy is the use of specific organizations, such as the United Nations, and the "broad masses of the people" to advance "constructive proposals on the requirements for settling international questions." Disarmament is particularly stressed in this regard. Finally, Levin makes the remarkably candid observation that Soviet diplomacy "sometimes uses the contradictions between imperialist states in order to prevent them from creating a united front against the U.S.S.R." Although the exploitation of contradictions is strongly embedded in Leninist theory, such a frank statement is unusual. All of these methods are considered legitimate and are currently used in Soviet diplomacy.

One of the principal devices that the Soviet decision-makers employed in the decade following the decline of Malenkov was what has sometimes been called the politics of summitry. While, theoretically, the stakes in the game of summitry included the negotiation of important political and economic questions dividing the East and the West, from the Soviet perspective they most often involved the question of national prestige. Since prestige is a significant element of national power, the game could be considered a serious one with potentially great results.

The use of summit meetings and calls for summit conferences began most earnestly in 1955. At that time the new leaders in the Kremlin needed time to consolidate their positions and to concentrate their energies on domestic reconstruction. A relaxation of international tensions could enable them to devote greater attention to internal affairs without creating undue risks. In addition, the bitter cold war years of 1948 through 1954 had isolated the Soviet Union and her satellites from much of the rest of the world, hampering normal channels of communications and commerce. In the last Stalinist years, the prestige of the U.S.S.R. was at a postwar low. In spite of the rapid development of nuclear power, the common image of the Soviet Union in the eyes of those beyond her control was generally one of a hard, closed system shielding its economic and social backwardness. As the potential destructiveness of thermonuclear warfare came to be recognized, Soviet strategists began to comprehend the urgency of reorienting foreign policy objectives and techniques. To accomplish this, the emphasis had to shift away from blind revolutionary militancy and toward economic and propaganda activities. This could most successfully be accomplished by raising the stature of the Soviet Union among the nations of the world and opening some doors in the iron curtain.

In a series of reversals of former policies, Moscow announced the removal of the Soviet naval base at Porkkala, Finland, the rapprochement with Tito's Yugoslavia, and, most significantly, the Austrian State Treaty. Such steps were not accomplished without sharp conflict among the members of the elite. Although there had been some indication of internal conflict in late 1954 and in 1955, it was not until the anti-party crisis of 1957 that official statements were released identifying Molotov as the leader of the opposition to the new policies. The former Foreign Minister was denounced for having opposed the restoration of state and informal party relations with Yugoslavia, the conclusion of the State Treaty with Austria, and the "normalization" of relations with Japan. Emphasis was placed on the fact that "Molotov repeatedly opposed the Soviet Government's indispensable new steps in defense of peace and security of nations. In particular, he denied the advisability of establishing personal contacts between Soviet leaders and statesmen of other countries, which is essential for the achievement of mutual understanding and better international relations."[3] The positions taken by Molotov were closely associated with the foreign policy of Stalin and are frequently reflected in the statements of spokesmen for the People's Republic of China.

It was not until the reformists had overridden Molotov in the spring of 1955 (though he remained in the post of Foreign Minister for several months longer), that the United States acceded to the formal request of Premier Bulganin for a summit conference in Geneva. Both Bulganin and Party Secretary Khrushchev attended the meeting and conducted themselves with decorum. Of the three major questions considered—German unification, disarmament, and East-West contacts—only the proposal to increase cultural, scientific, and educational exchanges proved possible of fulfillment. Indeed, at the subsequent meeting of foreign ministers to work out the details for an agreement on all three problems, Molotov was completely unyielding in his insistence that only the Soviet proposals on the status of Germany and on disarmament were acceptable. It is not yet clear whether Molotov's intransigence represented a change of opinion in Moscow due to a temporary rise in the Foreign Minister's influence or whether Khrushchev and his supporters had no intention of following the more harmonious path set at Geneva. Whatever may have been the actual case, the Geneva Conference of heads of state opened the door for Soviet spokesmen to venture into the non-Communist world as apostles of the "Spirit of Geneva."[4] Moscow appeared to be particularly anxious to establish firm and convincing proof that the U.S.S.R. could not be shunted aside as a freak or a second-rate power in world councils. Numerous statements of Soviet leaders and the Soviet press in 1954-1955 made clear the Kremlin's anxiety to secure recognition of the right of the Russian nation to sit in the councils of the great powers and to participate in the settlement of major international problems. This was an unequivocal assertion of the desire for national prestige, which in turn could be used to further the foreign policy objectives of the Soviet leadership.

Yet, if the Geneva Conference was wanted by the Soviet Union more to attain psychological and prestige advantages than to resolve outstanding points of contention between Moscow and Western capitals, the meeting was not without mutual benefit to both sides. Even though the tangible results of Geneva were disappointing to the free world, the conference of heads of state did demonstrate the possibility of conducting discussions with an air of civility—in sharp contrast to previous performances. The Geneva confrontation of President Eisenhower and Premier Bulganin helped to persuade both Washington and Moscow that neither side was the devil incarnate and that ideological differences did not preclude increased contacts and discussions.

The immediate discernible effect of the "Spirit of Geneva" on Moscow was the use of its new-found prestige to attract the interest of non-Communist leaders in the less developed and newly independent countries. Khrushchev and Bulganin toured southern Asia and invitations to visit Moscow were extended to the heads of governments of India, Iran, Syria, Greece, and other nations. An exceptionally lavish display of welcome was accorded Prime Minister Nehru of India.[5] International tensions temporarily eased and the Kremlin devoted more attention to internal change and economic growth. Then the events of 1956 intervened and upset the plans of the new ruling elite. With the crushing of the revolution in Hungary, Moscow found its carefully cultivated prestige severely damaged.

After spending the first months following the suppression of the Hungarian revolting re-establishing its grip on the east European satellite, the Kremlin once again determined to improve the Soviet Union's image in the world. The principal tactic was another summit meeting. From the spring of 1957 until August, 1958, Khrushchev and Soviet propaganda agencies repeatedly called for a meeting of heads of state, at first urging only a two-power conference. The latter suggestion indicated a desire not only to improve the Soviet Union's prestige but to undermine the already waning unity of the Western alliance. On December 10, 1957, Bulganin sent a letter to Eisenhower asking for a joint effort "to put an end to the 'cold war,' to terminate the armaments race, and to enter resolutely upon the path of peaceful coexistence."[6] In the meanwhile, the successful launching of Sputnik I in October, 1957, and the unilateral suspension of nuclear weapons tests in March, 1958, sharply raised the prestige of the U.S.S.R. Then, as tension rose in the Middle East and the Far East in the summer of 1958, the Soviet attitude toward a summit gradually changed. Khrushchev wrote to Eisenhower complaining that the West was placing unnecessary obstacles in the path of a summit meeting, and shortly thereafter the Soviet Foreign Ministry publicly revealed confidential documents concerning Western proposals for a summit. Furthermore, on June 16, news reached the West of the execution of Imre Nagy, an event which made it difficult for the United

States to accede to the demand for a conference.[7] However, as the Middle East crisis gained in intensity, Khrushchev renewed the call for a meeting of the heads of five powers, including India. Soon it appeared that the U.N. Security Council would be accepted as the place for a meeting, but Khrushchev suddenly renounced his ambition for a summit after conferring with Mao in Peking.[8] Stepped-up firing on Quemoy and Matsu by the Chinese and the first Berlin crisis since 1948 soon followed.

Recess from the game of summitry, however, was short-lived. While the Foreign Ministers' Conference was in progress in the summer of 1959, Soviet officials pressed for an invitation from Washington for a Khrushchev visit to the United States. The years 1958-1959 had witnessed economic setbacks in the Soviet Union leading to the repudiation of the existing five-year plan and the adoption of a new seven-year program of economic development. Armaments were proving costly to Soviet industrial advances and the potential threat from Marshal Zhukov and the Soviet Army was real enough to lead to the Marshal's replacement and the reshuffling of high-ranking military personnel. Tension had to be reduced to justify a reallocation of budget commitments. A Khrushchev trip to the United States served that purpose, besides increasing the stature of the Soviet Union and of the Premier. The visits of Mikoyan and Kozlov in January and June of 1959 helped to pave the way for an official invitation to Khrushchev to visit Washington, tour the United States, and hold an "unofficial" conference with President Eisenhower.

The "spirit of Camp David" which the Soviet press repeatedly noted after the Khrushchev-Eisenhower meeting never rivaled that of Geneva. Nevertheless, the occasion was used to lay the groundwork for an official summit meeting in the spring of 1960. Khrushchev spent the preceding months perfecting his own brand of personal diplomacy during a tour of southern Asia and a state visit to Paris. Then, on May 5, 1960, came the announcement that an American U-2 reconnaisance plane had been shot down over the U.S.S.R. In his first public statement on the incident, Khrushchev exonerated Eisenhower from responsibility and attributed such flights to "imperialists and militarists," naming Dillon, Nixon, and Herter.[9] Eisenhower's acceptance of responsibility undoubtedly placed the Soviet Premier in an awkward position among his own colleagues. He had needed a relaxation of tensions and was now confronted with a crisis not of his own making. It is especially significant that the period of conservative ascendancy in Soviet politics dates from this episode. The old-guard Minister of Defense, Rodion Malinovskii, accompanied the Premier to Paris and sat next to him as he made highly vituperative attacks on Eisenhower and the United States. Yet the Premier's subsequent addresses in East Berlin and Moscow were strangely conciliatory; he renewed his call for coexistence and even suggested once again that Eisenhower had not personally known of the U-2 flights.[10] On the other hand, after the Bucharest conference of ruling Communist party leaders, his attacks on the West became increasingly bitter, culminating in his shoe-pounding performance in the General Assembly of the United Nations. Following the election of Kennedy to the presidency, Soviet pronouncements once more became reserved in tone. On January 1, 1961, *Pravda* reported Khrushchev's New Year's Eve announcement that the new administration could not be held responsible for the U-2 affair and the policies of the Eisenhower government.

The motive behind Khrushchev's desire to meet President Kennedy appears to have come less from the pursuit of prestige than from an impulse to meet the new President personally in order to "size up" his chief rival. Soviet achievements in space and a generally impressive rate of domestic economic growth had by 1961 assured the U.S.S.R. of her rightful place as a powerful nation. Tension in Laos and a rapidly pyramiding crisis over Berlin provided ample grounds for consultation between the two heads of state. Furthermore, this time the causes of tension were more clearly shared by both sides in the cold war, for, while Khrushchev could be blamed for placing new pressure on Berlin, the West had to bear much of the responsibility for the outbreak of civil strife in Laos. (The problem grew out of the nullification of the 1958 elections under the prodding of Western officials.) Khrushchev may also have wanted to evaluate Kennedy for another reason—the growing dispute with China—for the first substantial evidence of the seriousness of the rift between Moscow and Peking had been reported in February, 1961, involving the events of the Bucharest conference the preceding June.[11] Finally, as is now known, claims of missile superiority were greatly exaggerated by the Soviet government during 1960-1961, and Khrushchev's oft-expressed confidence was at least in part a façade to deceive the West with the hope of discouraging any significant military moves by the United States or her N.A.T.O. allies. The actual state of Soviet military technology provided more than adequate grounds for the Soviet Premier's dissatisfaction with Chinese militancy. The combination of these factors existing in 1961 suggests that Khrushchev himself was uncertain as to what course his government should take.

In retrospect it is now possible to say that the shifting courses of action taken by the Kremlin between 1960 and 1963 in the political sphere resulted largely from dissension within the once seemingly monolithic Communist bloc, dissension within the high military circles in the U.S.S.R., and differences over the unevenness of economic advances in the domestic economy. In the midst of these uncertainties in 1961 (unknown to the West at that time), Khrushchev did not attempt to use the conference for news-making purposes and did not surprise Kennedy with any unexpected demands or startling new proposals. It was essentially a personal encounter. No great "Spirit of Vienna" propaganda campaign ensued. Since then, Soviet appeals for summit meetings have come much less frequently, although after the assassination of President Kennedy Khrushchev quickly felt out the possibility of a personal meeting with President Johnson. The Brezhnev-Kosygin leadership appeared to be uninterested in summit confrontations.

From 1955 until the abortive Paris conference of 1960, summitry was a game of politics with the Soviet leadership. In the initial stages of the period summit meetings served the purpose of improving the image of the U.S.S.R. without requiring it to compromise in hard negotiations. To what extent summitry was designed to increase the prestige of Khrushchev himself, as distinct from that of his country, cannot be determined. After the beneficial results of Geneva, summitry became both an aim and a tool of Soviet foreign policy. The global publicity heaped on the Soviet Union and her leaders was an inexpensive method of raising the prestige of the U.S.S.R., while the possibility always existed of attaining some specific concession at little or no cost. The split personality of the Soviet elite revealed itself quite openly. Cunning and crafty efforts to achieve particular objectives were combined with an apparently sincere effort to reduce international tensions.

In addition to summitry, Soviet officials sought personal exchanges with the leaders of many smaller nations and opportunities to present their case directly to the citizens of other countries. From 1955 until his fall from power, Khrushchev's personal visits took him to Geneva, India, Afghanistan, Burma, Indonesia, France, Great Britain, the United States, Egypt, and the Scandinavian countries. While participating in Khrushchev's governing coalition, Brezhnev made trips to Africa, the Middle East, and Italy, while Mikoyan visited Japan, Cuba, and numerous other countries. Kosygin, in his new role of Prime Minister, spent a week in the U.A.R. The speeches of these touring Soviet officials had much in common. From San Francisco to Accra and from New Delhi to Bandung, Moscow's spokesmen described how the Soviet system operates and told of the gigantic economic strides made by the Soviet Union. With frequent references to Lenin and the October Revolution, they emphasized the peaceful nature of the Soviet state, called for disarmament and an end to nuclear testing, asked for expanded agreements and for support of peaceful coexistence.[12] In addition, Moscow often attempted to capitalize on internationally renowned heroes of the U.S.S.R. The Russian cosmonauts, in particular, were sent on publicity missions to Europe, Asia, and Latin America as living reminders of the advanced state of Soviet technology.

Personal diplomacy involves not only visits of Russian dignitaries abroad but also visits of foreign officials to the Soviet Union. Elaborate welcoming ceremonies have been given to chiefs of state and other high notables from underdeveloped countries to demonstrate the friendship of the Soviet government. Sukarno of Indonesia, Nehru of India, Nkrumah of Ghana, Keita of Mali, Nasser of Egypt, a large official delegation from Somalia, and many others have received such accolades. After Nehru's trip to the Kremlin in 1961 to persuade the Soviet decision-makers not to resume nuclear testing, Premier Khrushchev managed to produce a joint communiqué in which the Indian Prime Minister endorsed universal disarmament and peaceful coexistence, while the Soviet Ministry of Defense continued to conduct nuclear test explosions; the purpose of Nehru's visit was thereby obscured and the meeting was turned into a Russian propaganda coup. Similarly, the visit of nine African ambassadors to Khrushchev's office prompted a lecture by the Premier on the rapid economic growth of his country and on the equality of races in the Soviet Union.[13] No opportunity was lost to instruct others in the virtues of the Soviet path or to exploit any event to the advantage of Moscow.

In January, 1966, Kosygin even undertook a conventional

role of personal diplomacy, that of mediator in the India-Pakistan controversy over Kashmir. After laying the groundwork during the previous autumn, the Soviet Prime Minister played host to President Khan and Prime Minister Shastri in Tashkent. The purpose of the meeting was to resolve issues left unsettled by the truce proclaimed in Kashmir after several military skirmishes. Although the Soviet press made propaganda out of the role of the U.S.S.R. as peacemaker, several tangible agreements were made by the two south Asian leaders. These included the withdrawal of all troops to positions occupied before the conflict began, the resumption of diplomatic relations, repatriation of prisoners, and provisions for future discussions of immigration and refugee problems as well as the expansion of economic and cultural relations.[14] Even though the Western powers underplayed the significance of the conference, the Tashkent meeting was widely acclaimed in Asia. The Soviet role indicated the willingness and ability of the new leadership to engage in conventional diplomacy.

It can be reasonably assumed that these personal encounters and foreign travels have had a two-way effect on Soviet leaders. Soviet officials have been exposed to much of the world that they had previously known only through biased secondhand reports. Although the precise impact of these exposures on the attitudes of Soviet leaders cannot be properly assessed, such cracks in the iron curtain helped open the way for new and broader exchanges between the U.S.S.R. and non-Communist states. The strong criticism of Molotov for his opposition to personal diplomacy and Khrushchev's public endorsement of personal meetings attest to the favor the modernist forces in the Kremlin attach to such procedures. Personal diplomacy appears to be appreciated not only for the prestige it may bring to the Soviet Union but also for enabling Soviet officials to observe and to learn as well as to preach.

THE POLITICS OF DIVIDE AND CONQUER

The general view of Kremlin strategists toward divisions among capitalist states reflects a relatively close correspondence between Leninist theory and actuality. According to Lenin's theory of imperialism inevitable contradictions—both external and internal—exist within the imperialist camp, owing in part to the uneven economic and political development of capitalist states. It has been frequently argued that this vision of a conflict of interests among the principal Western powers has resulted in two major tendencies in Soviet policy. First, it has made Communist leaders extremely sensitive to fluctuations in the balance of power in the Western world, and it has often led them to draw premature conclusions about the imminent outbreak of open conflict or the imminent collapse of governments in capitalist countries. Second, and more significant, this tenet of the doctrine has encouraged Soviet policy-makers to attempt to exploit the differences between capitalist states. The intensity of Soviet efforts to divide the nations of the West and Moscow's use of local Communist parties to encourage divisions are often thought to indicate the importance of ideological influence on Soviet policy. While Leninist theory may encourage a policy of divide and conquer, the strategy of dividing one's opponents was, of course, not invented by the Communists. Where theory and realpolitik converge, motives are difficult to assess.

Although Khrushchev insisted that the growth of Soviet power had made the contradictions between socialism and capitalism the "fundamental contradiction in the contemporary world," this circumstance was not thought to have greatly reduced the "deep antagonisms" within the capitalist "camp." Contemporary Soviet interpretations hold that centrifugal forces operating in the imperialist system result in the "intensification of rivalry and the outbreak of open conflicts first in one, then in another part of the capitalist world."[15] These economic conflicts are thought to result in political crises where parliaments and democratic forms cease to function effectively and are ultimately replaced by reactionary dictatorships.

In 1955-1964, according to Soviet interpretations, the chief source of conflict in the capitalist camp was the divergent positions of the United States and West Germany within the framework of N.A.T.O. Soviet strategy concentrated on driving wedges between these two powers and other members of the alliance. At every opportunity the Soviet Union sought to isolate West Germany. It was argued that France could play a larger role in European politics by serving as mediator between Great Britain and the United States on the one hand and the Soviet Union on the other. Before the extent of de Gaulle's independence became apparent, the Russians contended that France was destined to play a lesser role if she continued to be a member of a German-dominated N.A.T.O. and European Common Market. This policy was demonstrated shortly before the Geneva Summit Conference convened in 1955, when Molotov met with Faure and Pinay to try to persuade them to play the role of conciliator between the two opposing sides during the parley.[16]

After failing in this tactic, Soviet policy centered on convincing the French that German desire for revanche and for the forcible revision of frontiers had penetrated the N.A.T.O. alliance. On his visit to France in 1960, Khrushchev reminded Frenchmen of the numerous German invasions of their nation and bluntly warned them of the peril of forgetting the historic enmity of the two countries. Before the 22nd Party Congress in 1961, the Soviet Prime Minister referred to the Common Market as a "marriage of convenience" that could work only to the detriment of France. The United States and West Germany were said to have "inherited . . . the Nazi appetite for world domination" and planned to satisfy this hunger at the expense of Britain and France.[17] Following the conclusion of the French-West German Treaty and the refusal of de Gaulle to participate in the Nuclear Test Ban Treaty in 1963, the Kremlin's attitude toward French independence underwent a transformation. Suggestions that Soviet officials were beginning to disapprove of France's independent course appeared in the Soviet press, and it was vaguely hinted that Moscow might feel more comfortable if de Gaulle could be swayed a little more by Washington.[18] This shift in attitude appeared to stem from the Soviet Union's growing preoccupation with the split within the international Communist movement and with overcoming domestic economic problems. In order to concentrate on those issues, Moscow wanted the difficulties on her western front to be kept at a minimum, even if that meant greater coordination of the foreign policies of Western states.

The Soviets also attempted to drive a wedge between Great Britain and the United States. The appearance of harmony between the two English-speaking countries was generally treated as an illusion. According to Moscow leaders, potential conflict existed as a result of the way in which the United States had replaced Britain as the leading guardian of "colonialism" in the Middle East and as the director of the Baghdad Pact.[19] Contradictions in the alliance were deemed to be persistently reflected in the competition for control of the petroleum industries in the Arab states and were most sharply demonstrated by the Anglo-French-Israeli invasion of Egypt in 1956.[20]

The Suez crisis provided the Kremlin with an excellent opportunity to play on the differences between Britain and the United States. In this crisis the United Nations was the most conspicuous forum for Soviet attempts to divide and embarrass the Western allies. At the outbreak of the war, the Soviet Foreign Minister called on the Security Council to take immediate action against Britain, France, and Israel. When the Security Council met, the Soviet delegate introduced a resolution calling for an immediate cease-fire and withdrawal of forces. This was vetoed by France and Britain, but the United States was forced to announce an embarrassed abstention. To compound the predicament of Washington, the Russian Foreign Minister then submitted a resolution to the Secretary General which called on all members of the United Nations, *especially the U.S.A. and the U.S.S.R.*, to give military assistance to Egypt. When the measure failed, Moscow blamed the "Western power bloc" for preventing effective action against the colonialist aggressors.

The United Nations has been the scene of other efforts to split the Western alliance. After the U-2 incident in May, 1960, the Soviet delegation asked the Security Council to consider the aggressive acts of the United States. The debate that ensued was little more than an attempt to frighten Turkey, Pakistan, and Norway for having aided and abetted the U.S.A. The intention, of course, was to discourage those states from continuing to authorize American military bases on their territories. The same forum served as an effective stage for keeping anticolonial fears before the delegations of underdeveloped countries, in order to make communications between advanced Western states and less developed ones more difficult.[21] The Soviet Union professes to be the defender of the new states in the organs of the United Nations and claims that when "the imperialist powers have tried to expand their influence over the economies of the developing states through the apparatus of the U.N.," the U.S.S.R. has worked to protect their interests.[22]

Another topic that caused particular concern, and engendered a great deal of study by Soviet scholars, was the Common Market. The very foundation of this organization appeared to belie Soviet official statements on inevitable contradictions among capitalist states. Yet the operational plans of the Common Market provided a possible example for improving the relations among members of the Council of Mutual Economic Assistance. Soviet observers recognized the trend toward integration and admitted that groups of capitalist countries might partially succeed in merging some of their economic and cultural functions, but they predicted that one such group would then oppose another group.[23] The contradictions among groups were thought to be especially prevalent in the area of foreign trade, especially in G.A.T.T., in which the United States has a powerful voice, the Common Market, and the Outer Seven.

Such efforts to exploit the differences among Western states might be pursued by any rival power. In themselves they reveal no obvious ideological basis, nor can available empirical evidence prove that they were motivated by an ideological drive. It can be argued, of course, that the intensity of the Soviet drive to split the opponents' camp and its heavy reliance on propaganda devices stem from Communist doctrine. Furthermore, the existence of conflicts and rivalries within the Western alliance and successful Soviet attempts to dramatize such contradictions may appear to the Kremlin as confirmations of Marxist-Leninist dogma. There is no direct evidence to prove the extent to which ideology may determine Soviet behavior. But, whatever the motivation, Kremlin strategists evidently place great value on political techniques as a means of enhancing the position of the Soviet Union. Ideology may provide the Kremlin with a general frame of reference, especially as regards contradictions among capitalist states, but this is precisely the point where Leninist theory comes closest to corresponding with reality.

COMMUNIST PARTIES AND FRONT ORGANIZATIONS

Communist parties and Soviet foreign policy

In addition to government-to-government relationships, the Soviet Union has often been able to employ other national

Communist parties to its own advantage. This, in fact, has most clearly distinguished the Soviet conduct of foreign policy from that of Western countries. Until the mid-1950's the various national Communist parties were theoretically bound by the dictates of Moscow. They served as means of weakening or subverting the governments of their respective states in the interest of the international Communist movement or, more accurately, in the interest of the U.S.S.R. While members of the various national parties frequently served in national representative institutions during the Stalin era, their aim in doing so was "to expose the parliamentary illusions which the reformists sow among the workers." The immediate object of their participation was to destroy the effectiveness of parliamentary bodies.

In 1959, the Marx-Engels-Lenin Institute of Moscow published a "manual" entitled *Fundamentals of Marxism-Leninism* and designed as a guide for Communists throughout the world. The new line, expounded by Khrushchev in 1956, was reflected in the manual's evaluation of parliaments and the relation of Communists to them. While avowing the correctness of the old attitude toward bourgeois assemblies in the past, the text declared that the changing situation required a different evaluation of the usefulness of the machinery of parliamentary democracy in winning political power. The report stated that "broad anti-monopoly, anti-imperialist coalitions, uniting the majority of the nations, are now in process of formation in the capitalist world." The development of these coalitions creates "new types of popular power" which can use representative institutions as their forum for development.

> The parliamentary method of transition to socialism would give the working class a number of advantages. The formation of a new power by so traditional an institution as parliament is for many countries, would at once endow it with the necessary authority, facilitating the subsequent socialist transformation.[24]

No distinction was made in this appraisal between advanced and less developed countries.

Following these general directives from Moscow, the national Communist parties have attempted to draw workers and peasants into the world revolutionary struggle, to infiltrate trade unions and agricultural cooperatives, and to unite leftist parties and groups in other countries under Communist leadership. In addition to their effort to recruit discontented workers and others into Communist parties, the Soviet leadership has resorted on several occasions to the popular front strategy in an attempt to gain allies and to weaken existing governments. This strategy takes the form of Communist appeals to unite the numerous working class and peasant parties and, more broadly, to draw leftist elements of the bourgeoisie and intelligentsia into a broad alliance against the "exploiting groups."

The revival of the popular front strategy under Khrushchev's leadership appears to have had a different motivation from the anti-Fascist coalitions of the 1930's. The Stalinist tactic was purely negative; it was accepted only as a device to provide protection against a dangerous enemy with a powerful war machine. The modern rejuvenation of the popular front device has had a more positive basis. After the de-Stalinization campaign had come into the open, the Kremlin strategists apparently felt that the possibility of cooperation had been enhanced, and could be advanced by emphasizing the similarities between the economic and social goals and aspirations of Communists and Western socialists. Even though this strategy, if successful, would undercut the support of established governments, the aim of the Soviet directive was ostensibly the union of the proletarian and semiproletarian strata of society in a cooperative effort to implement social reforms and advance the victory of Communism through the device of peaceful coexistence.

The Khrushchev era witnessed three periods in which collaboration with the non-Communist left was a prime target. The first period was during 1955 and 1956. Then the Hungarian revolution brought an end to the possibilities of effective cooperation for over a year. In 1958, the Kremlin renewed its interest in encouraging a popular front strategy. This second campaign to establish closer ties with Western socialists lasted until the collapse of the Paris summit meeting in 1960. The French elections of November, 1962, the Italian elections of April, 1963, and the Chilean elections of September, 1964, marked the third revival of popular front strategies by national Communist parties supported by the C.P.S.U.

The first attempt to achieve accord with socialist parties outside the Communist system was the rehabilitation of Yugoslavia as a socialist country. The Soviet rapprochement with Tito in 1955 indicated tacit recognition of various forms of socialism. The changing Moscow line was further indicated by an abrupt reversal in policy on the part of the French Communist party.[25] For the first time since 1947, the Communist deputies in the French National Assembly supported a government with no Communist members on a vote of confidence. The next month, the French Communists formally invited the Socialists to align with them for election purposes, although Mollet quickly rejected the bid. Finally, Duclos, one of the most prominent leaders of the French Communist party, made a serious proposal for a Communist-Socialist-Radical popular front government, but this, too, was turned down. From these actions it became apparent that Moscow was encouraging the French party to broaden the base of Communist activity through the popular front stratagem.

Experimentation with the popular front technique during 1955 produced a formal announcement on the subject at the 20th Party Congress. Khrushchev expressed the belief that the changed conditions of the world made it possible for social democratic movements of Western democracies to become allies of the Communist party. Arguing that many of the world's misfortunes of the 1950's were due to a split in the ranks of the working class, he insisted that "cooperation with those circles of the socialist movement whose views on the forms of transition to socialism differ from ours is also possible and essential." Otherwise, he claimed, the split played "into the hands of the reactionary forces." The representatives of the working class should at least collaborate on achieving the goals of disarmament, raising the living standards of the people, and the settlement of international disputes by negotiation. The intent, of course, was to draw a large segment of the population of Western countries into the "Zone of Peace" in the hope of lessening the anti-Communist militancy of capitalist states.

Although implementation of the popular front strategy was promptly undertaken, it produced no notable results. The Socialist International Council quickly rejected all Communist overtures toward collaboration on the party level, even though it did recognize some possibility of cooperation on the government level.[26] The personal efforts of Khrushchev to establish closer relations with the left wing of the British Labor Party were also rebuffed.[27] Moscow extended a cordial welcome to a delegation of French Socialists in May, 1956, but strongly assailed the comments of members of the delegation who, on their return to France, suggested that the C.P.S.U. was guilty of anti-Semitism, ordering the arrest of political prisoners, and preventing the rise of a "second party" in Russia.[28] In spite of the failure to reach accord with Socialist parties in the Western states, Moscow continued to extend offers of cooperation until the forceful repression of the revolution in Hungary led the Kremlin elite to recognize the futility of such gestures during moments of international crisis and sharply reduced Soviet prestige.

After the lapse of more than a year, the popular front notion was revived in an even broader context than before. The announcement of the new goal was made in *Pravda* on January 7, 1958. In order to realize the aims of peaceful coexistence, the article declared, Communist parties "are prepared to cooperate . . . with Socialist, Catholic, liberal, radical and other bourgeois parties and organizations." Ideological conformity was not deemed essential for cooperation, but the primary responsibility for peace and social progress was placed on the Communists and Socialists in capitalist countries. Following this announcement, the C.P.S.U. made numerous contacts with Socialist parties in Italy, France, Germany, Britain, Norway, Denmark, the Netherlands, Belgium, Austria, and Japan.[29]

These efforts took three principal forms. First, there were personal exchanges of delegations from the C.P.S.U. and from Western socialist and other leftist parties. All of these exchanges were barren of result.[30] Second, the Central Committee of the C.P.S.U. officially corresponded with the comparable party organs of various socialist and workers' parties, particularly those in France, Italy, Great Britain, West Germany, Denmark, and Austria.[31] And third, Radio Moscow made numerous appeals in foreign language broadcasts directly to the membership of Western leftist parties. Most of the appeals were for an all-left front, but some merely called for support of specific Soviet policies such as the creation of a nuclear-free zone in central Europe.[32]

As a result of the failure of these contacts to produce tangible results, the Kremlin's strategists came to the conclusion that the chief obstacle to union of the parties of the left was the opposition of the right-wing element in the Western parties. The open "anti-Communist" position of party leaders like Mollet, Gaitskell, Brandt, and Spaak was interpreted as being the result of the ideological influence that the bourgeoisie had succeeded in bringing to bear on a segment of the working class. On the other hand, hope was still held that an accord could be reached with party leaders like Nenni, Bevan, and Mendes-France. However, after the Sixth Congress of the Socialist International in 1958 declined even to explore the possibilities of a popular front, *Pravda* bitterly attacked the "stubborn resistance" to progress, and for nearly three years thereafter efforts to establish popular fronts in Europe almost completely disappeared.

The popular front technique was impractical from the beginning in Great Britain and West Germany, where the Communist parties were small and ineffective. On the other hand, the potential for an alliance existed in France and Italy. The de Gaullist Fifth Republic maneuvered all but 10 of the 144 Communist deputies out of their seats in the first elections under the new regime, but in November, 1962, the French Communist party demonstrated its ability to obtain over 20 per cent of the popular vote and to increase its membership in the lower house of the Parliament to 44. Growing opposition to de Gaulle contributed to lowering the barriers to widespread electoral collaboration between Socialists and Communists in the second round of elections. For the first time since the last world war, the French Communist party withdrew candidates in favor of Socialists and Radical Socialists in some districts in return for the withdrawal of candidates of those parties in others. However, the cautious rapprochement between these parties was basically a negative anti-Gaullist move and appeared to have no significance other than a temporary electoral truce.

In April, 1963, the Communist party of Italy (C.P.I.) made important gains over the previous election of 1958. Claiming a membership of over 1.5 million, the C.P.I. polled over 25 per cent of the popular vote and elected 166 of the 630 deputies in the lower chamber. Under the imaginative leadership of Palmiro Togliatti, the C.P.I. worked effectively with the Socialist party of Pietro Nenni as the opposition to the Christian Democrats. After 1956, the close relationship between the two parties deteriorated and in October, 1963, Nenni displayed willingness to split his party if necessary in order to cooperate with the progressives in the Christian Democratic Party. In December, the non-Communist left-center alliance became a reality. The strong showing of the C.P.I. in the spring elections, therefore, did not result in enhancing the prospects of an "all-left" coalition. In fact, Togliatti's party became increasingly isolated as the democratic center party moved left to work with democratic socialists. The prospect of collaboration between the Communists and Socialists further declined after the death of Togliatti in 1964.

One of the most interesting developments concerning the relations between the C.P.S.U. and non-Communist parties was the exchange of communications between the Soviet party and the Socialist party of Japan (S.P.J.) in 1964. The Japanese Communist party was completely taken over by the pro-Chinese majority and launched a sharp verbal attack on the C.P.S.U.[33] Anastas Mikoyan, while on an official visit to Japan, conferred with leaders of the Japanese Socialist party and appeared to have established some measure of rapport with them on the question of increased communications between the C.P.S.U. and the S.P.J.[34] Harmonious exchanges of communications and delegations during the summer months of 1964 continued between the two parties. Rather than encouraging the creation of a splinter pro-Soviet Communist party in Japan, the leaders of the C.P.S.U. seemed to prefer to maintain a less formal but cordial relationship with the Socialists. This development raised a question that would have to remain unanswered for some time —just how evolutionary was the great "party of revolution" prepared to become?

In applying the coalition to the countries of Asia, the Middle East, Africa, and Latin America, the popular front was renamed and called the "national liberation movement." Of the independent countries of all of these areas, only in Indonesia did the Communist party represent a genuinely large and popular political force. Much of the Indonesian party's strength resulted from the leadership of D. U. Aidit, who insisted that his country was not ripe for socialism and that his party should support the nationalist government of Sukarno.[35] However, as Aidit ignored his own advice and became increasingly associated with the Chinese party, the Indonesian army decimated the leadership of the Communists in a bloody but brief civil war. Elsewhere, the national Communist parties were torn by dissension over the Moscow-Peking conflict and were generally ineffective in enhancing their political positions. The inability of the Communists to rule effectively in the Indian state of Kerala and their failure to seize power in Syria and Iraq in 1958 testify to the weak political position of the Communist movement in those states.

Nowhere were the frustrations and disappointments of the Kremlin more apparent than in the newly independent states of Africa. In 1963, Communist parties were virtually nonexistent in Libya, Ethiopia, Tanganyika, Kenya, Uganda, Mauritius, Portuguese Africa, Spanish Africa, Rhodesia, and Nyasaland. They existed only on paper or with tiny memberships in Tunisia, Sudan, Zanzibar, Basutoland, South Africa, Nigeria, and the Congo. They had been declared illegal in the two North African states to which Moscow had given the greatest assistance—Nasser's Egypt and Algeria. The much vaunted national liberation movements had given the Kremlin a strong, directing voice in no country on the African continent by the end of the Khrushchev regime, in spite of periods of Soviet influence in Ghana, Guinea, Mali, and Somalia. Furthermore, splits between pro-Moscow and pro-Peking factions of already small parties hampered the growth and effectiveness of African Leninism and reduced its immediate potential.[36] It was also significant that such influence as the Kremlin had been able to gain resulted from government-to-government contacts, not from national Communist party leadership. The propaganda boasts of Moscow during Khrushchev's leadership were, therefore, grossly disproportionate to the accomplishments of the popular front and national liberation strategies.

Front organizations and Soviet foreign policy

Besides having access to a network of Communist parties that can sometimes be employed for tactical political purposes, the Kremlin has attempted to make elaborate use of organizations that are not officially sponsored by either the Communist party or the Soviet government but are in fact dominated by their agents. These front organizations serve as distributors of propaganda designed to enhance the prestige of the Soviet Union and to increase the support of Soviet policies among the people of other countries. The World Peace Council, the World Federation of Trade Unions, the World Federation of Democratic Youth, and the Soviet Committee for Solidarity with Asian and African Countries are among the front organs that have been the most active. In addition, there are numerous other organizations for women, youth, and professional groups.

During the Khrushchev period, the World Peace Council, founded in 1949, maintained a perpetual campaign in behalf of Soviet proposals on disarmament and the cessation of nuclear testing. Holding international assemblies in Helsinki, Finland, in 1955 and Colombo, Ceylon, in 1957, the Council exploited the use of neutral countries for its meetings, called on the peoples of all nations to support the Soviet Union's disarmament proposals, condemned imperialism, and warned all new states to avoid joining military alliances with imperialist nations.[37] In 1962, a related organization, the World Congress for Disarmament and Peace, met in the Kremlin Palace to hear Khrushchev expound on the virtues of peaceful coexistence and the necessity of universal disarmament.

The World Federation of Trade Unions has been the channel for much pro-Soviet propaganda aimed explicitly at the working class. At its Fourth Congress in Leipzig in 1957, the international front organization claimed to represent 106,000,000 workers and to have delegates representing eighty countries in attendance.[38] Although these membership figures are deceptive, since the vast majority of members are from states within the Communist system, the Federation was considered important enough for Khrushchev himself to deliver the principal address before the Fifth Congress in 1961. The Soviet Premier's speech reminded the delegates that Communism will produce a worker's paradise and called on them to support the policy of peaceful coexistence.

The Kremlin has made particularly strenuous efforts to enlist the support of youth. The World Federation of Democratic Youth and the International Union of Students are among the most active of all the front organizations. They are sponsors of the periodic meetings of the World Youth Congress, the World Youth and Student Festival, and the World Youth Forum. The publicity organs of the Soviet Union paid great attention to the youth festivals held in Prague in 1947, Budapest in 1949, East Berlin in 1951, Bucharest in 1953, Warsaw in 1955, and Moscow in 1957. Even greater attention was devoted to these events when they were held outside the borders of the party-states in Vienna (1959) and Helsinki (1962). Since the Soviet propagandists exploit these gala occasions for their own purposes, the reports on them tend to be highly exaggerated. For example, *New Times* claimed that 34,000 students from 131 countries attended the Sixth World Youth and Student Festival.[39] In reporting on the Fourth World Youth Congress held in Kiev in 1957, the same periodical claimed that the World Federation of Democratic Youth had the unlikely total of 85 million members in 97 countries. After the Seventh World Youth Festival met in Vienna in 1959, *New Times* attacked the Western press for reducing the attendance figures below the organizations' estimate of 20,000 from 120 countries.[40] One aim of Soviet officials appears to have been to distort the actual importance of the festivals in order to inflate the value of the propaganda reports of such events. Part of this propaganda is in the form of messages sent to youth organizations throughout the world calling for disarmament, peaceful coexistence, and anticolonialism. Occasionally efforts to draw students into the front result in embarrassing failures, as they did at the Youth and Student Festival in Helsinki, in 1962. Sixty per cent of the students in attendance were citizens of the party-states, whereas the predicted attendance from other continents fell considerably short of expectations.[41]

The Third Afro-Asian Solidarity Conference held in Moshi, Tanganyika, in February, 1963, demonstrated in another form the propaganda setbacks and troubles of Moscow. While the delegates expressed approval of neutral foreign policies and roundly condemned imperialism, the speakers repeatedly warned against incursions by both Communist and capitalist powers and expressed fears of a "second scramble for Africa and Asia."[42] Soviet representatives faced a new experience at the conference when they were placed in the same category as Americans and forced to watch the Chinese Communists successfully exploit the racial issue to the disadvantage of the U.S.S.R. Similarly, in an Asian peace assembly staged in Japan in 1964 the Chinese Communists captured control of the session and forced the Russian delegates to leave.

Successful or not, all of the aforementioned Communist front organizations displayed particular concern for securing broader support for Soviet foreign policy objectives and for raising the prestige of the Soviet Union and of the Soviet brand of Communism. They are principally image-makers designed to serve the purposes of the Kremlin. Probably the most active fronts have been those associated with the peace movements sponsored by Soviet or pro-Soviet spokesmen and groups. By enlarging the popular support of the policy of peaceful coexistence and its related programs (such as total disarmament) the Kremlin has attempted to bring pressure on the governments of non-Communist states to pursue policies acceptable to the Soviet Union. The use of such political techniques, combined with economic programs involving foreign aid and increased trade, provided Moscow with the means of constructing a kind of cheap alliance system with underdeveloped states by encouraging their neutrality in the competition between the Soviet Union and the

United States. Such a system served the general policy objectives of the U.S.S.R. without resulting in heavy financial burdens comparable to those required for the maintenance of the more formal and elaborate alliances in which the United States has participated.

Political means that can be employed at relatively little cost to the Soviet policy-makers are favored to enhance the prestige of the nation and the nation's leaders, to attract support for particular Soviet policies, and to divide the opponents of Moscow. Personal diplomacy has provided an inexpensive means of improving the image of the U.S.S.R. in this regard. At the same time such diplomacy has very likely helped to enlarge the outlook of at least some of the Soviet spokesmen by exposing them to different cultures, values, and economic systems. Similarly, political tactics may be easily used to exploit differences among the allies of the United States, but Soviet officials have shown the capacity to recognize the possibility that there are times when divisions among their opponents may hamper the conduct of Soviet foreign policy by forcing the Kremlin elite to divert attention from pressing domestic problems or difficulties within the Communist system. The policy-makers have, therefore, been made aware of certain limitations on political techniques and have acquired a somewhat more sophisticated appreciation of them than was evident during the early cold war years of the late 1940's and early 1950's. In any case these political techniques have rarely been the exclusive property of Soviet Communists, for they have been among the methods commonly employed by other nation-states as well.

The Soviet Union does have one distinctly unique tool in its conduct of foreign policy that has no exact equivalent in non-Communist countries. That is the existence of national Communist parties in most nations, which maintain relations with the C.P.S.U. The notion of the monolithic nature of this international organization has now been dispelled. Nevertheless, the ability of the Kremlin to rely on many of those parties for information, political strikes, and political agitation designed to weaken anti-Communist governments is a uniquely Communist tool of foreign policy. Popular front and national liberation movements are thought to provide national Communist leaders with an opportunity to participate in government coalitions, steer national policy along lines beneficial to Moscow, and eventually, it is hoped, to establish a Communist regime. Much attention has been devoted in the West to these intentions and claims of Communists. Once again, however, the words have been much more alarming than the actions and their results. The fact remains that not one Communist regime has achieved power through this device. By obscuring evidence, claims have been made by Moscow that Czechoslovakia and Cuba fall within this category. Such claims are misleading. The Communists have no grounds to declare the successfulness of the popular front and national liberation stratagems, and the West has much less cause for fear than some Westerners have been prone to express.

Politics is important to the conduct of Soviet foreign policy just as politics is important to the policies of other nation-states. The style of the Soviet leaders in playing the game is much more highly rationalized in terms of political dogma than in the West but, with the exception of the now eroding system of national Communist parties, the political tactics pursued by the Soviet Union have actually differed very little from political tactics employed by other nation-states.

PROPAGANDA AND IDEOLOGY AND SOVIET FOREIGN POLICY

VII

While Soviet theorists have avowed that war can be eliminated as a means of resolving international disputes and that competition between capitalist and Communist states can be conducted on economic and political levels, they have never contended that peaceful coexistence means an absence of conflict and struggle. In the sphere of ideology the Soviet leaders insist that "there has never been nor can there ever be peaceful coexistence" between the two systems. In this area Communists "have always fought and will continue to fight for their ideas, for the revolutionary ideology of the working class as the most advanced and progressive ideology of our times."[1]

In order to propagate Soviet Communist doctrine and to persuade others to support Soviet policies and Soviet-sponsored organizations, the Kremlin has developed an elaborate propaganda apparatus that carries the ideological struggle around the world. This apparatus includes the national parties within the international Communist movement that are aligned with Moscow, the government ministries of Foreign Affairs, Culture, and Foreign Trade and the committees and programs related to them, Radio Moscow, numerous newspapers and periodicals, and front organizations that are ostensibly non-Communist. The confidence that the policy-makers place in the efficacy of global propaganda appears to represent in large measure an extension of their conviction that domestic propaganda and indoctrination are essential ingredients of Soviet rule. As propaganda helps persuade citizens to accept and support the right of the party elite to govern, so can it encourage citizens in other countries to accept and support Soviet policies.

THE DOMESTIC SIGNIFICANCE OF PROPAGANDA

The importance attached to propaganda and indoctrination within the Soviet Union is indicated by the level at which policies and programs are made and coordinated. The Section of Propaganda and Agitation is an organ attached to the Secretariat and Presidium of the C.P.S.U. It is, therefore, located at the very apex of the party hierarchy. This attests not only to the importance of propaganda operations in the Soviet system but also to the aim of integrating propaganda with overall policy. The Propaganda and Agitation Section may be viewed as the core of the indoctrination machine, associated with the party elite on the one hand and directly concerned with all forms of mass communications, cultural activity, and education on the other. Through such means the party organs strive to exclude divergent views and ensure that each medium for the conveyance of ideas acts in concert with the immediate and long-range objectives of the regime's decision-makers.

The Soviet propaganda apparatus has two prominent characteristics. First, it attempts to be all-inclusive: every aspect of mass communication—the press, radio, television, theater, motion pictures, literature, art, and music—are considered appropriate instruments of propaganda and are subject to control. Secondly, all means of propaganda are treated bluntly and openly as such. No effort is made to conceal the interest of the party elite in propaganda and agitation. Modern technological innovations in communications have consequently only served to increase the ability of the party organs to disseminate the official propaganda. Other purposes of the media of communications, such as entertainment or esthetic satisfaction, are often treated as secondary to the propaganda purpose.

The principal themes associated with Soviet propaganda can be classified under two categories. In the first place, there has been glorification of "the Soviet man." The idealization of the Soviet man embraces all of the basic virtues that the elite wish to engender among the masses. These virtues include an intense type of Soviet nationalism, belief in the perfection of the Soviet system, diligent and enthusiastic devotion to work, and total acceptance of Soviet society and the goals espoused by those who make policy. In the second place, propaganda characterizes the enemies of the Soviet state. The general enemy is imperialism (meaning capitalist and semicapitalist states) but the specific states counted as opponents may vary in name, number, and the intensity ascribed to their opposition. Definitions of the enemy and expositions on the aims of the enemy frequently serve to justify appeals for greater efforts in working to achieve domestic economic goals, which in turn are held to strengthen the Soviet state in dealing with its external opponents. Propaganda designed to justify the foreign policy of the regime is, therefore, related to domestic programs and is used as a cheap incentive to stimulate citizens to increase their labor in behalf of the nation. Domestic indoctrination thereby serves as a counterpart to what Harold Lasswell described as the strategic use of propaganda in international politics as a means of economizing in their struggle to establish an international Communist system.

THE PROPAGANDA ORGANS OF SOVIET FOREIGN POLICY

Until 1963, the voice of the Communist Party of the Soviet Union was a decisive factor in the affairs of nearly every Communist party in the world. In 1962, there were approximately 40 million party members, of whom only 4.5 million lived outside the party-states.[2] A large majority of these were in three states—Indonesia, Italy, and France. In spite of the small numbers of actual party members, however, the Soviet party has been able to rely on most of them to disseminate propaganda on the correctness of Moscow's course in foreign affairs and to engage in activities designed to promote the influence and prestige of the Soviet government. No other nation-state has had such a far-reaching nongovernmental mechanism so well disciplined in the arts of propaganda and subversion, constantly prepared to act in behalf of that nation's policies. Since the open breach in Communist ranks, the future effectiveness of this instrument may be seriously impaired, but in the past it has been a dependable tool of the Kremlin.

The Ministry of Foreign Affairs and related official institutions encourage their personnel to engage in similar activities. This has been especially true of Soviet delegates in the United Nations, who have become increasingly active in enlisting the support and sympathy of representatives from less developed countries.[3] One of the principal themes has been the "anti-imperialist" stance developed by Communist spokesmen, who pose as the champions of national independence. Another major tactic has been holding the Soviet Union as the example for all backward states whose leaders want to accomplish industrialization as rapidly as possible. On a more personal plane, the Soviet Committee for Cultural Relations with Foreign Countries operates under government auspices to welcome visitors from abroad and to entertain them with tours, speeches, and artistic exhibits and performances. Houses of culture are also maintained on a permanent basis in many countries. As the junior equivalent of this committee, the Sputnik International Youth Travel Bureau escorts young visitors to the Soviet Union, provides them with lodging at the Friendship Hotels of Moscow,

Leningrad, and Kiev, and entertains them with talks and discussion sessions.[4]

The ministries of Culture and Foreign Trade are responsible for promoting and arranging cultural and educational exchanges and trade exhibits designed to demonstrate the technological, scientific, and artistic achievements of the Soviet Union. In 1961, for example, the Soviet government conducted cultural exchange programs with thirty-six countries, including those in the Communist system of states.[5] These programs consisted of performances by the Bolshoi Ballet, the Soviet Army Chorus, and concert artists as well as art exhibits and film festivals. In addition, Soviet scientists are increasingly being encouraged to participate in international conferences and exchanges of specialized delegations. Russian citizens in these traveling groups apparently are expected to corroborate the official view of conditions in the countries visited, at least in public speeches and articles, for several returning representatives have been reprimanded for not doing so.

Another approach that sometimes yields propaganda dividends has been participation in trade fairs and industrial exhibitions. Between 1961 and 1963, the party-states sponsored from seventy to eighty trade fairs annually in neutral and Western nations. During that period the emphasis shifted away from the advanced nations while the members of the system concentrated their industrial and cultural exhibitions in Asia, Africa, and Latin America. The new states of Africa in particular were the recipients of much Soviet attention. By 1961, the U.S.S.R. had long-term scientific and cultural agreements with the U.A.R., Guinea, Ghana, Ethiopia, Mali, and Somalia.[6] These accords provided for the sending of over 400 Soviet scientists and teachers, the performance of Soviet artists, and the exhibition and distribution of Soviet films, brochures, and books. In return, the African states were encouraged to send students to receive training at universities and institutes in the party-states. The

Patrice Lumumba University of Friendship of Peoples was established in Moscow for the express purpose of training African nationals.

In spite of the great fanfare that has frequently accompanied the introduction of Soviet programs, Moscow has not accrued any significant gain as a result of cultural exchanges and propaganda appeals. The assertion that the large role played by government in the economies of many of the developing states proves the influence of Communism is highly misleading and inaccurate. The positive role of government in national economic life is a common feature of modern states on both sides of the political equator. Neither does the existence of one-party systems or one-man dictatorships necessarily imply the influence of Communism.

The Soviet propaganda campaign has been geared to evoke a response of anti-Western sentiment and official nonalignment in the "East-West" conflict. A more desirable response, from Moscow's perspective, is also to evoke toleration of local Communists and promote the programs of the national Communist party.[7] When measured by this standard, the Soviet program has not lived up to the initial expectations. Moscow's influence in Guinea was severely set back in 1961. Soviet prestige in Ghana and Mali declined in 1962-1963, and suffered great damage in the Congo in 1963, when the entire staff of the Soviet embassy was ordered out of the country. In Algeria and the U.A.R., countries strongly courted by the U.S.S.R., the Communist parties have been declared illegal. In none of the African states has a Soviet-controlled party threatened existing regimes. The student exchange program has also failed to produce the results Moscow expected. African students officially expressed dissatisfaction with their treatment in Bulgaria and actually staged a protest demonstration in the Kremlin.

In spite of difficulties, however, Moscow has cultivated its image as a rapidly rising industrial giant capable of helping economically backward states to imitate the successful Soviet course of development. Propaganda and exchange programs have probably helped to increase the awareness of people in other countries of the Soviet Union, but the leaders of most neutral states appear to believe that their countries benefit from the cold war by playing on the weaknesses of both sides. Despite "leftist" economic programs in many of these less privileged states, the governments of only a few have displayed any serious intention of blindly following the lead of either Washington or Moscow.

In addition to the formal organizational efforts of government and party in the area of foreign propaganda, the radio and press have major significance in the intricate complex of the Soviet propaganda apparatus. Although the cost of financing operations in this area is not known in the West, the time devoted to these media of communication and the volume of the output indicate the earnestness with which the Kremlin approaches the ideological struggle. The Soviet leaders quite frankly declare that radio and television are to be used as "heralds of the great truth of Communism. . . . The task is to place the whole great and effective force of radio and television completely at the service of the Communist education of the peoples."[8]

In line with this policy, Radio Moscow is beamed to all corners of the world. *Sovetskaia kultura* noted in 1961 that daily broadcasting from Moscow totaled 220 hours in 40 languages, while local stations in the republics and provinces broadcast 650 hours daily in 50 languages.[9] Although Western figures on Soviet broadcasting are not quite as large as those given in *Sovetskaia kultura,* they are still impressive. The United States Information Agency reported that the broadcast time of Radio Moscow averaged 1,128 hours weekly in June, 1962. Moscow directs most of these broadcasts to the countries of Europe, the Near East, South Asia, and Africa, but no populated continent is overlooked in the programming. During 1961-1962, broadcasts to Africa in four languages were increased by 80 per cent and those to Vietnam were doubled, indicating the growing importance the Kremlin attached to those areas. Soviet agents also concluded agreements with Cuba, Mali, and Guinea making them members of the International Radio and Television Organization, a program-distributing agency for the Soviet Union.

Radio Moscow is often skillfully used for propaganda purposes. Many of its foreign language broadcasts are simply anti-Western, particularly anti-American. Such programs are primarily designed to reduce the prestige of the United States and her allies. Broadcasts in Arabic, for example, usually concentrate on the close relationship of selected Western states to Israel and the domination of Western-owned oil companies in the Middle East. Programs beamed to Africa stress racial problems in the United States. During the riots in Birmingham, Alabama, in May, 1963, for example, reports and commentaries were broadcast to Africa in at least six languages. These broadcasts deplored the atrocities commited against Negroes and reported talks by Soviet citizens condemning the actions and attitudes of racists. One commentator claimed that incidents in Alabama represent "the true face of those who are making overtures to the black continent."[10] Similar claims were made in Spanish language broadcasts to Latin America which compared discrimination against Latin American people in the U.S.A. with that against Negroes and noted that more than 100 "armed sanctions" had been imposed by Washington on Latin American states.

Another class of broadcasts is designed to improve the image of the Soviet Union. These programs generally emphasize the strong "anti-imperialist" tradition of the U.S.S.R., the benefits brought to particular countries by Soviet aid and trade, and the advantages of educational and cultural exchange arrangements.

On occasion they appeal directly to the people to encourage their governments to support policies favored by Moscow at the moment. The sophistication of the programs appeared to have improved somewhat in the decade beginning in 1955, although there was still a tendency to triteness.

In addition to radio, the Soviet Union maintains the most extensive foreign language publishing and distributing house in the world—Mezhdunarodnaia Kniga. Books and pamphlets are produced in vast quantities and sold inexpensively throughout the world. The office of Mezhdunarodnaia Kniga reported in 1963 that it then sent books, periodicals, and journals in 49 languages to 80 countries. Annual displays of these publications are staged in several countries on all continents. In 1962, the report stated, over 10 million copies of 1,500 different books were distributed in countries outside the system of party-states. To supplement Soviet publications, the Kremlin purportedly assists in financing locally published periodicals, particularly in the less developed nations. In India there were 19 Communist periodicals, while in Argentina and Brazil, where the Communist party is officially outlawed, there were 21 and 29, respectively. Although the bulk of this material is sold openly in the receiving countries, some of it has been of such a nature that the local Communist party has resorted to fraud and smuggling. An interesting incident occurred in Argentina in 1962, involving the government confiscation of 630 pounds of Communist ideological material at the port of Rosario. The material was found on two East German ships and consisted of 740 publications in Spanish, 3,960 in German, English, and French, and also included photographs and flags. The Chilean newspaper that reported the incident complained that the Chilean-Soviet Cultural Institute at Arica had become a center of Soviet propaganda and commercial activity.[11] Moscow and the other party-states have engaged in similar activities in order to assure the distribution of propaganda materials. Radio programs and printed literature have been extensively utilized to accomplish this purpose.

All of the means available to increase the stature of the Soviet Union and that part of the Communist movement under Moscow's control have been utilized by the Kremlin. Whether the specific piece of propaganda stems from a Soviet disarmament proposal or the achievement of a Gagarin or a Titov in space, Moscow freely uses it to the advantage of the Soviet state. As *Kommunist* has pointedly noted, it must be made clear in waging the ideological struggle that the scientific and industrial accomplishments of the Soviet Union have been the result of the Soviet system. "All these successes weigh in the balance the competition between socialism and capitalism, they all have political significance since they strengthen the prestige of Communism."[12]

A possible shift in emphasis came late in 1963, when, for the first time, disillusionment was expressed over the effectiveness of international propaganda warfare. During a "scientific conference" on the ideological struggle, it was suggested by one of the principal participants that the Kremlin was not pleased with the fruits of its propaganda. The West was accused of stealing slogans and it was noted that propaganda is now carried out by governments rather than by special parties, which are less restricted in their choices of tactics. Strangely, after insisting that the ideological struggle could never be diminished in the period of coexistence, the 1963 conference criticized the United States for spending over 500 million dollars on overseas propaganda annually and curiously condemned the "imperialists" who are "trying to make psychological warfare 'total' and global'. . ."[13] The entry of the United States into the propaganda sphere and the resulting competition for Moscow had apparently caused some second thoughts.

IDEOLOGY AND SOVIET FOREIGN POLICY

The attention given by Soviet strategists to propaganda often raises the question of the extent to which ideolgy serves as a directive that the decision-makers follow. It is generally conceded that the members of the elite recognize the importance of ideology as an internal control device. Assuming this to be the case, it can also be contended that the effectiveness of indoctrination in reducing domestic discontent and channeling popular thought has encouraged the Soviet leaders to apply the same technique to foreign policy. The link between propaganda and ideology and between propaganda and the national aspirations of other countries can be discerned by content analysis of the propaganda itself. But this leaves unanswered and unexamined the question of the extent to which Marxism-Leninism, either as theory or as belief system, influences the policy-makers in the Kremlin.

The relationship between Leninist doctrine and the formulation of Soviet foreign policy has been the subject of much debate among Western scholars ever since the Bolsheviks first seized power in 1917. The inconclusiveness of this debate has stemmed largely from two factors: first, the lack of relevant data concerning the decision-making processes in the Kremlin and the background characteristics of the political elite (which makes it impossible to analyze the thought processes of members of the elite); and second, the personal commitment of the analyst either to belief in the total commitment of the Kremlin strategists to Leninist dogma or to the assumption that the struggle for power is self-motivating and operates irrespective of theoretical concepts. With existing limitations on collection of data and the unreliability of interviews with Soviet officials on the question of motivation, a conclusive answer based on objective evidence is quite impossible. Interpretation is nonetheless necessary, and in dealing with specific policies already in effect may yield rewarding results. Yet the way in which the holders of power see the world, their attitudes toward their own purposes and the purposes of others, cannot rightly be minimized, for the intellectual framework within which analyses of national power and of the international situation are made may be expected to color, if not actually to direct, policy choices. The precise extent of this influence cannot be empirically determined. The following interpretation, admittedly not definitive, is based on official Soviet statements regarding international events and trends.

Lenin's emphasis on the international system of monopoly capital, seeking profits by extending spheres of influence and establishing colonial rule over foreign territories, and the expectation of rivalry among capitalist powers for control of colonies, together with their reliance on military force to sustain and enhance their positions, have been continuing features of the official Soviet view of imperialism, whoever the man at the helm of the party has been. The attitude of Soviet Communists toward individual capitalist nations and "the international system of imperialism" is important not because it spells out particular policies for the Soviet Union to follow, but because it may condition Soviet expectations of and responses to the foreign policies of Western states. Insofar as the theory of imperialism influences these expectations and responses, the concept makes the Soviet leaders especially sensitive to some policies of their opponents, such as emphasis on military strength, and dulls their vision of other policies, such as occasional voluntary withdrawal from colonial countries.

According to the set of preconceived assumptions contained in the theory of imperialism, the desire of monopolies supported by the military establishment to expand their holdings and increase their profits is the major motivating force of capitalist states. This leads the Kremlin to anticipate hostile activity against the Communist system. Knowing that a proletarian revolution would deprive them of their position and wealth, the leaders of monopolies and of the military combine to exert pressure on capitalist governments to pursue policies based on anti-Communism and "positions of strength."[14] Consequently, the most powerful capitalist nations, Khrushchev told the 20th Party Congress, can be expected to exert economic and political pressures "to win supremacy, to suppress the working class and the democratic and national-liberation movements." They also aspire to create military alliances which will enable them to conduct hostile actions against the socialist camp from foreign bases.

In the eyes of Soviet analysts these general expectations have been borne out by postwar trends which indicate the reliance of capitalism on the state and the national military apparatus. More than ten "small" wars have occurred since the last world war, in such distant places as Korea, Vietnam, Laos, Suez, Algeria, and Cuba, as a result of the internal laws of state-monopoly capitalism, according to Kremlin analysts. The only moderating force on the aggressive alliance system of the imperialists is the "fear of proletarian revolution in the wake of military defeat and of the relative increase in the strength of the socialist world. . . ."[15] Recent history must be interpreted, therefore, in terms of the relations, and particularly of the conflicts, between the camp of imperialism and the camp of socialism.

There are periods, however, when the populace of capitalist states rises in opposition to war danger resulting from reckless policies and forces governments to modify aggressive designs. During these intervals the tensions of the cold war lessen and the possibility of conducting successful negotiations and making accommodations between the leaders of the two camps increases. But the monopolists and militarists inevitably attempt to re-assert their power, for peaceful accommodation is not desirable from their point of view. "The contradictory nature of the concrete actions of U.S. foreign policy" is accounted for by this alternating influence of the masses and the wielders of economic power. Basically, however, the ambitious drives inherent in imperialism, according to contemporary Soviet theoreticians, govern the policies of capitalist states.

The Soviet analysis of Western policies in the Middle East, for example, includes all the basic assumptions of the theory of imperialism. The anticipated rivalry among capitalist powers for spheres of influence is seen in the assumption of leadership by the United States over Great Britain in the Baghdad Pact. In turn, this alliance is characterized as "a bloc designed to serve the interests of the colonialists."[16] American intervention in Lebanon conformed to the interests of monopolists who derive economic advantages from an increase in military spending. Comments from the *New York Herald Tribune*, the *Journal of Commerce*, *Steel*, *U.S. News and World Report*, and the *Wall Street Journal* are cited to confirm this impression.[17] As the Soviet efforts to consolidate gains in the area met with repeated rebuffs between the summers of 1958 and 1959, Moscow laid the responsibility for its own failures on "provocateurs" acting under orders of imperialist circles which seek to undermine the friendly relations between the Soviet Union and Arab republics. Finally, in summarizing the basic elements of "the colonialists' traditional policy" in the Middle East during this period, *Pravda* emphasized the reliance of the West on "corrupt feudal leadership," use of the "divide and rule" tactic, and direct economic and military intervention.[18] All of these tactics were thought to be embodied in the Eisenhower Doctrine and were interpreted as part of the design of the United States oil magnates to reap huge profits by making the Arab states dependent on Western capital for further development.

A similar appraisal was given the activities of West Germany in Africa and the Middle East during and after the crisis over

Lebanon in 1958. The *New Times* noted with great alarm the expansion of German capital into Africa. Declaring that "the Common Market and Eurafrica schemes open up new vistas for German penetration," the periodical expressed fear of the revival of German militarism and colonialism. As a result of mutual imperialist interests in the Middle East, Germany was later held responsible for assisting the United States and Great Britain in the military intervention in Lebanon.[19] With the revival of the German economy, the Soviet press claimed that a Bonn-London-Washington alliance was aiming to dominate the world. These claims came as West German participation in N.A.T.O. was being broadened and as the Berlin crisis of 1958 was gaining momentum.

Khrushchev and the Soviet press gave the same type of interpretation to the U-2 incident and the subsequent collapse of the summit conference in Paris. Although the Soviet Premier displayed grave concern for the national sovereignty of the Soviet Union, charging that the admitted espionage was "insulting to the dignity of the people and the government," he also dwelt on the economic advantage the West would purportedly receive from a new exacerbation of world tensions. "It is easier," he insisted, "for the monopolies of the U.S.A. to inflate war production and make colossal profits when the atmosphere is troubled and tense."[20] Before the Romanian Party Congress Khrushchev avowed that the events leading to the failure of the Paris conference were "no accidental developmental," but represented "the tactics of imperialism." This interpretation appeared to be vindicated, according to the *World Marxist Review*, by the ensuing arms buildup which the "political and ideological advocates of aggressive imperialism" force on their countries.[21]

Yet, in spite of the relative consistency in the verbal expression of the theory of imperialism from Lenin to Brezhnev, its application in terms of policy has undergone subtle but meaningful change. While Lenin and Stalin could make temporary agreements with capitalist states on the ground that the weakness of the Soviet Union demanded it, Khrushchev's proposals of coexistence came at the height of Soviet prestige and strength and suggested a much longer-term existence of a world divided into two different social systems. Indeed, the Chinese contention that coexistence and the noninevitability of war thesis imply that profound changes have occurred in imperialism itself is quite accurate. The implication clearly exists, even though the Kremlin cannot be expected to voice such an admission. Moverover, the conclusion of the test-ban agreement, the continuation of cultural exchange programs, the heightened emphasis on borrowing technological innovations from the Western states at a time when the Kremlin claims to be outdistancing the United States, and especially the different assessments of the character and intentions of "imperialist" leaders all raise legitimate questions concerning the seriousness with which the Soviet elite takes the theory of imperialism. To what degree does the theory actually influence policy decisions and to what degree are the published statements merely an application of the terminology of imperialism to a postmortem analysis of given events? The most that can be said at the present is that recent Soviet behavior does not consistently reflect a firm commitment by the elite to a single view of imperialism.

The Soviet Union is engaged in a "competition of ideas" on a colossal scale. The Kremlin treats propaganda as an important part of the strategy of peaceful coexistence. Considering the difficulties of the international Communist movement in the decade of Khrushchev's leadership, it is doubtful that either Khrushchev or his colleagues seriously believed that victory could be attained for the Soviet variety of Communism through the force of ideas alone. But they did act as though they were genuinely convinced that the ideological struggle would contribute to such a victory. The Bolshoi Ballet might not have been expected to win battles, but it might have been used to help weaken the image of the less commendable aspects of Soviet life and to create a more favorable picture of Soviet culture.

In some of the propaganda the achievements in culture and science have been treated as Russian accomplishments, thereby stressing the national awareness of the Kremlin elite. At other times such achievements have been attributed to the Soviet Communist system; the ideological element has been underscored, but even then there has been at least implicit emphasis on *Soviet* Communism. This has been particularly true in Asia and the Middle East, where the Soviet propaganda machine has emphasized the ideological determinant of Russia's industrial and scientific advances more frequently than elsewhere. Officials who have taken personal tours of south Asia and propaganda organs have often linked the image of a vibrant advancing Soviet Union with the Communist system. In those nations where the economic and social structure was still in a state of flux, the Soviet tacticians apparently believed that the competition of ideologies was most crucial.

The place of ideological struggle in the strategy of peaceful coexistence may be partially explained by the fact that it is easier, and less dangerous, to expound the myths of revolutionary Leninism than actually to implement a policy of revolutionary commitment. Furthermore, a clear distinction is required between propaganda designed to glorify an interpretation of the theoretical foundations and goals of Communism and that designed to persuade others to accept some general policy line of the Soviet Union which may have no direct relationship to the theoretical foundations of the regime. The ideological struggle of the post-Stalin era, therefore, has been only partly expressive of the revolutionary beginnings of the Soviet republic, for the propaganda followed no consistent nationalistic or ideological pattern. Rather, in schizophrenic fashion, it switched from one to the other, never fully embracing either.

COEXISTENCE AMONG THE PARTY-STATES

> If the Chinese comrades wish to apply their efforts to normalizing the Albanian Party of Labor's relations with the fraternal parties, it is doubtful whether there is anyone better able to facilitate accomplishment of this purpose than the Communist Party of China. . . .
>
> —N. S. Khrushchev

CONFLICT WITHIN THE SYSTEM OF PARTY-STATES

VIII

IN THE PARLANCE of the Kremlin, the term "coexistence" applies only to relations between states with different social systems. Relations among states within the system of party-states are excluded by definition. Yet, as with so many favorite phrases of Marxism-Leninism whose meanings have undergone transformation, events have made it necessary to apply a kind of coexistence policy to relations among Communist states. The rift within the Communist world has made it possible to speak of coexistence within the system, as the Yugoslavs frankly do, and has also had an impact on the relations of individual party-states with non-Communist countries.

In 1919, the Communist International set forth twenty-one conditions for membership. Those conditions provided the theoretical justification for giving the leaders of the Communist Party of the Soviet Union the final voice in interpreting Communist doctrine and in directing the international Communist movement. The U.S.S.R. was to serve as the "base" of the impending world revolution. Throughout the Stalin era the practical consequence of this policy was the requirement of rigid conformity to the Russian model in the domestic and foreign policies of other Communist-ruled states. The inflexibility of Stalin's policy eventually resulted even in defining proletarian internationalism, a venerable phrase of orthodox Marxism, in terms of undeviating allegiance to the will and the way of Moscow. This meant that there was only one road to socialism—the Soviet road. It was on the basis of an alleged deviation from this path that Yugoslavia was expelled from the Cominform in 1948.

Yet the emergence of other Communist states after World War II eventually led to a re-evaluation of theoretical premises regarding relations among socialist states. The Khrushchev regime inherited the complex task of making the necessary innovations in theory and practice. A beginning was made in 1955 by the attempt to re-establish friendly relations with Yugoslavia. In 1956, at the 20th Party Congress, Khrushchev announced the modification of the Soviet base thesis by extending official recognition to the possibility of achieving socialism through different roads as well as to effecting the transition to socialism by peaceful means. The assumption appeared to be that economic and cultural ties and overall unity in ideological commitment would be sufficient to hold the party-states together. Nationalism was dying, Khrushchev insisted, and would soon cease to compete for loyalty with the interests of the international proletariat. The policy of demanding strict adherence to the Soviet pattern was, therefore, modified to permit a small, but undefined, degree of deviation from the Soviet model, while proletarian internationalism was redefined to stress cooperation rather than absolute uniformity. The trend toward domestic experimentation and increased divergencies among the party-states was further aggravated by the widespread circulation of Khrushchev's anti-Stalin speech in 1956. The parallel developments of anti-Stalinism and the acceptance of different roads to socialism did not create the difficulties that were soon to plague the system, but they did make it possible for latent problems to manifest themselves in a sudden and unexpected manner. As these difficulties became manifest, the Chinese Communists, never very dependent on the Soviet Union, began to challenge the leadership of the Kremlin in the revolutionary movement.

Our principal concern here is with the apparent reasons for the malady of disintegration and with the principal charges hurled by the competing party-states against each other.

FOUNDATIONS OF THE RIFT

In his secret speech at the conclusion of the 20th Party Congress, Khrushchev denounced Stalin's "shameful role" in the Yugoslav affair of 1948 and accused him of magnifying Yugoslavia's errors "in a monstrous manner." On March 20, 1956, *Borba,* the mouthpiece of the League of Communists of Yugoslavia, printed excerpts from Khrushchev's address with favorable comment.[1] In April, the last obstacle to increased party contacts between the C.P.S.U. and the Yugoslav League was removed when the Cominform, which had been officially responsible for the expulsion of Yugoslavia from the Communist system, was disbanded. Earlier, Tito had been willing to establish cordial governmental ties between Moscow and Belgrade, but had not displayed any interest in restoring cooperation between the parties, particularly if such a step required the submission of the League of Communists to the Soviet party.

With the advent of the anti-Stalin campaign and the abolition of the already moribund Cominform, Tito was encouraged to discuss the restoration of relations between his party and the C.P.S.U. during a visit to Moscow in June, 1956. At the reception for the Yugoslav Premier in the Soviet capital, Khrushchev spoke of the "grief and harm" resulting from the 1948 break. He applauded the meeting with the Yugoslav leader as demonstrating the "monolithic unity" of the socialist camp. Tito affirmed his country's friendship with the U.S.S.R., but he cautiously added that he did not want "to spoil its relations with other states," as renewed party ties might have done.[2] The following day, the Moscow Declaration was released. Signed by Khrushchev and Tito, acting as heads of their respective parties, the document stated that favorable political conditions had been created for cooperation between the two parties. In addition, the Declaration declared that:

> Abiding by the view that the roads and conditions of Socialist development are different in different countries, that the wealth of the forms of Socialist development contributes to their strengthening, and starting with the fact that any tendency of imposing one's own views in determining the roads and forms of Socialist development are alien to both sides, the two sides have agreed that the foregoing cooperation should be based on complete freedom of will and equality, on friendly criticism and on the comradely character of the exchange of views in disputes between our parties.[3]

This statement of the C.P.S.U. and the Yugoslav League appeared to demonstrate that the Soviet elite fully endorsed the resolution of the 20th Party Congress recognizing different roads to socialism in practice as well as in theory. At the very least, the Declaration confirmed a sharp policy reversal on the part of the Soviet party, which had been approved over the strong protests of Molotov and perhaps other representatives of the old guard as well.

Moscow's rapprochement with Belgrade came at the time that Poland and Hungary were completing the most difficult stage of industrialization and collectivization. To reformists in those countries, even to reformists in the ruling Communist parties, the Soviet Union appeared to have given its stamp of approval to Yugoslav revisionism, which included decentralization of the control of industry and de-emphasis on state ownership of farms. Furthermore, the recognition of the possibility of different roads to socialism that was suggested at the 20th Party Congress appeared to have been confirmed by the June Declaration. This encouraged the moderate elements of the Communist parties in Poland and Hungary to press for the consideration of broader policy alternatives than acceptance of the

Soviet base thesis had theretofore allowed. But the event which evoked the greatest reaction was the widespread distribution in eastern Europe of the anti-Stalin speech of Nikita Khrushchev.

The unrest that followed Khrushchev's speech in 1956 was foreshadowed by Palmiro Togliatti's report to the Central Committee of the Italian Communist Party in June. Togliatti openly challenged the theory of the Soviet base by calling for a "polycentric system, corresponding to the new situation . . . [which required] new types of relations among the Communist parties themselves."[4] The leader of the Italian Communist Party proceeded to demand the "full autonomy" of the individual parties and the establishment of bilateral relations among them. Finally, he asked for an official explanation of what had made possible the "serious errors" of Stalinism and demanded guarantees against their repetition. These comments came during the Tito visit to Moscow and were reported in the Polish press at the same time as the C.P.S.U.-League of Communists Declaration was reprinted. The Soviet leadership had failed to make clear the extent to which Moscow would be willing to tolerate differences, and Togliatti appeared to be asking for a "test case."

The initial Soviet response to Togliatti was delayed, but appeared conciliatory in tone. *Pravda,* a week after the Italian party leader's speech and also a week after the Khrushchev-Tito Declaration, declared that "under present conditions all Communist parties base their actions upon the national peculiarities and conditions of each country, giving the fullest possible expression to the national interests of their people."[5] After the riots that occurred soon thereafter in Poznan, Poland, however, the leadership and official press of the Soviet Union began to stress the demand for unity among national Communist parties. *Pravda* reminded party leaders in the east European party-states that they were moving "*toward one* goal, toward communism." While continuing to recognize the importance of "creatively applying Marxism-Leninism" to the conditions of each nation, the editorial asserted that the national interests of the working class "cannot contradict their international socialist interests."[6] There were different roads to socialism, the Soviet elite was prepared to admit, but they had to be "Marxist-Leninist roads" and could, therefore, not be too different.

The crisis quickly reached a climax in Poland. Reformers within the Polish Communist party advocated the restoration to power of Wladyslaw Gomulka, a man who had been imprisoned under Stalin for his revisionist ideas. While the Politburo of the Polish party was in session, Khrushchev, Molotov, and Kaganovich appeared in Warsaw. The fact that the First Secretary was accompanied by two of his strongest critics suggested that the difficulty in Poland was viewed by the old guard as a failure of Khrushchev's policy toward the party-states and evidenced a temporary decline in Khrushchev's power. Exactly what occurred in the Warsaw meeting is not known but some of the effects are clear. The Soviet troops and tanks near the outskirts of the Polish capital were recalled, Gomulka became the First Secretary of the Polish party, and the Soviet General Rokossovskii was removed from the Politburo. The moderation of these measures indicated that Khrushchev's policies were not to be reversed, despite the presence of Molotov. Moreover, the general terms of the bargain reached by Gomulka and the Soviet officials were also moderate. Revealing the terms to the Polish people on October 24, Gomulka noted that in domestic affairs Poland would be free to build socialism according to the means "most suitable" to national conditions without being bound by the Soviet model, but in foreign affairs the socialist states must "act together and on a single front."[7]

Gomulka conferred with Soviet leaders in Moscow from November 15 to November 18. The talks resulted in the joint Polish-Soviet Declaration. This statement accented the importance of unity in foreign affairs and explained the rights of Soviet troops in Polish territory. In addition, a 700-million-ruble loan and 1,400,000 tons of grain were granted the Polish government. Gomulka, in return, agreed to follow the Kremlin's line in foreign policy. Only once did he openly fail to abide by that agreement—Poland abstained on the Indian resolution urging Hungary to admit observers of the United Nations while all other party-states represented in the United Nations voted against it.[8]

Hungary's revolution was far more violent and the reformers attempted to go much further in terms of both domestic and foreign policies than Gomulka had dared to go. Imre Nagy, recalled to party leadership after the first wave of violence and after the Soviet troops had withdrawn from Budapest, was caught up in the swift tide of revolutionary fervor and was unable to be the cautious leader of events that Gomulka had been in Poland. As the reforms promised by Nagy reflected an increasingly radical departure from the policies of the preceding regime, the Kremlin dispatched Mikoyan and Suslov to the Hungarian capital to assess the situation. The decision to launch the decisive second intervention apparently was made before Nagy announced his intention to withdraw Hungary from the Warsaw Pact and to pursue a course of neutrality in foreign policy, thus indicating that there was a limit on the kinds of domestic innovation that the dominant faction in Moscow was prepared to tolerate.[9] It is also possible that Nagy warned Mikoyan and Suslov that further Soviet interference would compel him to declare the neutrality of his government in the hope of attracting the active support of the United States. In either case, whether the Soviet decision was made in reaction to domestic or to foreign policy shifts in Hungary, the second Soviet intervention was overpowering—tanks and troops moved on Budapest as the U.S.S.R.'s might was used to crush the revolution and to restore a kind of Communist control more acceptable to Moscow.

The Soviet press justified the second intervention on the

ground that "foreign imperialist reactionary groups" had instigated the revolution in order to restore the "bourgeois order."[10] Jacob Kadar, the new leader of the Hungarian Workers' Party, however, recognized that the roots of the revolution were much deeper. Addressing the Hungarian public by radio, Kadar said that the cause of the revolution lay in the "grave errors and crimes which were committed to the detriment of the working people . . . by the Rakosi clique, which had decisive influence on the leadership of the country and Party."[11] He further insisted that the indignation of the people was "perfectly legitimate," that the Soviet Union did not need the "servile and obsequious measures" of the Rakosi government, and that "slavish imitation" of the U.S.S.R. was improper for the Hungarian people. Significantly, Kadar's speech was reprinted in full in *Pravda*. Once again, the Kremlin was willing to allow a Communist reformer to take the reins of a subservient government but, as in the case of Poland, the reforms could be only in domestic policy and then only within the currently accepted general framework of Marxism-Leninism. The foreign policy of the members of the Communist system had to be uniform, according to Moscow. The experience of both Poland and Hungary also revealed that the Soviet Union would tolerate reform movements only if they came through the party and not if they were inspired by non-Communist leadership.

The toleration of reforms was perhaps most clearly demonstrated in regard to the decollectivization of agriculture and to religion. Imre Nagy reported that as early as 1953 Molotov had indicated willingness on the part of the Soviet government to revise the rigid attitude toward forced collectivization by saying: "The farm cooperatives must not be disbanded by fiat, but, should they choose to disband voluntarily, they shouldn't be hindered."[12] The same year that Molotov was voicing this concession, Yugoslavia abandoned its Soviet-inspired agricultural program and permitted restoration of private ownership of farms. But even though the permissibility of private ownership of land was discussed in the early post-Stalin years among the members of the system and openly accepted by Tito, the attempt to collectivize agriculture was not discontinued in Poland and Hungary until after the events of 1956. Following those events, 87 per cent of the cultivated land area of Poland and a smaller percentage in Hungary were restored to private hands.[13] *Kommunist* officially bestowed its approval on the Polish course in 1961 and, later, sharp attacks were made on Stalin's forced collectivization of agriculture in the Soviet Union.[14] A greater degree of toleration was also revived in Poland and Hungary toward the Roman Catholic Church. Some religious instruction was reintroduced and greater liberty was granted the clergy. Consequently, de-Stalinization and the acceptance of different roads to socialism had a significant impact on the domestic policies of Poland and Hungary, and even the Soviet Union began to consider more objectively a number of the policies adopted in Yugoslavia.

Another important effect of the crisis of 1956 was the intensification of efforts to bind the economies of the east European states more closely to the Soviet economy and to eliminate some of the features that had characterized the Stalinist exploitation of the satellites. The principal instruments for effecting these ends were coordinated long-range plans, greater specialization in production, extension of Soviet economic aid, and the expansion of trade among the members of the party-state system. The Council on Mutual Economic Aid stressed that the international division of labor was advanced by specialization of production and would eventually eliminate the different levels of development in the socialist states.[15] The separate states would thereby be bound together economically in the world socialist system.

While the Soviet decision-makers went about their task of restoring satisfactory relations with the east European members of the system, they also sought a convenient scapegoat for the crisis. The Soviet leadership's first reaction to the revolutionary turmoil was to cast most of the blame for the troublesome affair on Tito. In the eyes of Moscow, the Yugoslav dictator had acquitted himself badly. Although he had supported the use of Soviet troops against Nagy, Tito described the first Soviet intervention in Budapest in his famous speech at Pula as a "fatal error."[16] Tito then proceeded to criticize the Soviet Union by declaring that "the cult of personality is, in fact, the product of the system." He also praised developments in Poland and assailed the attitude toward Gomulka of "Stalinist" leaders in other party-states. From this point onward relations between Moscow and Belgrade continued to deteriorate until 1961, although Soviet attacks on Yugoslav "revisionism" were rarely as savage as those levied by the Chinese Communists.

Having discounted Tito as a dependable source of support, the Kremlin strategists turned to Peking for more forthright assistance in restoring order in the shaken system of international Communism. According to reports released by Peking in 1963, the Chinese Communists had encouraged the Poles to make a show of independence before the crisis that was precipitated by the Poznan riots. Whether or not this was true, Moscow felt called on to invite China, whose leaders had accepted the anti-Stalin campaign with reluctance, to send a representative to Poland and Hungary to help restore party harmony. Chou En-lai's acceptance of this invitation brought China into east European politics openly for the first time. Chou's speeches in Budapest and Warsaw dutifully stressed one theme—the need for unity among all party-states and for Soviet leadership of the Communist system. While recognizing the possibility of domestic differences, Chou insisted on unity in foreign policy and singled out the Yugoslavs for severe criticism for following an independent course in foreign relations.[17] The Chinese Foreign Minister was, therefore, publicly endorsing the position taken by Moscow during the Polish-Soviet and Hungarian-Soviet negotiations. For the time being an element of unity had been attained, although Yugoslavia had been temporarily excluded from membership in the party-state system.

The events in east Europe in 1956 came as a shock to the Soviet leadership. They compelled the elite to face up to the fact that nationalism did not end with socialism and that recognition of different roads to socialism and de-Stalinization had only encouraged Poland and Hungary to steer independent courses, and was causing difficulties in the domestic affairs of other party-states. Khrushchev and his supporters had chosen economic interdependence and ideological unity as the principal means of tying the Communist countries together under the assumption that these two factors would be sufficient to accomplish that purpose. To employ these means successfully, it was belatedly realized, required the leadership of the Soviet Union and the reassertion of its pre-eminence in the system of party-states. There was a major practical obstacle in the way, however—if the system had ever been monolithic, it was clearly no longer so solidly unified. Moscow, Peking, and Belgrade all claimed to speak for international Communism and all three capitals had played important roles in the east European crisis of 1956.

ISSUES OF DISSENSION WITHIN THE INTERNATIONAL COMMUNIST SYSTEM

In spite of the widespread belief in the monolithic nature of the Communist movement, there have actually been relatively few factors uniting the system of states governed by Communist parties. Jan F. Triska, in a research project of the Stanford Institute of Political Studies, found four major factors contributing to the unity of the system. These were the "quasi-identical political, economic, social, and legal systems," general acceptance of a Marxist-Leninist belief system, the military pre-eminence of the Soviet Union within the system, and "the geographical contiguity" of the member-states except Cuba.[18] Besides serving as elements of unity, however, the same factors, as the author points out, may also provide cause for dissension. There is no official organization of the various national Communist parties, much less one that is capable of exercising some degree of authority to coerce dissident members. Indeed, there is no organization on the governmental level embracing all of the members of the system. The largest such organizations, the Warsaw Pact and Comecon, are essentially east European organizations. The structure of the Communist state system is, therefore, a very loose one, with no definite rules of fair play and no executive officer or policy-making body with the authority to resolve conflicts.

In the absence of any recognized means of resolving differences, the rift within the system apparently grew from unpublicized notes between governments to more open debate conducted through third parties; then to a polemical "dialogue" between the principal centers of conflict, and finally to unofficial but open schism. The reasons for the breakup of the Third International are enumerated by Soviet authorities as "errors" of the Communist Party of China. These errors consist of (1) ignoring the Marxist-Leninist characteristics of the present epoch; (2) incorrectly assessing the role and place of the socialist system in the world revolutionary process; (3) claiming the necessity of world war for the final victory over imperialism; (4) denying the class nature of peaceful coexistence; (5) ignoring the conclusions of the Moscow Declaration of 1960 concerning the new third stage in the development of the social crisis of capitalism; (6) misunderstanding the current stage of the working class movement—the role of the anti-imperialist struggle of the masses in capitalist countries—and disagreeing with the Declaration of 1960 on the ways and forms of effecting the transition to socialism; and (7) denying the significance of national liberation revolutions and their contribution to the strength of the forces of progress.[19] These points of difference need to be supplemented by other issues rarely noted in the official criticism of the Chinese Communists by the C.P.S.U. Such additional questions include territorial disputes and certain domestic political and aconomic trends in Communist countries. These issues can be generally grouped into three categories: those pertaining to the operational mechanics of the international Communist movement and to its leadership, those concerned with domestic practices and aims of the separate Communist states, and those involving interpretations of the non-Communist world and the appropriate policies of the party-states toward it.

Issues concerning the international Communist movement

The convocation of the representatives of Communist parties from sixty-four countries in November, 1957, indicated that the party leadership in the Soviet Union was conscious of the growing complexity of coordinating the Communist movement. The principal purpose of the meeting was to restore the unity of the separate parties by reducing the divisive influence of Titoism in the party-states, especially in Poland, and to set a general course acceptable to all parties, particularly to those in power. The Declaration of Ruling Communist Parties was the main product of the conclave. It referred to the Soviet Union only as "the first and mightiest Socialist power" and noted that all differences between socialist countries should be settled through "comradely discussion." The statement pointedly singled out revisionism as the "main danger" to the solidarity of Communists and declared that "factions and groups sapping unity" were a hindrance to the international movement. Gomulka, under pressure from the Kremlin, had no choice but to accept the

Declaration, although Tito refused to sign anything more than the vague Peace Manifesto introduced by Poland and endorsed by all sixty-four delegations. The accent of the session was on unanimity rather than on majority decision, and the content of the Declaration suggested that the leaders of the C.P.S.U. genuinely wanted to avoid the impression of dictating the terms of the statement, even though the powerful presence of the Soviet representatives undoubtedly influenced the delegates from most, if not from all, of the other parties.

Although the Moscow conference succeeded in creating the appearance of unity (sans Yugoslavia), events of the preceding eighteen months had already laid the foundation for dissension between key members of the system. Khrushchev's policies had not turned out well and Peking had been brought in at Moscow's request to heal the wounds. A situation of dual leadership had been created. If the assumptions of Leninist theory were truly valid, then proletarian internationalism would clearly triumph and no problem could be expected to develop. On the other hand, if the revolutionary commitments of the two largest Communist states were shaded by their respective national distinctions, class ties might not prevent competition for leadership of the international Communist movement from deepening to the point of reviving the ancient differences between China and Russia as well as exacerbating differences of both a pragmatic and an ideological nature.

Sources of tension between the two Communist giants and indications of uneasiness in their relations with each other began to appear in 1956. One of the points of disagreement from the very beginning appeared to be how decisions of mutual interest to the various Communist parties, and especially to the ruling parties, could be attained and what method would be used to determine what parties and states legitimately belonged in the Communist system. Initially the dispute centered on the status of Yugoslavia and the League of Communists. After the adoption of the Program of the League of Yugoslav Communists in May, 1958, *Jen Min Jih Pao*, the Chinese Communist party equivalent of *Pravda*, hurled violent criticisms at the document and insinuated that the Cominform had been correct in its charges against Tito in 1948.[20] The words from Moscow were critical, though less antagonistic, but the actions of the Kremlin indicated reluctance to provoke Belgrade into another dispute of the proportions of the 1948 controversy. Representatives of the two countries continued to negotiate over the terms of soviet economic aid to Yugoslavia for more than two months after the adoption of the revisionist program before Moscow finally canceled them. More overtly, the Kremlin moved to reestablish its position as the principal guardian of Leninist thought in order to prevent the ideological leadership of the C.P.S.U. from further deteriorating. A series of articles published in *World Marxist Review* by noted Communist leaders from Czechoslovakia, Poland, and Hungary recognized the leading role of the Soviet Union in all affairs concerning the relations of party-states. In one of the articles Kadar declared that the test of the internationalism of any working-class party should be "its attitude toward the Soviet Union."[21] By speaking through party leaders in the east European states, the Soviet Union informed the Chinese politely but firmly that the U.S.S.R. had no intention of abdicating leadership of the Communist movement in favor of Peking.

In the summer of 1960, a conference of Communist leaders was convened, apparently at the instigation of Soviet party leaders, to try to resolve the growing conflict among the party-states. The Chinese delegate, Peng Chen, spoke before Khrushchev. His address, as reported in Peking, did nothing to smooth the dispute.[22] The Chinese, he said, were inspired by "the general line, the great leap forward, and the peoples' communes." Peng stressed his government's support of certain policies of Moscow, but all policies specifically listed were those in which the Kremlin had taken a strong stand against "U.S. aggression." Peng took particularly sharp exception to Khrushchev's policy in Algeria, coming periously close to accusing him of selling out the Algerian Communists in return for a trip to Paris to visit de Gaulle. He further insisted that the "aggressive and predatory nature of imperialism will never change." Khrushchev's officially reported address was a reasoned defense of the policy of coexistence and the innovations formally incorporated into Marxist-Leninist theory at the 20th Party Congress. But subsequent reports contended that at the private meetings the First Secretary of the C.P.S.U. became belligerent and attacked Mao by name as an unreconstructed Stalinist.[23] The 1957 conference of representatives from Communist parties had failed to provide the means by which conflicts could be authoritatively resolved. The violent nature of the unofficial meeting in Bucharest made necessary another attempt to find a unanimously accepted program.

In the same month as the Bucharest conference, the Soviet Union issued its most comprehensive denunciation of Chinese interpretations of peaceful coexistence, the inevitability of war, and the possibility of peaceful transition to socialism in a long article purportedly commemorating the publication of Lenin's *Left-wing Communism: An Infantile Disorder*.[24] The article pointedly cited Lenin's reference to Blanquists who wanted "to skip all intermediate stages to communism," an attitude to which Lenin referred as "childish naiveté." After vigorously condemning dogmatism, the statement reminded others of the support given coexistence, peaceful transition to socialism, the elimination of war as an objective necessity, and unity in the socialist system by the 1957 Declaration and by the 21st Congress of the C.P.S.U. Moscow's inability to force Peking to heed such indirect criticisms of its policies was indicated shortly after the Bucharest conference. On August 13, 1960, Radio Peking broadcast the contention that "modern revisionists" were parroting the imperialists and had become "apologists for imperialism." Moscow demonstrated its concern for the growing division by removing the old Stalinist, Molotov, from his post as ambassador to Outer Mongolia. The implication of the Soviet move was that Molotov was suspected of encouraging the Chinese to assail the official policies of the U.S.S.R.

Before the differences became more acute, Khrushchev moved to resolve them through another party conference similar to the one held in 1957. The Moscow Conference of eighty-one Communist parties convened in November, 1960. Reliable information is not available concerning the intensity of the debate, but the content of the Declaration that resulted from the conference supports the view that Moscow and Peking were unable to reach a firm accord.[25] The Declaration generally supported the Soviet line, including the policy of peaceful coexistence, the support of "national-democratic" governments in new states, and the possibility of peaceful transition to socialism. The Chinese were probably more pleased with the strong condemnation of imperialism, recognition of the possibility of violent transition to socialism, and the attack on Tito and revisionism as the "main danger." Although Khrushchev won support for most of the foreign policy to which the members of his coalition subscribed, the final product was far too vaguely worded and subject to various interpretations to have supplied the ideological unity that was needed within the system. That the differences remained unsettled quickly became evident when Enver Hoxha, leader of the Albanian Party of Labor and bitter opponent of Khrushchev's attempted reconciliation with Tito, returned to Tirana and announced that busts of Stalin and Mao would be erected—a direct slap at the Soviet Premier.

Just before the opening session of the 22nd Congress of the C.P.S.U., the Soviet Union announced "growing Yugoslav friendship" and the expectation of further expansion of trade between the two countries. Albania, having climbed into the lap of Peking as a result of disillusionment with the amicable relations developing between the U.S.S.R. and Yugoslavia, declined to send a delegation. Khrushchev sharply told the Congress that it was imperative for "each party to observe the joint decisions adopted collectively and likewise not to permit any actions that could undermine the unity of the Communist ranks. . . ."[26] The Soviet Premier then went further than anyone expected by publicly chastising Albania for its divisive attitude. Chou solemnly rebuked Khrushchev by reminding him that "open unilateral condemnation of a fraternal party does not make for solidarity, does not help settle issues." Only American imperialists and the Yugoslav revisionists, he charged, could be interested in driving a wedge "into the progressive forces and undermining their solidarity."[27]

Earlier, in his report to the party gathering at the Marx-Engels-Lenin Institute in January, 1961, Khrushchev had contended that the U.S.S.R. did not want to be recognized in any way as having a paramount position over other communist parties. He suggested that the party conferences in 1957 and 1960 had been called in order to give all parties a voice in the declarations, that the statements on ideology were not dictated, but were the expression of the general consensus of the delegates. Soon after the 22nd Congress and the Soviet break with Albania, however, *Pravda*, on January 18, 1962, asserted the right of the C.P.S.U. to "purify" the world Communist movement. Comparing Khrushchev's attack on Albania with Lenin's deliberate and successful attempts to split the party in 1912, the editorial declared that the elimination of left-opportunists from the party on that occasion had in fact "strengthened its ranks."

Ignoring Peking's antipathy to Tito, Khrushchev proceeded to move toward another rapprochement with Yugoslavia and to recognize Yugoslavia as a party-state which legitimately belonged in the system of socialist states. In October, 1962, Leonid Brezhnev went to Belgrade on a state mission that resulted in two agreements. First, a joint communiqué on policy was issued which expressed the accord of the two governments on the policies of peaceful coexistence, disarmament, and a German peace treaty. Second, a new and expanded trade agreement was signed. Tito was subsequently given the honor of addressing the Supreme Soviet, a rare gesture of respect toward any foreign dignitary. In a speech before the East German Communist Party Congress, Khrushchev insisted that "Yugoslavia is Socialist," not merely "Leftist," and declared that just because the leadership of one socialist state disagreed with that of another was no reason "to spend our time excommunicating others from socialism."

The report of the Central Committee of the C.P.S.U. on the Chinese Communist accusations against the Soviet leadership was delivered by Mikhail Suslov in February, 1964.[28] Suslov attacked the Chinese "claim to the role of 'supreme arbiters' in the socialist community" and singled out their "excommunication" of Yugoslavia for criticism. The statements issued from Peking, Suslov's report asserted, had been "in defiance of the facts." "Tomorrow it may occur to the C.P.C. [Communist Party of China] leadership to do as much with regard to other socialist countries." In addition, the Chinese were charged with having "disruptive aims" by discrediting the role of Comecon and "attempting to sow discord among the socialist countries." In pursuing such policies the Chinese leaders were deemed guilty of "subversive activity against the Leninist unity of the world Communist movement" by deliberately following a campaign to split the movement.

The Suslov report shed unexpected light on the events of the 1960 Moscow conference, indicating that the split had in fact reached serious proportions by that date. The report charged that the Chinese government, on the eve of the 1960 conference, demanded a revision of all agreements previously concluded with the U.S.S.R. on economic, scientific, and technical cooperation, and that the Chinese themselves had been responsible for the sharp reduction in trade between the two states by turning down "a considerable part" of the planned deliveries of Soviet equipment. It was also noted that Mikoyan had officially informed the Chinese in November that "if China really needed Soviet specialists and if they were provided normal conditions for work, we were prepared to send them back to the C.P.R. [Chinese People's Republic]" Khrushchev was also reported to have communicated this proposition to Chou En-lai at the conclusion of the 22nd Party Congress. However, "the Chinese leaders did not reply to all these proposals, while continuing to exploit the question of Soviet specialists for their unseemly ends." Even allowing for Suslov's bias, it is fair to assume that the Chinese government's demands on the Soviet government at a moment when representatives from the various parties were attempting to find a commonly acceptable statement of principle deeply influenced the debates over what appeared to be ideological questions.

The Central Committee report, however, found the Chinese guilty of much more during the 1960 conference than merely obstinate demands on the Soviet government. Suslov claimed that the Chinese delegates attempted to prevent the inclusion of a statement from the 1960 Declaration of Communist Parties regarding "the impermissibility of factional activity within the world Communist movement." Even though the Chinese effort failed, shortly after the conference representatives of the Chinese party were held to have formulated a theoretical basis "for their refusal to carry out a common decision." "They put forward the concept of 'majority and minority,' which claims that the minority has a right not to comply with collectively adopted decisions and to combat the common line approved." More recently, Suslov charged, the Chinese had conducted a campaign for the "recruitment of adherents in the ranks of fraternal parties, and the formation of factional groups composed of them." These "splitting" activities had also extended to "the congresses and conferences of peace fighters and of women's, youth and other international associations for disruptive sorties." The intention of the Chinese, asserts the Soviet report, is the formation of a "bloc of their fellow-thinkers that will have its own platform and group discipline and with its center in Peking."

The strongest language of the Suslov report indicted the Chinese leaders for "petty-bourgeois, nationalist, neo-Trotskyist deviation." "Factionalism comprised the 'soul' of Trotskyism." The "factionalism" of the Chinese operates under "super-revolutionary" slogans and the thesis that revolutionary war is the " 'most decisive means' of putting an end to the contradiction between two social systems." The latter thesis is condemned as the "petty bourgeois" essence of Trotskyism. Furthermore, the report found that "nationalism is inexorably gaining the upper hand in the entire policy of the Chinese leaders, that it is becoming the mainspring of their actions." The Soviet accusations against the elite in Peking thus singled out nationalism as the driving force behind the Chinese attempt "to overtake all the socialist countries and occupy a dominating position in the world socialist system." Having recognized the nationalistic flavor of China's position, the Soviet observers were no doubt aware of the significance of Russian nationalism to their own position. The Soviet elite could not allow the Chinese to define the goals of the movement and prescribe the tactics when they were likely to upset the expectations of the Soviet decision-makers for their own nation and perhaps even to threaten the security of the U.S.S.R. and the entire system of party-states.

The struggle for pre-eminence among the party-states and also among the nonruling Communist parties had, therefore, burst into open conflict. Peking could claim the support of Albania and perhaps North Korea and North Vietnam. Moscow claimed the allegiance of most of the other Communist-ruled states but the degree of allegiance varied widely. Romania quickly learned to play one side against the other, increasing its contacts with Western states and even challenging the territorial rights of the Soviet Union to former Romanian territory. At the same time it remained one of the most Stalinist states in its domestic policies. In regard to the nonruling parties, the Chinese temporarily proved to be an even more serious challenge to Moscow's leadership by attracting the sympathies of many party leaders in Asia, Africa, and Latin America who were frustrated by the policy of peaceful coexistence. The Brezhnev-Kosygin leadership, aided by unwitting Chinese mistakes, managed to restore some of Moscow's lost prestige among the party leaders of developing nations. But a factor that probably contributed to the fall of Khrushchev was the assertion of independence by the influential nonruling parties of Italy and France. Despite the change in Soviet leadership, the trend toward polycentrism appeared to be irrevocable.

Disagreement over domestic policies

In addition to different approaches toward the coordination of the international Communist system, the Soviet and Chinese leaders disagreed over several domestic programs and national claims. The most noteworthy of the disagreements centered on the question of the construction of communism, priorities of allocations to domestic construction and international revolution, the cult of the personality, and the question of territorial claims put forth by the Chinese.

In 1958, the Chinese Communists announced the construction of a national system of communes as part of the "great leap forward." The commune scheme could be interpreted as an effort to bypass the Soviet Union by permitting claims that China had already entered the stage of "building communism" while even the U.S.S.R., at that time, had made no comparable assertion. Acceptance of the Chinese claim would have placed the

People's Republic of China in a more advanced stage of domestic construction than the Soviet Union and would probably have increased the prestige of the Chinese regime at the expense of the U.S.S.R. The Kremlin was silent at first, sending out no editorial comment to refute the Chinese contention. However, Mikoyan, visiting the United States, openly derided the commune plan by noting that the Soviet Union had abandoned such schemes "years ago."[29] In January, 1959, the only reference in Khrushchev's report to the communes was that "the Communist Party of China is employing many original forms of socialist construction."[30] Notably, he did not say "Communist construction." Explaining how the Seven-Year Plan foreshadowed the construction of communism, the Soviet Premier noted, no doubt for China's benefit, that the socialist phase of development cannot be "violated or bypassed at will." The Soviet leadership was temporarily able to persuade China to modify its claims, for *Hung Ch'i*, the organ of the Central Committee of the C.P.C., applauded the aims of the Seven-Year Plan and agreed that the transition from socialism to communism could not be achieved until a high level of production existed.[31] In spite of the momentary truce, the issue had been created and the Chinese leadership demonstrated willingness to compete with the Soviet Union for prestige among both the ruling and the nonruling Communist parties of the world.

Disagreements also became manifest over the treaty obligations of the two countries. The 1957 treaty of assistance had included a Soviet pledge of assistance in the development of nuclear power in China. Only a year later the Soviet Union broke this accord and declined to help the Chinese create a nuclear arsenal of their own.[32] Treatment of Soviet scientists and technicians became a matter of dissension in other parts of the assistance program and trade agreements between the two Communist powers began to go unfulfilled. Apparently one of the principal criticisms the Chinese made was that Soviet aid was too little and that the Kremlin refused to meet some of the requests of the Chinese government. The Suslov report of 1964 condemned the Chinese leaders for attacking the effort of the Soviet policy-makers to improve the standard of living in the U.S.S.R. Suslov condemned the contention that "the improvement of the living standard is making Soviet people 'go bourgeois,'" and sharply denounced the assertion that "the principle of material incentives 'results in people seeking personal gain and enrichment inducing the itch for profit and a growth of bourgeois individualism, and injuring socialist economics.'" In rebuttal the report claimed that "neither Marx nor Lenin have anywhere even remotely hinted that the rockbottom tasks of socialist construction may be realized by the methods of 'leaps' and cavalry charges, overlooking the degree to which the socio-economic and spiritual premises of the advance have matured and ignoring the task of improving the living standards of the people." The refusal of the Soviet elite to retard the growth of their own nation in order to stimulate the growth of other party-states has, therefore, been another manifestation of nationalism.

Controversy over the border between the Soviet Union and China added another dimension to the range of differences between the two Communist states. Western observers had often noted that tension existed over territory along the Sinkiang-U.S.S.R. boundary. However, it was not until 1964 that Soviet and Chinese statements confirmed the extent of the dispute. The Chinese contended that in 1957 their government had asked the government of the Soviet Union to confer on the question of "unsettled" borders. On September 2, 1964, *Pravda* declared that the Chinese had made claims against Soviet-held territories as early as 1954 and had demanded government-to-government negotiations. This question may, indeed, have been one of the primary causes of the growing coolness between Moscow and Peking in 1957-1962. Charges and countercharges of nationalism were probably intensified as a result of the Chinese desire to reclaim the ancient territorial borders of their empire and of the Russian desire to maintain possession of land already under their domain.[33]

Questions of war, peace, and revolution

The leadership of the Communist parties of the Soviet Union and of China have made different assessments of the international situation as well as of relations among the party-states and of trends in the domestic life of the other's country. These differences stem from conflicting perceptions of the contemporary status of the principal "imperialist" states, of the appropriate form of relations between the party-states and industrially advanced non-Communist states, and of the role of the Communist movement in "national-liberation" revolutions and in the newly developing countries of Asia, Africa, and Latin America.

Different policies officially pursued by the governments in Moscow and Peking toward the Western powers could be detected as early as the spring and summer of 1958. During the Middle East crisis and the United States intervention in Lebanon, Soviet officials reaffirmed their belief in peaceful coexistence and called for a summit meeting to resolve the Soviet-American conflict over interests in the Middle East.[34] The Western powers agreed to a meeting of heads of state in the U.N. Security Council, but after a surprise trip to Peking, Khrushchev rejected the idea of a summit conference.[35] Peking cheered the decision to pursue a tougher policy toward the West and stepped up its bombardment of the islands of Quemoy and Matsu off the Chinese mainland.[36]

The different approaches of the two governments toward relations with Western powers inevitably became entangled in the competition for leadership in the Communist movement. These differences were, therefore, expressed in ideological terms. Mao, long highly regarded as a Communist theoretician, published a tract on imperialism. Declaring that the sun was "rapidly" setting on the imperialist countries, he claimed that "imperialism and all reactionary forces, which appear strong but are actually weak, are paper tigers."[37] *Hung Ch'i*, on the anniversary of the October Revolution, commented on the reactionary nature of imperialism and the necessity of being prepared for violence in the transition to socialism.[38] This strong dissent from the Soviet view of the enemy was concurrent with Mao's announcement of China's "great leap forward" to the building of communism through the creation of communes.

Difficulties between the two centers of Communism were aggravated by the repetition of official statements from Moscow endorsing the possibility of coexistence and by Peking's policy toward India. Khrushchev's decision to journey to the United States in 1959 appeared to be a direct slap at the Chinese leadership, especially as the trip was preceded by an announcement that the Soviet government had no intention of providing the C.P.R. with an atomic bomb or technical data concerning the development of nuclear capabilities. Peking's reaction to this statement was not known in the West until August 15, 1963, when the Chinese accused Khrushchev of willfully breaking the Sino-Soviet technical aid accord of 1957.[39] *Pravda*, on September 10, 1959, took an equally cold attitude toward the Chinese provocations along the Indian border, saying that "it would be wrong not to express regret that the incident took place." The Kremlin refused to endorse the Chinese action, and the Chinese defied Premier Khrushchev by publishing an article in *Hung Ch'i* explaining the impossibility of coexistence.[40] The Soviet Premier, however, was not deterred from insisting on a more realistic appraisal of the "imperialist" powers. Soon after returning from the United States, Khrushchev traveled to Peking and delivered a lecture to the Chinese on the policy of coexistence.[41] The Soviet leadership appeared to be pressing the Chinese leaders to take a more realistic approach and to exercise greater caution in regard to relations with Western states. The Chinese contended that the policy of coexistence was in fact an admission that the very nature of imperialism had changed and that the conservatism of Soviet policy was tantamount to renouncing the revolutionary purpose of the Communist movement.

Chinese disapproval of Soviet policy toward India and Algeria indicated the different assessments given by the leaders of the two states to the national liberation movement. Moscow's conservative policy of fostering neutralism by providing economic assistance to underdeveloped countries and by crediting the leaders of many new states with prestige far in excess of their national power was repudiated by Peking. Nowhere was this more clearly demonstrated than during the Sino-Indian border war of 1962-1963. The Soviet government voiced its disapproval of the Chinese attack, and even announced that a new technical cooperation agreement with India had been approved while the war was still in progress.[42] In his report to the Supreme Soviet, Khrushchev commented on the Soviet Union's friendship with India and noted that history had proved that Lenin had been wiser in signing the Brest-Litovsk Peace than Trotsky had been in opposing it. Both references were obviously intended for China to digest. During the same period, the Cuban crisis occurred, ending with the withdrawal of Soviet missiles and Kosygin's speech on the wiseness of compromise and the correctness of Soviet policy. The Chinese were equally disturbed by the Soviet Union's sympathy for India and by the decision to withdraw the missiles from Cuba.[43] These policy differences had resulted in an exacerbation of the rift and contributed to the inability of the Chinese and Soviet delegations to restore harmony during the Moscow negotiations in the summer of 1963.

The Suslov report reaffirmed the disagreements of the two largest Communist parties on the issues of war, peace, and revolution. It charged the Chinese with thinking that war was necessary to provoke revolution and that war provided "the only means of settling the contradictions between capitalism and socialism." Particularly strong criticism was directed at the C.P.R. for extending the Sino-Indian conflict during the tense moments of the Cuban crisis and for opposing efforts to obtain disarmament. Suslov announced that the Soviet elite considered it "inexpedient" to help the Chinese produce nuclear weapons because such a course would lead to the acquisition of nuclear power by West Germany and Japan. The Chinese were deemed guilty of ignoring "the immense variety of conditions in which the countries of Asia, Africa, and Latin America exist." "Chinese representatives speak of nothing but the necessity for waging an armed struggle in those countries." The Suslov report held that "such tactics are particularly harmful now" and that the only interest of the C.P.C. leadership was "to establish control over the national liberation struggle in order to make it an instrument for the implementation of its hegemonic plans." The Chinese were accused of forming separate organizations in the less developed world to compete with older organizations supported by the Soviet Union; they had, moreover, attempted to set "the Eastern peoples apart on a nationalist and even racial basis." According to the official Soviet interpretation, the Chinese therefore denied the Leninist practice of uniting all the anti-imperialist forces of all countries in a solid front against the governments of capitalist states.

Although the Chinese concentrated their attacks as much on Khrushchev's leadership as on Soviet policy in general, the removal of Khrushchev in October, 1964, resulted in no more than a temporary truce. Many of the issues that divided Moscow and Peking remained. In fact, the question of Sino-Soviet relations was probably a less important reason for Khrushchev's removal than domestic considerations. Furthermore, the controversy with Peking was only the most dramatic illustration of the dissolving unity of the world Communist movement. At the 23rd Party Congress the Soviet leaders indicated no new approach toward the problems of the international movement and expressed hope for better relations with both the United States and China. However, in August, 1966, the Brezhnev-Kosygin leadership returned to the pattern set by Khrushchev by issuing a strong public denunciation of Chinese policies. In addition, Soviet troops began to install themselves along the Chinese border in camps that appeared to be intended for long-term use. Despite these moves, the strategic interests of the U.S.S.R. continued to center more on Europe and the Mediterranean area than on the Far East. Relations with the east European party-states and the prestige of the U.S.S.R. with the governments and Communist parties of western Europe remained the primary strategic concern of the Soviet elite.

The first rapprochement of the Soviet Union with Yugoslavia in 1955-1956 resulted in formal recognition of the possibility of different roads to socialism. This development was widely interpreted by the more "liberal" Communists in the east European states as a softening of Moscow's requirement of rigid conformity to the Soviet model in other party-states. The concurrent reduction in military and police control in eastern Europe and the corresponding emphasis on ideology and economic ties among the party-states as the principal instruments for maintaining unity placed a tremendous burden on ideology, and aggravated government-to-government relations.

The enormity of the burden placed on common ideological commitment was apparently not recognized by the Soviet leadership until the events in Poland and Hungary in 1956. Yet even then the Soviet policy-makers declined to employ force against the Poles in October and resorted to use of the army in Hungary only after the "counter-revolutionary" leadership was swept by popular dissatisfaction toward domestic and foreign policies that would probably have taken Hungary outside the Soviet orbit of influence altogether. The Kremlin's initial reaction to Imre Nagy's actions was to declare that they had been directed by "imperialists" from western Europe and North America. It was only after the revolt had been suppressed and emotions had calmed that the Soviet authorities admitted that "errors" of the Rakosi government had been largely responsible for the public unrest. But even after the revolts, the inadequacy of unity through ideology was not fully appreciated by the Kremlin.

The development of three independent sources of power within the system of party-states—Moscow, Peking, and Belgrade—and others less independent but no longer servile further complicated matters for the Soviet Union by increasing the possibility of different interpretations of Marxism-Leninism. Still clinging to the belief that ideology and economics were the keys to unity among socialist states, the Soviet leaders called the party conferences of 1957 and 1960 in the hope of producing a statement of principles that would guide all national Communist parties and, through Comecon, coordinate the plans of the east European states with those of the U.S.S.R. While seeking to exercise leadership of the system and at the same time permitting greater flexibility and relying more on consultation and persuasion, the Soviet leaders attempted to build ideological unity without issuing ex cathedra edicts from Moscow.

This approach not only encouraged greater goodwill, but reduced the financial burden of maintaining control through the secret police and the army. The reaffirmations of friendship with Tito after 1961 and the increasingly varied domestic programs of the east European states demonstrated the continuing commitment to recognizing different roads to socialism. However, good relations between Belgrade and Moscow were due to basic agreement on foreign policy, and the conflict between Moscow and Peking stemmed largely from differences on international questions. The Soviet elite was prepared to tolerate significant differences in domestic programs, but insisted on commitment to a single foreign policy among members of the socialist commonwealth. Not until 1964 did the Kremlin reluctantly acquiesce in the partial reassertion of independence in foreign affairs by Romania and other members of the system.

The disposition of Communists to conduct arguments in ideological terms should not be permitted to obscure the fundamental reasons for their differences. The right to interpret doctrine confers power on the interpreters. In the domestic power struggles of the Soviet Union, the conflicts between Stalin and Trotsky, Stalin and his other opponents of left and right, and Khrushchev and his various opponents never prevented the winner from adopting the policies of the defeated. The struggles after Lenin were usually less the result of fights for specific policies than of fights to be able to declare policy. The post-Stalin period witnessed the opening of the policy-making process to operational groups within the Soviet society, with the result that functional interests as well as personalities competed for a voice in public decision-making.

A similar development was taking place within the international Communist movement, stimulated by differences in national concepts of power and purpose. The polycentric tendencies within the system of party-states were manifestations of different economic and cultural levels, territorial disputes, conflicts over treaty obligations, and different assessments of particular national interests. The more the national party elites reflected the social structure of their respective states, the more they conceived of their nations' purposes in terms that were likely to contradict the views of other national elites. Thus each Communist country tended to assess differently its role in the Communist system, its evaluation of potential enemies, and its foreign policy objectives. That the Soviet and Chinese elites reached different conclusions about themselves and the nature of their enemies and the proper policies toward their adversaries is, therefore, not surprising. Because of the nature of these differences, whatever individuals gain power in the U.S.S.R. and the C.P.R., it is extremely unlikely that the reasons for the rift in the Communist world will disappear unless both countries undergo a profound transformation, and perhaps not even then.

The fact of dispute with China is probably not quite so bad in the eyes of the Soviet leaders as the *openness* of it. The undisguised struggle for dominance within the system of party-states has reduced the alternative policies toward the East European members of the system open to Soviet decision-makers, for the formerly subservient satellites are now in a position to play Moscow against Peking. Domestic economic and political problems combined with the disintegrating forces at work within the system have encouraged the introspective tendencies of the Soviet leadership and discouraged the reopening of bitter international rivalries with the United States.

Diversity has long been a prerequisite for economic and social growth in civilized societies. The leaders of Communist parties have been discovering that even Leninism could not prevent its resurgence.

CONCLUSION

I sometimes think that we are too much impressed by the clamor of daily events . . . it is the profound tendencies of history, and not the passing excitements, that will shape our future.

—John F. Kennedy

CONCLUSION

THE FORMATION of Soviet foreign policy is influenced by many factors. Perhaps the most important, also the most difficult to ascertain, is the internal conflict of groups that have acquired functional interests in the operation of the system. The interests most closely associated with foreign policy objectives have been the military establishment and the principal national economic sectors—heavy industry, light industry, and agriculture. As in most other countries, the military in the Soviet Union is not a monolithic establishment but is fragmented by different service orientations. The modernists and the traditionalists are separated in outlook and interest by different degrees of acceptance of modern weapons technology and of conventional forces. The different perceptions of the Western world by modernists and traditionalists correspond closely to their differences over basic military concepts. Similarly, in the development of military strategy, the alternatives considered closely parallel the operational interests of those who advocate them, and decisions reflect the status of each group in the power structure. The divisions over resource allocation, budgetary priorities and the role of the party in the economy also suggest that there is a high correlation between the functional interest of each group and the policies that it supports. Personalities are of course required to articulate positions, but the glamour of personalities should not be permitted to obscure more basic conflicts within the Soviet elite.

No single group holds a majority in the higher councils of the party and the state; a majority can be based only on a coalition of different interests. The majority is, therefore, fluid, and may shift from issue to issue or from one period to another. Policy shifts have come primarily on the basis of one of two criteria or a combination of the two, namely: (1) through the failure of existing policy to achieve the results expected by the decision-makers, or (2) through a change in the composition of the dominant coalition that can be accomplished only by the adoption of new policy. Alternative policies—whether on involvement in revolutionary situations in other countries, disarmament negotiations, trade expansion, personal diplomacy or other problem areas—have been evaluated and accepted or rejected by shifting aggregations of group interests and influential individuals. Serious setbacks have often resulted in the decline of the group associated with one policy and the rise of the advocates of another.

There have also been external influences on the formulation of foreign policy and of closely related areas of domestic policy. Relations with other party-states and the desire for unity within the Communist movement have exerted cross-pressures on the Soviet elite. The objectives articulated by Western leaders and the foreign policies of Western states have also, naturally, affected the choices of the Soviet leaders. This can be seen in Soviet policy not only toward Western states but toward the nonaligned nations, which Soviet decision-makers wish to keep nonaligned by foreign aid and trade programs and by cultivating their leaders.

At no point does it appear that Leninist theory excludes a significant range of policy choices from being considered by the Soviet leadership. Indeed, the theoretical modifications of Leninism formally enunciated during the Khrushchev period came after new trends in policy had already made their appearance. Peaceful coexistence had been suggested during the late Stalin period and had been used as a major theme during the Malenkov interregnum and at the Geneva Conference in 1955. Khrushchev, however, was responsible for shaping the military, economic, ideological and political aspects of coexistence and for defining their substantive content. The adoption of more flexible tactics toward the underdeveloped countries also began before theoretical modifications were formally made to stress the continuation of economic colonialism, the progressive potential of nationalism in new states, and National Democracy as a means of effecting the transition to socialism. The relaxation of Stalinist controls over other Communist states likewise began before the Soviet base theory and proletarian internationalism were modified to place emphasis on cooperation and coordination rather than on dictation. Also, all of the recent theoretical innovations had antecedents in earlier Leninist concepts and tactics, except those recognizing the noninevitability of war and the possibility of peaceful transition to socialism. Khrushchev's coalition defined and polished the ideas to give them greater substance and to adapt them to the needs of the Communist movement and the system of party-states in the nuclear and space age.

This is not to contend that Marxism-Leninism has an utterly meaningless relationship to Soviet policy. There is evidence to suggest that the concept of imperialism may play a definite role in the conceptual framework for analyzing developments in international politics. This theory leads the Kremlin leaders to anticipate certain behavior from capitalist states and to interpret events in the light of the assumptions of the theory. The notion of the imperialist enemy conditions the attitudes of Soviet decision-makers, encouraging them to view the West with hostility and suspicion and to exonerate themselves from what might otherwise be considered immoral behavior. The inability of Moscow to conduct a meaningful discourse with the leaders of the West can be traced in part to the Leninist theory of imperialism. However, as the test ban treaty illustrates, even this lack of consensus can be overcome under the weight of military and budgetary considerations and the mutual desire to survive.

On the other hand, the policy lines associated with peaceful coexistence reveal important nonideological influences. Although Khrushchev and his supporters insisted that the sole reason for modifying the theory of inevitable war was the conviction that the strength of the party-states was sufficient to deter capitalist aggression, realization of the destructiveness of nuclear war and of the retaliatory power of the United States appear to have been the dominant reasons for changing the theory. These considerations, rather than ideological precepts, guided Soviet behavior in Berlin, Cuba, and the conferences on disarmament and arms control. The persistent concern over the status of Germany represents a question of genuine national interest to the Soviet Union. Agreement with the West may be made difficult by the suspicion and distrust stimulated by tenets of the ideology, but protection of the national interests of the U.S.S.R. takes precedence over the immediate advancement of Communism when the Soviet Union is confronted with the possibility of a military response or any other form of threat to its own security.

The most important continuing function of ideology appears to be domestic. The premises of Marxism-Leninism provide the ruling elite with their principal means of rationalizing existing patterns of authority. Particularly since the decline in the use of terror, normative theory has served an enlarged purpose. It has provided the rulers with an instrument for indoctrinating the masses, thereby serving as a means of channeling public sentiment and of generating public enthusiasm in the struggle to achieve the goals of the Communist utopia. But ideology has not noticeably hampered its pragmatic consideration of policy alternatives in foreign and military affairs.

The impact of Marxism-Leninism on recent Soviet foreign

policy can be ascertained only in two general ways. In the first place, the concept of policy in terms of struggle persists in the present era. The formulation of many domestic economic goals on the basis of competition with the United States, with the hope of surpassing American output, reflects this tendency. The emphasis on struggle is closely related to the concept of imperialism. In the second place, the Kremlin rulers have been more prone to approach foreign policy in terms of a general strategy than leaders of Western states. The Leninist theory of colonialism, which sees the former colonial countries of the East as the surest path to control of the West, may well have contributed to the growth of Moscow's interest in the countries of Asia, the Middle East, Africa, and Latin America, particularly from 1958 through 1961. The Kremlin's campaign for influence in those nations has thus far been directed less toward securing military alliances than toward encouraging them to follow the Soviet model of rapid economic development and to remain independent of Western alliances. Indeed, the grand strategy of coexistence, developed under Khrushchev and continued under his successors, has been characterized by cautious attempts to reach a détente with the West in central Europe while concentrating Soviet resources on the developing states in order to enable them to increase their independence of their former colonizers. On the other hand, the existence of a powerful N.A.T.O. alliance in Europe left the Kremlin free to compete with the West on more favorable terms only in these less developed areas, so that practical considerations cannot be discounted as having influenced general policy plans.

Certainly, many of the particular policies associated with this grand strategy have not borne the stamp of Leninist doctrine and do not support the general strategy. The foreign aid program was taken from the American example and not from the pages of Communist scripture. Under this program, money has been lent to neutralist governments which have often imposed strong controls on local Communist parties. Government-to-government relationships have been established at the expense of national Communist parties. Specific policies, political, economic, and ideological, have frequently been intended to enhance the prestige of the Soviet Republic.

Apparently having expected more spectacular results than were forthcoming, the Soviet elite began to reduce their foreign policy campaign after the Cuban crisis of 1962. Domestic economic difficulties and internal problems within the system of party states undoubtedly played a large role in bringing about this retrenchment from foreign commitments in 1963-1965. In addition, serious problems over the appropriate and legitimate procedure in effecting the resolution of policy conflicts within the Soviet hierarchy were a major reason for the increasingly introspective outlook in the Kremlin. In fact, if the statements issued by the French and Italian Communist parties after the consultation of their leaders with Khrushchev's successors can be accepted as accurate reflections of the events that led to the downfall of the Soviet Premier, procedure in resolving controversies over major policy problems was more crucial than any disagreement over a specific policy in helping to forge the alliance of greatly varied interests that forced Khrushchev from power. The editorial comments of *Pravda* and *Izvestiia* two years after Brezhnev and Kosygin assumed Khrushchev's posts indicated that the ruling alliance had been able to agree temporarily on who would occupy the top positions but had not reached agreement on basic policy direction. All things were promised to all factions, a pledge that was impossible of fulfillment. Since decisions would have to be made about establishing priorities, a continuation of the interplay of coalitions and the resulting shifts in policies was likely to persist. Uncertainty in domestic politics would probably increase the tendency toward preoccupation with internal affairs. The promise of consumers' goods and improved welfare programs may eventually encourage the regime, whoever its leaders may be, to pay more attention to the problems of life at home and less to the issues of international politics except where those issues directly affect the national interests of the U.S.S.R.

What can Western leaders expect of Soviet intentions and actions during this period of change? The answers given in the past no longer suffice. The view that education and a high literacy rate in the Soviet Union lay the groundwork for reforms in the style of Western liberalism is unproved and unlikely. In fact, the notion smacks of ethnocentrism insofar as it is based on the belief that educated people anywhere will ultimately construct a political and economic system comparable to that familiar to the prognosticator. To expect the shifts in Soviet culture to result in the development of a liberal society is to expect far too much.

On the other hand, to expect the present regime to be able to perpetuate itself indefinitely without significant changes in both the structure and the style of its sociopolitical system is to attribute for greater power to the Soviet elite than it is capable of exercising. To accept Moscow's boasts as evidence both of what the leaders of the U.S.S.R. aim to do and of what they can do is to grant greater omniscience to Communist dogma than it has ever merited. To expect the Soviet Union to remain as it was under Joseph Stalin in 1935 or in 1950 is as misleading as to claim that it will someday and somehow turn into a liberal democracy. There is nothing in history to enable us to conclude that either side has attained such perfection as to be self-perpetuating and permanently stable.

What can be expected is change. If there is a law of social development it is this—technological innovations engender cultural change. New ideas and new means of implementing them induce alterations in cultural patterns. The weakening of the iron curtain that once protected East from West and West from East has enabled Moscow and Washington to begin to conduct a discourse, at least on some important topics. Exchanges of delegations of specialists, expanded trade, increased tourist traffic, broadened communications links of various kinds, supported by an ever-widening range of technological accomplishments, have opened the doors to other types of discourse and influence. The revival of pluralism in the system of party-states, the growing recognition of pluralism in the modern world of nation-states, and the existence of various group interests within national systems foreshadow the diversity that marks human civilization of whatever cultural origin. Pluralism itself, of course, does not breed security; it may indeed increase the number of differences that cause divisions of opinion and occasionally armed conflicts among men. But it is also a major factor in keeping open the doors to creativity and cultural growth. Perhaps the recognition of its desirability will someday enable man to harness its most explosive aspects.

The Soviet Union is not immune to the pressures brought by diversity. Changes will occur, but these changes will be made within the context of Soviet culture. The foreign policy of the U.S.S.R. can be expected to reflect those changes, but it can also be expected to pursue policies consonant with the interests of the Soviet Republic. So long as the nation-state system exists, national policies can be expected to reflect national concerns. Nicely organized, harmonious world systems are still the expression of utopian theories, not descriptions of reality. Nor are they likely to become so.

BIBLIOGRAPHY

NOTES

INDEX

SELECTED BIBLIOGRAPHY

Since many good, annotated bibliographies are available, it is not our intention to duplicate those efforts here. The need to do so is further diminished by the presentation of complete citations in the notes to this volume. Consequently, references to Soviet periodicals, translation series, public documents, and Western periodicals are omitted from the following list of suggested readings. The list is intended as a general guide to the reader who is interested in acquiring additional insight into Soviet foreign policy. In no way is it intended to be a complete presentation of available works on this wide-ranging and complex subject.

The only additional works to which the author wishes to call attention are the monograph series of Sidney I. Ploss of the Foreign Policy Research Institute of the University of Pennsylvania and the series prepared under the direction of Jan F. Triska of the Stanford Studies of the Communist System.

Armstrong, John A., *The Politics of Totalitarianism*, New York: Random House, 1961.

Aubrey, Henry G., *Coexistence: Economic Challenge and Response*, Washington: National Planning Association, 1961.

Barghoorn, Frederick C., *The Soviet Cultural Offensive*, Princeton: Princeton University Press, 1960.

Barghoorn, Frederick C., *Soviet Foreign Propaganda*, Princeton: Princeton University Press, 1964.

Berdyaev, Nicolas, *The Origin of Russian Communism*, Ann Arbor: University of Michigan Press, 1960.

Bergson, Abram, and Kuznets, Simon, *Economic Trends in the Soviet Union*, Cambridge: Harvard University Press, 1963.

Berliner, Joseph S., *Soviet Economic Aid*, New York: Praeger, 1958.

Black, Cyril E., and Thornton, Thomas P., *Communism and Revolution: The Strategic Uses of Political Violence*, Princeton: Princeton University Press, 1964.

Bornstein, Morris, and Fusfeld, Daniel R., eds., *The Soviet Economy*, Homewood, Ill.: Richard D. Irwin, Inc., 1962.

Bromke, Adam, ed., *The Communist States at the Crossroads*, New York: Praeger, 1965.

Brown, J. F., *The New Eastern Europe*, New York: Praeger, 1966.

Brzezinski, Zbigniew K., *Ideology and Power in the Soviet Union*, New York: Praeger, 1962.

Brzezinski, Zbigniew K., *The Soviet Bloc: Unity and Conflict*, Cambridge: Harvard University Press, 1960.

Champassak, Sisouk Na, *Storm over Laos*, New York: Praeger, 1961.

Conquest, Robert, *Power and Policy in the USSR: The Study of Soviet Dynamics*, London: Macmillan, 1961.

Crankshaw, Edward, *Cracks in the Kremlin Walls*, New York: Viking, 1951.

Crankshaw, Edward, *Khrushchev's Russia*, Baltimore: Penguin Books, 1963.

Dallin, Alexander, ed., *Soviet Conduct in World Affairs*, New York: Columbia University Press, 1960.

Dallin, Alexander, *The Soviet Union and the United Nations*, New York: Praeger, 1962.

Dallin, David J., *Soviet Foreign Policy After Stalin*, Philadelphia: Lippincott, 1961.

Deutscher, Isaac, *Stalin: A Political Biography*, New York: Random House, 1960.

Dinerstein, Herbert S., *War and the Soviet Union*, rev. ed., New York: Praeger, 1962.

Economic Commission for Europe, *U.N. Economic Survey of Europe in 1962*, E/ECE/493, 1963.

Embree, G. D., *The Soviet Union between the 19th and 20th Party Congresses, 1952-1956*, The Hague: Martinus Nijhoff, 1959.

Garthoff, Raymond, *Soviet Strategy in the Nuclear Age*, 2nd ed., New York: Praeger, 1962.

Gibney, Krank, *The Khrushchev Pattern*, New York: Duell, Sloan & Pearce, 1960.

Goldwin, Robert A., ed., *Beyond the Cold War*, Chicago: Rand McNally, 1965.

Goodman, Elliot, *The Soviet Design for a World State*, New York: Columbia University Press, 1960.

Kellen, Konrad, *Khrushchev: A Political Portrait*, New York: Praeger, 1961.

Kirkpatrick, Evron M., ed., *Target: The World*, New York: Macmillan, 1956.

Kirkpatrick, Evron M., ed., *Year of Crisis*, New York: Macmillan, 1957.

Kulski, Wladyslaw Wszebor, *Peaceful Coexistence*, Chicago: Regnery, 1959.

Laqueur, Walter Z., *The Soviet Union and the Middle East*, New York: Praeger, 1959.

Laqueur, Walter, and Labedz, Leopold, eds., *Polycentrism*, New York: Praeger, 1962.

Lederer, Ivo J., ed., *Russian Foreign Policy*, New Haven: Yale University Press, 1962.

Levin, D. B., *Diplomatiia*, Moscow: Gosudarstvennoe Izdatel'stvo, 1963.

Mackintosh, J. M., *Strategy and Tactics of Soviet Foreign Policy*, London: Oxford University Press, 1962.

Mander, John, *Berlin: Hostage for the West*, Baltimore: Penguin Books, 1962.

Meyer, Alfred G., *Leninism*, New York: Praeger, 1962.

Meyer, Alfred G., *Marxism: The Unity of Theory and Practice*, Cambridge: Harvard University Press, 1954.

Meyer, Alfred G., *The Soviet Political System*, New York: Random House, 1965.

Moore, Barrington, Jr., *Soviet Politics—The Dilemma of Power*, Cambridge: Harvard University Press, 1950.

Mezhdunarodnye otnosheniia i vneshniaia politika SSSR, Moscow: Gosudarstvennoe Izdatel'stvo, 1961.

Nove, Alec, *Communist Economic Strategy*, Washington: National Planning Association, 1959.

Page, Stanley W., *Lenin and World Revolution*, New York: New York University Press, 1959.

Penkovskiy, Oleg, *The Penkovskiy Papers*, trans. Peter Deriabin, New York: Doubleday, 1965.

Pentony, Devere E., ed., *Soviet Behavior in World Affairs: Communist Foreign Policies*, San Francisco: Chandler Publishing Co., 1962.

Pethybridge, Roger, *A Key to Soviet Politics*, New York: Praeger, 1961.

Pistrak, Lazar, *The Grand Tactician: Khrushchev's Rise to Power*, New York: Praeger, 1961.

Pokrovsky, G. I., *Science and Technology in Contemporary War*, trans. Raymond L. Garthoff, New York: Praeger, 1959.

Polezhaev, V. N., and Yakobson, G. M., *Mezhdunarodnye ekonomikie organizatsii i soglasheniia*, Moscow: Vneshtorgizdat, 1961.

Reshetar, John S., *Problems of Analyzing and Predicting Soviet Behavior*, New York: Doubleday, 1955.

Rimalov, V., *Economic Cooperation Between the USSR and Underdeveloped Countries*, Moscow: Foreign Languages Publishing House, 1962.

Ritvo, Herbert, *The New Soviet Society*, New York: The New Leader, 1962.

Robinson, Thomas W., *A National Interest Analysis of Sino-Soviet Relations*, The Rand Corporation, P-3319, 1966.

Rostow, Walt Whitman, *The Dynamics of Soviet Society*, New York: Norton, 1953.

Rotmistrov, P. A., ed., *Istoriia voennogo iskusstva*, tom 2, Moscow: Voennoe Izdatel'stvo Ministerstva Oborony SSSR, 1963.

Rush, Myron, *The Rise of Khrushchev*, Washington: Public Affairs Press, 1958.

Sbornik: torgovykh dogovoro, torgovykh i platezhnykh soglashenii, i golgosrochnykh torgovykh soglashenii SSSR s inostrannymi gosudarstvami, Moscow: Vneshtorgizdat, 1961.

Schuman, Frederick L., *The Cold War: Retrospect and Prospect*, Baton Rouge: Louisiana State University Press, 1962.

Seton-Watson, Hugh, *From Lenin to Khrushchev*, New York: Praeger, 1957.

Shulman, Marshall D., *Stalin's Foreign Policy Reappraised*, Cambridge: Harvard University Press, 1963.

Sokolovskii, V. D., *Soviet Military Strategy*, translated, analyzed and annotated by H. S. Dinerstein, Leon Goure, and Thomas W. Wolfe, Englewood Cliffs, N. J.: Prentice Hall, 1963.

Spanier, John W., and Nogee, Joseph L., *The Politics of Disarmament*, New York: Praeger, 1962.

Sultanov, A. F., ed., *Sovetsko-Arabskie druzhestvennye otnosheniia*, Moscow: Gosudarstvoe Izdatel'stvo, 1961.

Tanham, George K., *Communist Revolutionary Warfare*, New York: Praeger, 1961.

Ul'ianvoskii, R. A., *Neokolonializm SShA i slaborazvitye strany Azii*, Moscow: Izdatel'stvo Vostochoi Literatury, 1963.

U.S. Department of Defense, *The Communist Economic Offensive*, DOD Pam 4-84, November, 1961.

U.S. Department of State, *Background of Heads of Government Conference 1960. Principal Documents*, 1955-1959, D/S 6972, Washington: Government Printing Office, 1960.

Zagoria, Donald S., *The Sino-Soviet Conflict: 1956-1961*, Princeton: Princeton University Press, 1962.

NOTES

2. THE THEORETICAL FOUNDATIONS OF COEXISTENCE

1. For different interpretations of the role of Marxism-Leninism in the Soviet system, see Alexander Dallin, *Soviet Conduct in World Affairs*, New York: Columbia University Press, 1960; Barrington Moore, Jr., *Soviet Politics: The Dilemma of Power*, Cambridge: Harvard University Press, 1950; Zbigniew Brzezinski, *Ideology and Power in the Soviet Union*, New York: Praeger, 1962; Alfred G. Meyer, *The Soviet Political System*, New York: Random House, 1965 .

2. Stalin, *Foundations of Leninism*, New York: International Publishers, 1939, p. 29.

3. Lenin, "Zadachi soyuzov molodezhi," *Sochineniia*, 31, p. 269.

4. Lenin, "Left-Wing Communism: An Infantile Disorder," *Selected Works*, London: Lawrence and Wishart, Ltd., 1938, X, p. 138.

5. Lenin, "Dve taktiki sotsial-demokratii v demokraticheskoi revolutsii," *Sochineniia*, 9, p. 67.

6. This view is concisely stated in a paragraph Lenin wrote as an insert to an article by V. Kalinin. See *Sochineniia*, 9, p. 423.

7. Stalin, *Leninism: Selected Writings by Joseph Stalin*, New York: International Publishers, 1942, pp. 41-42.

8. Lenin, *Sochineniia*, 9, pp. 35-36.

9. Lenin, *State and Revolution*, New York: International Publishers, 1932, p. 17.

10. Stalin, *Leninism: Selected Writings*, pp. 424-426.

11. P. Fedoseev, *Bolshevik*, No. 14 (July, 1948). On this general subject, note Cyril E. Black and Thomas P. Thornton, *Communism and Revolution: The Strategic Uses of Political Violence*, Princeton: Princeton University Press, 1964. In particular see the first three essays by Cyril E. Black, Andrew C. Janos, and Thomas P. Thornton, pp. 3-74.

12. Lenin, *Imperialism—The Highest Stage of Capitalism*, New York: International Publishers, 1939, pp. 120-121.

13. Stalin, "Marxism and the National Questions," *Collected Works*, 1946 edition, II, p. 328.

14. VI Congress of the Communist International, *Handbook of Marxism*, Emile Burns, ed., New York: International Publishers, 1935, p. 990.

15. Lenin, "Rech na sobranii aktiva moskovskoi organizatsii RKP(b)," *Sochineniia*, 31, pp. 426-427.

16. *Resolutions of VI Congress*, Vol. 8, No. 84, New York: International Publishers, 1930, p. 1590.

17. *Pravda*, May 8, 1947. Stalin also expressed this view in interviews with Roy M. Howard in *The New York Times*, March 5, 1936, and with Alexander Werth in *The Times* (London), September 25, 1946.

18. For a slightly different interpretation of Stalin's concept of coexistence, see Marshall D. Shulman, *Stalin's Foreign Policy Reappraised*, Cambridge: Harvard University Press, 1963, pp. 51-79, 176-198.

19. For an excellent discussion of this transformation in Lenin's thought, see Stanley W. Page, *Lenin and World Revolution*, New York: New York University Press, 1959, p. 135ff.

20. See Stalin, "The National Question," reprinted in *Marxism and the National and Colonial Question*, New York: International Publishers, 1935, pp. 195-199. This article stresses the importance of a broad revolutionary front and of attracting mass peasant support. Also see "The Political Tasks of the University of the Peoples of the East," in the same volume, pp. 206-220.

21. *Pravda*, October 29, 1961.

22. "Khrushchev's Secret Speech," reprinted in *The New Communist Manifesto and Related Documents*, 2nd ed., Daniel N. Jacobs, ed., Evanston, Ill.: Row, Peterson, 1962, pp. 86-87.

23. N. S. Khrushchev, "Za novye pobedy mirovogo kommunisticheskogo dvizheniia," *Kommunist*, No. 1 (January, 1961), p. 20. This article is the official text of Khrushchev's report on the 1960 conference of Communist party leaders to the meeting of Soviet party workers on January 6, 1961. The meeting was a C.P.S.U. Central Committee project that included the Higher Party School, the Academy of Social Sciences, and members of the Institute.

24. See the editorial on morality in *Pravda*, April 4, 1955, and the article by A. Alyoshin, "The Source of Our Strength," in *New Times*, No. 37 (September, 1961), p. 7.

25. E. Varga, "*Kapital* K. Marksa i sovremennyi kapitalism," *Kommunist*, No. 17 (November, 1961), p. 43. Also see *Fundamentals of Marxism-Leninism*, Moscow: Foreign Languages Publishing House, 1961, pp. 294-369.

26. See Karen Brutents, "The Doom of Colonialism," *New Times*, No. 44 (October, 1961), p. 10, and Dmitry Volsky, "The 'Gradual Withdrawal' Tactic," *New Times*, No. 46 (November, 1961), p. 11.

27. A. Belyakov and F. Burlatsky, "The Leninist Theory of Socialist Revolution and Our Times," *Kommunist*, No. 13 (September, 1960), p. 10ff. *Current Digest of the Soviet Press*, XII, 39, p. 10.

28. Khrushchev, *Report to the 20th Party Congress*, Moscow: Foreign Languages Publishing House, p. 45.

29. A. Sobelov, "O parlamentskoi forme perekhoda k sotsialismu," *Kommunist*, No. 14 (September, 1956), pp. 31-32.

30. See B. Ponomarev, "Concerning the Nation-Democratic State," *Kommunist*, No. 8 (May, 1961), p. 33ff. *Current Digest of the Soviet Press* XIII, 22, p. 5. Also note *Kommunist*, No. 13 (September, 1962), pp. 89-109.

31. *Pravda*, June 22, 1960.

32. *Izvestiia*, January 17, 1963.

33. Y. Arbatov, "The Dialectics of Militarism," *World Marxist Review*, III (June, 1960), p. 9.

34. Khrushchev, *Report*, pp. 41-42.

35. L. Moskvin, "Tvorcheskii marksizm-leninizm i vneshniaia politika SSSR," *Mirovaia ekonomika i mezhdunarodnye otnosheniia*, No. 3, 1964, p. 7.

36. D. Aleksandrov, "Mirnoe sosushchestvovanie i sud'by chelovechestva," *Mirovaia ekonomika i mezhdunarodnye otnosheniia*, No. 11, 1963, p. 9.

37. N. S. Khrushchev, "O mire i mirnom sosushchestvovanii," *Kommunist*, No. 7, 1964, pp. 3-5.

38. *Pravda*, August 12, 1960.

39. C. I. Beglov, "Razvitie leninskikh printsipov mirnogo sosushchestvovaniia v trudakh N. S. Khrushcheva," *Voprosy Istorii*, No. 4, 1964, p. 18.

40. Quote from Khrushchev, ibid., p. 16.

41. Khrushchev, "O mire i mirnom sosushchestvovanii. . . .", p. 5.

42. Belyakov and Burlatsky, "The Leninist Theory . . . ," p. 6.

43. *Decisions of the 21st Extraordinary Congress of the* VPSU, Moscow: Foreign Languages Publishing House, 1959, p. 29.

44. L. Moskvin, "Tvorcheskii marksism-leninism . . . ," p. 6.

45. Khrushchev, "O mire i mirnom sosushchestvovanii . . . ," p. 7.

46. S. I. Beglov, "Razvitie leninski. . . . ," p. 13. Also see A. Popov and A. Sergeev, "Mirnoe sosushchestvovaniie general'nyi kurs sovetskoi vneshnei politiki," *Kommunist*, No. 18 (December, 1961), pp. 54-62.

47. *Pravda*, November 1, 1959.

48. See O. Nakropin and V. Sukhodeev, "Mirovaia politika i bor'ba dvukh ideologii," *Mirovaia ekonomika i mezhdunarodnye otnosheniia*, No. 9, 1963, pp. 3-14. This article is a response to Chinese criticism and defends the conclusion of agreements with non-Communist states.

49. See the detailed amplification of this theme in the essays contained in A. A. Gromyko, ed., *Mirnoe sosushchestvovanie—leninskii kurs vneshnei politiki sovetskogo soiuza*, Moscow: Izdatel'stvo IMO, 1962.

3. THE REVOLUTION IN SOVIET MILITARY DOCTRINE

1. H. S. Dinerstein, *War and the Soviet Union*, rev. ed., New York: Praeger, 1962, and R. L. Garthoff, *Soviet Strategy in the Nuclear Age*, 2nd ed., New York: Praeger, 1962.

2. See *Krasnaia zvezda*, January 25, 1956, April 26, 1956, and May 12, 1957.

3. See the account of the anti-party crisis by Roger Pethybridge, *A Key to Soviet Politics*, New York: Praeger, 1962.

4. *Izvestiia*, May 12, 1955.

5. *Pravda*, August 7, 1956.

6. I. Bagramyan, "The Glorious Fighting Path," *Kommunist*, No. 2 (February, 1958), p. 34ff. *Current Digest of the Soviet Press*, X, 1, p. 10.

7. *Izvestiia*, January 15, 1960.

8. Penkovski was tried for "betraying the homeland" by providing agents of Western governments with "secret, top secret" information, some of which "constituted state and military secrets of the Soviet Union." See *Pravda*, May 12, 1963.

9. For the modernist position, see Colonel P. Sidorov, "Neustanno krepit' oboronosposobnost' strany," *Kommunist vooruzhennykh sil*, No. 12 (June, 1961), pp. 59-65, and Colonel N. Sushko et al., "Razvitie marksistso-leninskogo ucheniia o voine v sovremennykh usloviiakh," *Kommunist vooruzhennykh sil*, No. 18 (September, 1961), pp. 19-29. For the traditionalist view, see Marshal A. A. Grechko, "Voennaia istoriia i sovremennost'," *Voenno-istoricheskii zhurnal*, No. 2 (February, 1961), pp. 3-12, and General P. Kuruchkin, "Ob izuchenii istorii voennogo iskusstva v sovremennykh usloviiakh," *Voenno-istoricheskii zhurnal*, No. 8 (August, 1961), pp. 3-12. Also note *Krasnaia zvezda*, April 5, 1961, in which Colonel A. M. Iovlev stressed the need for mass armies despite the changing means of conducting modern warfare.

10. See the studies of Sidney I. Ploss, "On the Conflict in Moscow" (May 16, 1963) and "A New Phase of the Soviet Policy Debate" (October 16, 1963), Center of International Studies, Princeton University. Also note the sharp distinction drawn between American "realists" and "rightists" in B. Dmitriev, "SShA: ugroza sprava," *Mirovaia ekonomika i mezdunarodnye otnosheniia*, No. 10, 1962, pp. 27-38.

11. *Pravda*, January 26, 1961.

12. *Vooruzhennye sily NATO*, Moscow: Voennoe izdatel'stvo Ministerstva oborony SSSR, 1962, pp. 20-24, 61-75, and 103-110.

13. *Pravda*, May 2, 1963.

14. *Pravda*, April 7, 1964.

15. The conflicts involving Kozlov and Podgorny have been closely followed by Sidney I. Ploss in his studies on the shifting alignments in the Soviet elite. See 'Some Political Aspects of the June 1963 CPSU Central Committee Session" (August 28, 1963) and "Recent Alignments in the Soviet Elite" (March 16, 1964), pp. 23-28. Also note Roman Kolkowicz, "Conflicts in Soviet Party-Military Relations, 1962-1963," The Rand Corporation RM-3760-PR (August, 1963).

16. Sydney Gruson reporting in *The New York Times*, April 5, 1963.

17. Morris Bornstein and Daniel R. Fusfeld, eds., *The Soviet Economy*, Homewood, Ill.: Richard D. Irwin, Inc., 1962, p. 17.

18. Abram Bergson and Simon Kuznets, *Economic Trends in the Soviet Union*, Cambridge: Harvard University Press, 1963, p. 359.

19. See the thoughtful and provocative article by Lynn Turgeon, "The Enigma of Soviet Defense Expenditures," *The Journal of Con-*

flict Resolution, Vol. VIII, No. 2 (June, 1964), pp. 116-120. Turgeon notes: "To assume that an economic system which turns out less than half of our total product could support a defense establishment which in real terms is equal to ours, and still maintain rates of industrial growth which are over twice as great as ours, is to attribute greater efficiency to the overall operations of the Soviet system than seems warranted" (p. 119).

20. Quoted in Sidney I. Ploss, "A New Phase of the Soviet Policy Debates" (October 16, 1963), p. 8.

21. *Izvestiia*, October 15, October 20, and November 17, 1963.

22. *Izvestiia*, October 26, 1963.

23. Khrushchev, "O mire i mirnom sosushchestvovanii," *Kommunist*, No. 7, 1964, p. 6.

24. *Pravda*, April 18, 1964.

25. V. D. Sokolovskii, *Soviet Military Strategy*, translated, analyzed, and annotated by H. S. Dinerstein, Leon Goure, and Thomas W. Wolfe, Englewood Cliffs, N.J.: Prentice Hall, 1963. Future references and quotations are to this edition.

26. Ibid., p. 158. This attention devoted to American works on military strategy is further illustrated in interesting fashion in M. Mil'shtein, "O nekotorykh voenno-strategicheskikh kontseptsiakh amerikanskogo imperializma," *Mirovaia ekonomika i mezhdunarodnye otnosheniia*, No. 8, 1962, pp. 85-95.

27. *Krasnaia zvezda*, May 9, 1963.

28. Sokolovskii, p. 419. Also note the display of rockets designated as antimissile missiles in the parade for the celebration of the 46th anniversary of the October Revolution. See *Pravda*, November 8, 1963.

29. P. A. Rotmistrov, ed., *Istoriia voennogo iskusstva*, tom 2, Moscow: Voennoe Izdatel'stvo Ministerstva Oborony SSSR, 1963, p. 707. A degree of ambivalence between old and new concepts is particularly apparent in the conclusion. See pp. 708-711.

30. See Sokolovskii, editor's introduction, p. 11.

31. *Pravda*, July 30, 1959.

32. Khrushchev, "Za novye pobedy mirovogo kommunisticheskogo dvizheniia," *Kommunist*, No. 1 (January, 1961), p. 20.

33. *Pravda*, January 17, 1963.

34. *Pravda*, October 1, 1959. *Current Digest of the Soviet Press*, XI, 39, pp. 21-22.

35. Khrushchev, "Za novye pobedy . . . ," pp. 17-18.

4. MILITARY ENGAGEMENT AND DISARMAMENT IN SOVIET POLICY

1. See Walter Z. Laqueur, *The Soviet Union and the Middle East*, New York: Praeger, 1959, pp. 235-240.

2. David J. Dallin, *Soviet Foreign Policy after Stalin*, Philadelphia: Lippincott, 1961, p. 476.

3. Zbigniew K. Brzezinski, *The Soviet Bloc: Unity and Conflict*, Cambridge: Harvard University Press, 1960, pp. 253-260.

4. Ferenc A. Vali, *Rift and Revolt in Hungary*, Cambridge: Harvard University Press, 1961, p. 360. For the Eisenhower announcement, see *The New York Times*, November 1, 1956.

5. See the soundly reasoned arguments in Arnold L. Horelick, "The Cuban Missile Crisis: An Analysis of Soviet Calculations and Behavior," *World Politics*, Vol. XVI, No. 3 (April, 1964), pp. 363-389.

6. V. Gantman et al., "Tekushchie problemy mirovoi politiki," *Mirovaia ekonomika i mezhdunarodnye otnosheniia*, No. 1, 1963, p. 6.

7. *Vital Speeches of the Day*, August 1, 1962, pp. 626-629. Also see Roger Hagan and Bart Bernstein, "Military Value of Missiles in Cuba," *Bulletin of the Atomic Scientists*, XIX (February, 1963), pp. 8-13.

8. Dallin, *Soviet Foreign Policy . . .*, p. 415, and Laqueur, "*The Soviet Union . . .*," p. 235.

9. Jan F. Triska, *Pattern and Level of Risk in Soviet Foreign Policy-Making:* 1945-1963, Research Paper No. 4, Stanford Studies of the Communist System, 1965.

10. Victor P. Karpov, "Soviet Stand on Disarmament," *The Journal of Conflict Resolution*, Vol. VII, No. 3, p. 333CR.

11. Ibid., p. 334CR.

12. See the anonymous article "On Thermonuclear Coexistence," in *Survey*, No. 39 (December, 1961), pp. 3-16.

13. U.N. Document DC/SC.1/26/Rev.2, Annex 15 (May 10, 1955), p. 19.

14. Ibid., p. 20.

15. Izvestiia, December 30, 1955.

16. U.N. Document DC/SC.1/PV.73 (March 27, 1956), pp. 10-11.

17. U.N. Document DC/SC.1/41, Annex 5 (March 27, 1956), pp. 6-7.

18. See U.N. Document DC/SC.1/PV.87 (March 18, 1957), p. 23; U.N. Document DC/SC.1/PV.109 (April 30, 1957), pp. 2-30; U.N. Document DC/SC.1/65/Rev.1, Annex 4 (August 27, 1957), pp. 1-31; U.N. Document DC/SC.1/PV.151 (August 27, 1957), pp. 2-32.

19. United Nations, General Assembly, Fourteenth Session, Plenary, *Official Records*, 799th Meeting (September 18, 1959).

20. Karpov, "Soviet Stand on Disarmament . . .", p. 334CR.

21. Ibid., p. 335CR.

22. United Nations, General Assembly, Fourteenth Session, Plenary, *Official Records*, 799th Meeting (September 18, 1959), p. 37.

23. Some authors assign propaganda the highest priority among the reasons that both sides participate in disarmament negotiations. Joseph L. Nogee suggests that the objectives in the "propaganda duel" have been: "(1) To maneuver the other side into a public recognition of the necessity and legitimacy of its principal position. For the Soviet bloc that meant getting the Western powers to endorse general and complete disarmament. For the Western powers that involved obtaining a recognition from the Soviets of the necessity for adequate control. (2) To portray its own plan as realistic and concrete; and conversely to expose the unreasonableness and unfairness of the opposition proposals. (3) To divide or reinforce divisions within the opposing team." See Joseph L. Nogee, "Propaganda and Negotiation: the Case of the Ten-Nation Disarmament Committee," *The Journal of Conflict Resolution*, Vol. VII, No. 3, pp. 513CR-514CR. Also note Joseph L. Nogee and John W. Spanier, *The Politics of Disarmament*, New York: Praeger, 1962. Nogee and Spanier contend that the history of disarmament negotiations is a study of gamesmanship in which each party deliberately creates a "joker" in order to make its proposal unacceptable to the other. This interpretation has been seriously challenged in an exceptionally well-documented article by Lloyd Jensen, "Soviet-American Bargaining Behavior in the Postwar Disarmament Negotiations," *The Journal of Conflict Resolution*, Vol. VII, No. 3, pp. 522CR-541CR. Jensen argues that the inclusion of a proposition that is legitimately considered a vital interest to one party, though it is unacceptable to the other party, cannot be properly described as a "joker." Therefore, the problem essentially remains one of conflicting vital interests.

24. See the cogently presented arguments of Walter C. Clemens, Jr., "Ideology in Soviet Disarmament Policy," *The Journal of Conflict Resolution*, Vol. VIII, No. 1 (March, 1964), pp. 7-22. Clemens

concludes that "it is the West's distrust of Communist Russia which is probably the greatest area of influence on the disarmament negotiations exercised by Soviet ideology. It is the influence that may be the most difficult to overcome." (p. 19).

25. United Nations General Assembly, Twelfth Session, Plenary, *Official Records*, 697th Meeting (October 2, 1957), pp. 235-237.

26. U.N. Document DC/SC.1/73, Annex 12 (September 5, 1957), p. 20.

27. *Pravda*, November 12, 1957.

28. *Izvestiia*, April 1, 1958.

29. *Izvestiia*, December 24, 1957.

30. *Izvestiia*, April 1, 1958.

31. U.N. Document A/4078, S/4145, Annex 15 (December 18, 1958).

32. E. Alekseev et al., "Tekushchie problemy mirovoi politiki," *Mirovaia ekonomika i mezhdunarodnye otnosheniia*, No. 7, 1962, p. 11.

33. *Izvestiia*, April 25, 1962.

34. Jensen, "Soviet-American Bargaining Behavior . . . ," p. 541CR.

35. *Izvestiia*, April 1, 1958.

36. See *Izvestiia*, October 3, 1958, and *Pravda*, August 31, 1961, for the announcements of the resumption of testing.

37. *Izvestiia*, January 22, 1963.

38. See *Pravda*, December 4, 1962. Also note Sidney I. Ploss, "Some Political Aspects of the June 1963 CPSU Central Committee Session," Center of International Studies, Princeton University (August 28, 1963), pp. 23-24.

39. *Pravda*, August 3, 1963.

40. N. Sergeeva et al., "Tekushchie problemy mirovoi politiki," *Mirovaia ekonomika i mezhdunarodnye otnosheniia*, No. 10, 1963, pp. 80-81.

41. Ibid., p. 79.

5. SOVIET ECONOMICS AND THE POLITICS OF FOREIGN AID AND TRADE

1. *Vneocherednoi XXI S'ezd Kommunisticheskoi Partii Sovetskogo Soiuza*, Moscow: Government Printing House, 1959, p. 63.

2. "Economic Development of the Socialist Countries," Supplement, *World Marxist Review* (January, 1961).

3. Ibid., pp. 107 and 115.

4. *Izvestiia*, December 27, 1960.

5. "The Soviet Economy in 1963," *New Times*, No. 51 (December, 1962), p. 3.

6. "Soviet Economic Progress in 1962," *New Times*, No. 5 (February, 1963), p. 12.

7. *Izvestiia*, January 24, 1964. The Economic Commission for Europe of the United Nations noted that the growth rate of the U.S.S.R. fell from 8 per cent in 1960 to 6 per cent in 1962. The 1963 rate was probably closer to 4 per cent. See Economic Commission for Europe, *U.N. Economic Survey of Europe in 1962*, E/ECE/493, 1963, p. 1.

8. See A. M. Alexeyev, "The Soviet Union in 1980," *New Times*, No. 35 (August, 1961), p. 5.

9. See *Decisions of the Twenty-first Extraordinary Congress of the C.P.S.U.*, Moscow: Foreign Languages Publishing House, 1959.

10. See Roger Pethybridge, *A Key to Soviet Politics*, New York: Praeger, 1962, pp. 74-76.

11. See Robert Conquest, *Power and Policy in the USSR: The Study of Soviet Dynamics*, London: Macmillan, 1961, pp. 292-328.

12. *Izvestiia*, March 30, 1957.

13. *Pravda*, December 1, 1962.

14. *Pravda*, December 9, 1962; also see *Partiniia zhizn*, No. 2 (January 18, 1963), p. 18.

15. *Izvestiia*, December 19, 1962.

16. *Pravda*, December 6, 1962.

17. *Pravda*, December 4, 1962.

18. *Izvestiia*, April 24, 1963.

19. Quoted in Sidney I. Ploss, "Some Political Aspects of the June 1963 CPSU Central Committee Session," Princeton Center of International Studies (August 28, 1963), p. 17.

20. A. Tolkachev and V. Kudrov, "Kliuch k resheniiu vozhneishikh narodnokhoziaistvennykh problem," *Mirovaia ekonomika i mezhdunarodnye otnosheniia*, No. 2, 1964, p. 9 and p. 11.

21. Yu. M. Kozlov, "Sootnoshenie kollegial'nosti i edinonachaliia v sovetskom gosudarstvennom upravlenii na sovremennom etape," *Sovetskoe gosudarstvo i pravo*, No. 2, 1964, p. 29.

22. Ibid., p. 31.

23. G. I. Khaids, "V. I. Lenin ob osnovnykh polozheniiakh sotsialisticheskogo narodnokhoziaistvennogo planirovaniia," *Sovetskoe gos-*

udarstvo i pravo, No. 4, 1964, p. 40. The author attempts to bolster Khrushchev's position at the November 1962 Plenum by citing the works of Lenin to demonstrate that he ostensibly took a similar position by demanding that "people of science and technology constantly take part in the organizations of planning and economic work. . . ." (p. 42). Another author stresses the roles of state committees and Gosplan in the central planning processes, almost completely ignoring the Supreme Economic Council. See Ts. A. Yampol'skaia, "O razvitii strukhturno-organizatsionnykh form gosudarstvennogo upravleniia," *Sovetskoe gosudarstvo i pravo,* No. 6, 1964, pp. 31-40.

24. Khaids, "V. I. Lenin ob osnovykhu . . ." p. 43. Also note the support given the decisions of the November 1962 Plenum of the Central Committee in A. S. Malenkin, "O nekotorykh voprosakh deiatel'nosti organov partiino-gosudarstvennogo knotrolia Ukrainy," *Sovetskoe gosudarstvo i pravo,* No. 3, 1963, pp. 36-44, and in I. A. Zenin, "O proisvodstvennom kooperirovanii," *Sovetskoe gosudarstvo i pravo,* No. 5, 1964, pp. 61-68.

25. In particular see "Party Guidance of the Economy," *Kommunist,* No. 16, 1963, pp. 3-12; *Current Digest of the Soviet Press,* XV, 50, pp. 13-15. The articles previously cited in *Sovetskoe gosudarstvo i pravo* also endorse the utilitarians' view of the role of the party in economic functions.

26. V. N. Polezhaev and G. M. Yakobson, *Mezhdunarodnye ekonomikie organizatsii i soglasheniia,* Moscow: Vneshtorguzdat, 1961, p. 185.

27. Ibid., p. 186.

28. *New Times,* No. 3 (January, 1958), p. 5.

29. See Viliam Siroky, "Economic Foundations of the Peaceful Policy of the Socialist Countries," *World Marxist Review* (April, 1959), p. 17.

30. "Economic Development of the Socialist Countries," p. 128.

31. See N. Volkov and A. Netrusov, "Strukturnye uzmeneniia v ekonomike stran narodnoi demokratii," *Mirovaia ekonomika i mezhdunarodnye otnosheniia,* No. 9, 1962, p. 12. A promising preliminary study of the roles of the various national academies of sciences in Comecon is presented by Arthur M. Handardt, Jr., and William A. Welsh, "The Intellectuals—Politics Nexus: Studies Using a Biographical Technique," *American Behavioral Scientist,* Vol. VII, No. 7 (March, 1964), pp. 3-7.

32. *Pravda,* June 17, 1962.

33. *U.N. Economic* Survey of Europe, p. 1.

34. N. S. Khrushchev, "Vital Questions of the Development of the World Socialist System," *Kommunist,* No. 12 (August, 1962), pp. 3-26. *Current Digest of the Soviet Press,* XIV, 35, pp. 5-6.

35. N. Volkov and A. Netrusov, "Strukturnye uzmeneniia v ekonomike . . . ," p. 7.

36. M. Senin, "SEV na sovremennom etape," *Mirovaia ekonomika i mezhdunarodnye otnosheniia,* No. 3, 1963, p. 5.

37. N. Fadeev, "Strany SEV krepiat ekonomicheskoe sotrudnichestvo," *Mirovaia ekonomika i mezhdunarodnye otnosheniia,* No. 10, 1963, pp. 10-11.

38. "Communist Economic Policy in the Less Developed Areas," U.S. Department of State Publication 7020 (July, 1960), p. 13.

39. V. Rimalov, *Economic Cooperation Between the USSR and Underdeveloped Countries,* Moscow: Foreign Languages Publishing House, 1962, p. 43.

40. See D. Degtyar and A. Kutsenkov, "Cooperation of the Socialist States with the Economically Underdeveloped Countries," *World Marxist Review* (June, 1962), pp. 37-38.

41. See N. Kondrat'ev, "Industrializatsiia Indii i ekonomicheskaia rol' gosudarstva," *Mirovaia ekonomika i mezhdunarodnye otnosheniia,* No. 4 1964, pp. 25 and 29.

42. *Pravda,* January 30, 1960, and *New Times,* No. 33 (August 15, 1962), p. 25. See Walter Z. Laqueur, *The Soviet Union and the Middle East,* New York: Praeger, 1959, pp. 229, 264-279.

43. *Soviet Weekly* (London), July 11, 1963. Also see *Pravda,* July 13, 1959; *Izvestiia,* March 10, 1960; *Izvestiia,* August 27, 1959, *Izvestiia,* August 30, 1960; *Pravda,* March 19, 1961; and *Izvestiia,* October 4, 1963.

44. *Izvestiia,* March 21, 1961. Also see *Pravda,* July 20, 1960; *Pravda,* December 25, 1960; *The New York Times,* February 26, 1961; *Pravda,* September 22, 1960; and *Izvestiia,* April 8, 1961.

45. *Three-Monthly Economic Review* (London), No. 39 (November, 1962), p. 7.

46. M. Lavrechenko, "Za rasshirenie ekonomicheskikh sviazei, za polnuiu likvidatsiio kolonializma," *Mirovaia ekonomika i mezhdunarodnye otnosheniia,* No. 2, 1964, pp. 61-62.

47. R. A. Ul'ianvoskii, *Neokolonializm SShA i claborazvitye strany Azii,* Moscow: Izdatel'stvo Vostochnoi Literatury, 1963, pp. 138-180.

48. See A. F. Sultanov, ed., *Sovetsko-Arabskie druzhestvennye otnosheniia*, Moscow: Gosudarstvoe izdatel'stvo, 1961, pp. 18, 30-31.

49. O. Tuganova, "Rol' molodykh gosudarstv v mezhdunarodnykh otnosheniakh," *Mirovaia ekonomika i mezhdunarodnye otnosheniia*, No. 2, 1964, pp. 16-17.

50. Ibid., p. 17.

51. See David J. Dallin, *Soviet Foreign Policy After Stalin*, Philadelphia: Lippincott, 1961, pp. 332-333.

52. Degtyar and Kutsenkov, "Cooperation of the Socialist States . . . ," p. 43.

53. *The Communist Economic Offensive*, DOD Pam 4-84, Department of Defense, November, 1961.

54. *Pravda*, December 11, 1959; *Izvestiia*, March 30, 1963.

55. See *Sbornik: torgovykh dogovorov, torgovykh i platezhnykh soglashenii, i golgosrochnykh torgovykh soglashenii SSSR s inostrannymi gosudarstvami*, Moscow: Vneshtorgizdat, 1961.

56. Rimalov, *Economic Cooperation between USSR and Underdeveloped Countries . . . ,"* pp. 77-78. The author as much as concedes this point in his survey of Soviet trade.

57. *New Times*, No. 13 (April, 1963), p. 17.

58. Note the Soviet concern for the impact the Common Market was having on Asian and African countries in "Obshchii rynok—novaia forma kolonializma," *Narody Azii i Afriki*, No. 4, 1962, pp. 3-12; "Obshchii rynok—kollektivoe nastuplenie kolonizatorov," *Narody Azii i Afriki*, No. 5, 1962, pp. 60-69. Anxiety over inroads made by the members of the Common Market into the trade of Asia, Africa, and Latin America and opposition to trade associations of underdeveloped countries are expressed in V. Kollontai and Ya. Etinger, "Ugroza ekonomike osvobodivshikhsia stran," *Mirovaia ekonomika i mezhdunarodnye otnosheniia*, No. 1, 1963, pp. 73 and 78.

59. V. Pavlat, "EES i torgovlia mezhdu vostokom i zapadom," *Mirovaia ekonomika i mezhdunarodnye otnosheniia*, No. 11, 1963, p. 91.

60. *Ezhegodnik Bolshoi Sovetskoi Entsiklopedii*, Moscow, 1962. See pages 204, 216, 235, 238, 245, 256, and 260.

61. An exception to the importation of Soviet oil is Britain, where agricultural goods and raw materials have been the main items purchased from the members of Comecon.

62. See *Pravda*, January 29, 1963 and February 2, 1963; and *New Times*, No. 11 (March, 1963).

63. *British Record,* New York: British Information Service (April 2, 1963), p. 2.

64. *Soviet Weekly* (London), October 10, 1963. It should be noted that a large percentage of Soviet-British trade occurs outside the formal quota agreement of the two countries. See *Three-Monthly Economic Review,* No. 40 (February, 1963), p. 10.

65. *Soviet Oil in the Cold War,* prepared by Halford L. Hoskins and Leon Herman, Committee of the Judiciary, U.S. Senate, 87th Congress, 1961.

66. *Izvestiia,* March 24, 1963.

67. See Soviet references indicating this policy in *Pravda,* October 5, 1962; *Izvestiia,* October 16, 1962; *Pravda,* January 18, 1963; *Izvestiia,* February 7, 1963; and *New Times,* No. 12 (March, 1963), p. 15, and No. 13 (April, 1963), p. 17. Also note *Three-Monthly Economic Review,* No. 40 (February, 1963), pp. 11-12.

68. Sections of this chapter are reprinted with permission of the editor from Michael P. Gehlen, "The Politics of Soviet Foreign Trade," *The Western Political Quarterly,* Vol. XVIII, No. 1 (March, 1965), pp. 104-115.

6. POLITICAL METHODS OF SOVIET POLICY

1. D. B. Levin, *Diplomatiia,* Moscow: Gosudarstvennoe izdatel'stvo, 1963, p. 126.

2. Ibid., p. 128. The succeeding quotations are from pp. 130-133.

3. Radio Moscow, July 3, 1957. Also see the comments of Robert M. Slusser on Molotov in Ivo J. Lederer, ed., *Russian Foreign Policy,* New Haven: Yale University Press, 1962, pp. 236-238.

4. See "The Spirit of Geneva," *New Times,* No. 32 (August, 1955), pp. 1-3; "There Must Be No Return to the Cold War," *New Times,* No. 43 (October, 1955), pp. 1-2; S. Menshikov, "A Meeting of Benefit to the Whole World," *New Times,* No. 39 (September, 1959), pp. 5-7.

5. See J. M. Mackintosh, *Strategy and Tactics of Soviet Foreign Policy,* London: Oxford University Press, 1963, pp. 131, 136.

6. Department of State, *Background of Heads of Government Conference* 1960, *Principal Documents,* 1955-1959. D/S 6972, Washington: Government Printing Office, 1960, p. 115.

7. *The New York Times,* June 17, 1958.

8. Reported in *The New York Times,* August 5, 1958.

9. *Izvestiia,* May 6, 1960.

10. *Pravda*, May 29, 1960.

11. *The New York Times*, February 12, 1961. According to documents that had just come into the hands of Western governments, Khrushchev swore at the Chinese and called Mao a "megalomaniac warmonger."

12. See, for example, *Izvestiia*, November 22, 1955; *The New York Times*, September 21, 1959. Khrushchev's article in *Foreign Affairs*, "On Peaceful Coexistence," XXXI (October, 1959).

13. *Pravda*, August 1, 1961.

14. *Izvestiia*, January 11, 1966.

15. L. Leontiev, "Krisis mirovogo kapitalisma," *Kommunist*, No. 15 (October, 1961), pp. 120-122.

16. See *The New York Times*, June 10, 1955.

17. Enrique Lister, "The Aggressive Triangle," *World Marxist Review* (September, 1960), p. 29. The author of this purely propaganda piece went so far as to suggest that the Pentagon intended to use Franco's army in an American-German-Spanish assault on France.

18. See A. Solonitskii, "Frantsuskii neokolonializm v deistvii," *Mirovaia ekonomika i mezhdunarodnye otnosheniia*, No. 1, 1964, pp. 34-43.

19. *Pravda*, July 31, 1958. Also see *Pravda*, May 5, 1955. This issue noted that German industrialists were already cutting into the traditional markets of the British. In a statement obviously designed for British consumption, it commented that "after remilitarization and the revival of the Hitlerite Wehrmacht, the West German monopolies will begin talking to their rivals, including Britain, in a very different language."

20. See the consideration of Western economic colonialism in the Middle East in *Mezhdunarodnye otnosheniia politika SSSR*, Moscow: Gosudarstvennoe Izdatel'stvo, 1961, pp. 451-465.

21. See Alexander Dallin, *The Soviet Union and the United Nations*, New York: Praeger, 1962, pp. 182-213.

22. L. Stefanov, A. Gurov, "OON i ekonomicheskoe razvitie osvobodivshikhsia stran," *Mirovaia ekonomika i mezhdunarodnye otnosheniia*, No. 5, 1963, p. 6. By the same token, the Soviet Union sees the rise of the new states as aiding the Soviet position in the U.N., for by swelling the membership they have erased the "mechanical majority" of the United States in the General Assembly (see p. 4).

23. A. Mileikovskii, "Mezhimperialisticheskie protivorechiia segodnia," *Mirovaia ekonomika i mezhdunarodnye otnosheniia,* No. 12, 1963, pp. 27-28.

24. *Fundamentals of Marxism-Leninism,* Moscow: Foreign Language Publishing House, 1960, pp. 660-661.

25. See *Pravda,* November 6, 1955, for Premier Faure's statement on his trip to Moscow and also for Duclos's press conference concerning the attitude of the French Communists toward the government.

26. *The New York Times,* March 5, 1956. For the Communist version, see *Pravda,* March 4, 1956.

27. See *The New York Times,* April 26, 1956, for Khrushchev's appearance at a Labor Party dinner and May 17, 1956, for Hugh Gaitskell's announcement that a Communist-Socialist popular front was quite impossible. Also note David J. Dallin, *The Soviet Union and the United Nations . . . ,*" pp. 237-239.

28. *Pravda,* July 28, 1956. See David J. Dallin, *The Soviet Union and the United Nations . . . ,*" pp. 239-244.

29. For a review of these moves, see Luciano Gruppi, "For Communist-Socialist Co-operation," *World Marxist Review* (October, 1958), pp. 34-36.

30. Using the British Labor Party as an example, note the Western press reports on the visit of Suslov to London and of Gaitskell and Bevan to Moscow in *The New York Times,* March 18, 1959, March 19, 1959, and September 15, 1959. The Soviet interpretation of the same exchange of delegations is found in *Pravda,* March 6, 1959, March 17, 1959, March 18, 1959, March 19, 1959, and September 4, 1959. Particularly note the editorial comment in *Izvestiia,* September 11, 1959, under the heading "Agreement Is Possible."

31. See *Pravda,* May 3 and May 6, 1958, for reports of correspondence to the French Socialist Party and the Radical Socialist Party. These statements also praised the efforts of the French Communist Party to form a united front. See *Pravda,* May 10, 1958, for the text of letters from the C.P.S.U. to Social Democratic parties of other countries noted above. Particularly strong appeals were made for the union of the Communist and Socialist parties of Italy. See *Pravda,* May 21, 1958.

32. Radio Moscow, May 5 and May 7, 1958, called on the German and Austrian Socialist Party members to oppose the arming of West German forces with nuclear weapons.

33. See *Partiinaia zhizn*, No. 14, 1964, for the reply of the Central Committee of the C.P.S.U. to the charges of the Japanese Communist Party. *Pravda*, May 24, 1964, reported the expulsion of pro-Soviet leaders from the C.P.J.

34. See *Izvestiia*, May 24, 1964.

35. See D. U. Aidit, *Indonesian Socialism and the Conditions for Its Implementation*, Djakarta: Aliarcham Academy of Social Science, 1962.

36. See Walter Z. Laqueur, "Communism and Nationalism in Tropical Africa," *Foreign Affairs*, Vol. 35 (July, 1961), pp. 610-621, and Robert A. Scalapino, "Sino-Soviet Competition in Africa," *Foreign Affairs*, Vol. 42 (July, 1964), pp. 640-654.

37. See *Communist Propaganda, A Fact Book*, 1957-1958, U.S. Information Agency, Washington: Government Printing Office, 1959, p. 22, and "The World Assembly for Peace," Document, *New Times*, No. 28 (July, 1955).

38. *New Times*, No. 40 (October, 1957), pp. 14-15.

39. See *New Times*, No. 33 (August, 1957), pp. 1-2. The delegates were welcomed by editorials entitled "Welcome, Dear Friends," and "Let's Be Friends," *New Times*, No. 30 (July, 1957), pp. 6-7.

40. *New Times*, No. 30 (July, 1959), p. 23.

41. Rolf Ekmanin, "Disenchantment in Helsinki," *Bulletin*, published by the Institute for the Study of the USSR, Vol. IX (November, 1962), pp. 17-27.

42. *African Digest* (London), Vol. X, No. 5 (April, 1963), pp. 173-174.

7. PROPAGANDA AND IDEOLOGY AND SOVIET FOREIGN POLICY

1. L. Ilyichov, "Peaceful Coexistence and the Struggle of Two Ideologies," *World Marxist Review* (November, 1959), p. 14.

2. *World Strength of the Communist Party Organizations*, Intelligence Report No. 4489 R-15, Washington: Bureau of Intelligence and Research, 1963, p. 2.

3. See Alexander Dallin, *The Soviet Union and the United Nations*, New York: Praeger, 1962, pp. 182-213.

4. For one of the most extensive examinations of the techniques and purposes of foreign propaganda, see Frederick C. Barghoorn,

Soviet Foreign Propaganda, Princeton: Princeton University Press, 1964.

5. *Sovetskaia kultura*, October 14, 1961, p. 2. Also note Khrushchev, *Happiness and Peace for the Peoples*, Moscow: Foreign Language Publishing House, pp. 193-195, 253-256, and 291-292.

6. I. Potekhin, *Afrika, 1956-1961*, Moscow: Gosudarstvennoe Izdatel'stvo, 1961, pp. 313-318.

7. B. N. Ponomarev, "Mezhdunarodnoe kommunistcheskoe dvezhenie po novom etape," *Kommunist*, No. 15 (1958), pp. 12-30.

8. *Sovetskaia kultura*, May 6, 1961, p. 1. A year before this statement was made, the Central Committee of the Communist Party complained of a lack of "militant, aggressive" broadcasts. See *Partinaia zhizn*, No. 4 (February, 1960), pp. 26-34.

9. *Sovetskaia kultura*, May 6, 1961, p. 1. Also see Simon Costilyan, USIA Report, *Twelve Years of Communist Broadcasting, 1948-1959*, Washington: Government Printing Office, 1962.

10. Radio Moscow, May 12, 1963.

11. *Correo de la Tarde* (Santiago), August 7, 1962.

12. G. Frantrov, "What Lies Behind the Catch Phrase 'Ideological Disarmament'?" *Kommunist*, No. 13 (September, 1962), pp. 110-119. *Current Digest of the Soviet Press*, XIV, No. 42, p. 5.

13. Scientific Conference, "The Ideological Struggle and Present International Relations," *International Affairs* (Moscow), No. 8 (August, 1963), p. 8. Also note p. 27.

14. See N. Inozemtsev, "U.S. Foreign Policy: Trends and Perspectives," *World Marxist Review* (July, 1960), pp. 11-15. Soviet references to the "positions of strength" policy are based on a statement of Secretary of State John Foster Dulles to the effect that the United States must conduct its foreign policy in the cold war from "situations of strength."

15. E. Varga, "The Capitalism of the 20th Century," *Kommunist*, No. 17 (November, 1959), pp. 36-52. *Current Digest of the Soviet Press*, XII, 4, p. 6.

16. *Pravda*, July 31, 1958.

17. *Izvestiia*, August 8, 1958.

18. *Pravda*, June 18, 1959. For a more extensive interpretation, see *Mezhdunarodnye otnosheniia i vneshniaia politika SSSR*, Moscow: Gosudarstvennoe izdatel'stvo, 1961, pp. 451-465.

19. *New Times*, No. 6 (February, 1958), pp. 8-9 and *New Times*, No. 42 (October, 1958), pp. 3-4.

20. *Pravda*, May 29, 1960.

21. Yu. Zhilin and V. Zagladin, "International Developments," *World Marxist Review* (September, 1960), p. 31.

8. CONFLICT WITHIN THE SYSTEM OF PARTY-STATES

1. Reported in Zbigniew K. Brzezinski, *The Soviet Bloc: Unity and Conflict*, Cambridge: Harvard University Press, 1960, p. 183.

2. *Pravda*, June 20, 1956.

3. *Pravda*, June 21, 1956.

4. "Palmiro Togliatti's Report," *The Anti-Stalin Campaign and International Communism*, New York: Columbia University Press, 1956, pp. 230-231.

5. *Pravda*, July 2, 1956. *CDSP*, VIII, No. 24, p. 8.

6. *Pravda*, July 16, 1956. *CDSP*, VIII, No. 29, p. 3.

7. *Pravda*, October 25, 1956.

8. *The New York Times*, November 22, 1956. The Soviet report failed to mention Poland's abstention. See *Ivestiia*, November 23, 1956.

9. See Ferenc Vali, *Rift and Revolt in Hungary*, Cambridge: Harvard University Press, 1961, p. 360. Also note *Pravda*, November 4, 1956, and November 5, 1956. The latter reference expressed particular concern over the foreign policy course endorsed by Nagy.

10. *Pravda*, November 3 and November 4, 1956.

11. *Pravda*, November 13, 1956. *CDSP*, VIII, 45, p. 14.

12. Imre Nagy, *On Communism*, New York: Praeger, 1957, p. 153.

13. See K. A. Jelenski, "Poland," reprinted in Walter Laqueur and Leopold Labedz, eds., *Polycentrism*, New York: Praeger, 1962, pp. 70-71.

14. G. Nalivaiko, "Sel'skokhozaistvennaia nauka i proizvodstvo," *Kommunist*, No. 17 (November, 1961), pp. 54-60. L. Bogdenko, *Voprosi istorii*, No. 5 (May, 1963), pp. 19-35.

15. *Pravda*, June 17, 1962. Also note N. S. Khrushchev, "Vital Questions of the Development of the World Socialist System," *Kommunist*, No. 12 (August, 1962), pp. 3-26. *CDSP*, XIV, No. 35, pp. 3-7.

16. *The New York Times* (text), November 17, 1956.

17. *Pravda*, January 19, 1957.

18. Jan F. Triska, *The Rift in the Communist World*, Stanford Studies of the Communist System, 1964.

19. T. Timofeev, "Tvorcheskii marksizm-leninizm i problemy rabochego dvizheniia," *Mirovaia ekonomika i mezhdunarodnye otnosheniia*, No. 8, 1963, p. 10.

20. Reprinted in *Peking Review*, Vol. I (May 13, 1958), pp. 6-8.

21. J. Kadar, "On the Experience of the Class Struggle in Hungary," *World Marxist Review* (February, 1959), p. 17. Antonin Novotny, "For the Triumph of Peace and Socialism," *World Marxist Review* (September, 1958), p. 10, and T. Daniszewski, "Under the Banner of Proletarian Internationalism," *World Marxist Review* (January, 1959), p. 57.

22. Radio Peking, June 22, 1960. A much condensed version appeared in *Pravda*, June 24, 1960.

23. See Donald Zagoria, *The Sino-Soviet Conflict: 1956-1961*, Princeton: Princeton University Press, 1962, p. 325.

24. *Pravda*, June 12, 1960.

25. For a conjectural reconstruction of the 1960 conference see William E. Griffith, "The November 1960 Moscow Meeting: A Preliminary Reconstruction," reprinted in Laqueur and Labedz, *Polycentrism* . . . , pp. 107-126.

26. *Pravda*, October 18, 1961.

27. *Pravda*, October 20, 1961.

28. *Pravda*, April 3, 1964. The report was delivered on February 14.

29. *The New York Times*, January 13, 1959.

30. *Pravda*, January 28, 1959.

31. Reported over Radio Peking, February 16, 1959.

32. See Zagoria, *The Sino-Soviet Conflict* . . . , pp. 189-194.

33. See Vadim Medic, "Sino-Soviet Central Asia: National Unification vs. Political Division," *The Russian Review*, Vol. 22 (January, 1963), pp. 56-67.

34. *Pravda*, July 20, 1958.

35. *The New York Times*, August 7, 1958. The Soviet press held the West responsible for blocking a summit conference. *Pravda*, August 7, 1958.

36. See *Peking Review*, Vol. I (August 19, 1958), pp. 8-11.

37. Reprinted in *Pravda*, November 4, 1958.

38. *Pravda*, November 6, 1958.

39. *Christian Science Monitor*, September 9, 1963.

40. *Peking Review*, Vol. II (September 22, 1959), pp. 6-11.

41. *Pravda*, October 1, 1959. *CDSP*, XII, No. 39, pp. 21-22.

42. *Pravda*, November 15, 1962.

43. Radio Peking, November 1, 1962. The broadcast was actually a reading of an editorial from *Hung Ch'i* that repeated the "paper-tiger" theme and concluded with the words "The United States imposes blockade, oppose it! The United States attacks, repulse them!"

INDEX